PREVENTING INTIMATE PARTNER VIOLENCE

VIOLENCE

Interdisciplinary perspectives

Edited by Claire M. Renzetti, Diane R. Follingstad, and Ann L. Coker

P

First published in Great Britain in 2017 by

Policy Press
University of Bristol
1-9 Old Park Hill
Bristol
BS2 8BB
UK
t: +44 (0)117 954 5940
pp-info@bristol.ac.uk
www.policypress.co.uk

North America office:
Policy Press
c/o The University of Chicago Press
1427 East 60th Street
Chicago, IL 60637, USA
t: +1 773 702 7700
f: +1 773-702-9756
sales@press.uchicago.edu
www.press.uchicago.edu

© Policy Press 2017

British Library Cataloguing in Publication Data
A catalogue record for this book is available from the British Library

Library of Congress Cataloging-in-Publication Data
A catalog record for this book has been requested

ISBN 978-1-4473-3307-4 paperback
ISBN 978-1-4473-3305-0 hardcover
ISBN 978-1-4473-3308-1 ePub
ISBN 978-1-4473-3309-8 Mobi
ISBN 978-1-4473-3306-7 ePdf

Cover design by Soapbox Design
Front cover image: istock
Printed and bound in Great Britain by CPI Group (UK) Ltd, Croydon, CR0 4YY
Policy Press uses environmentally responsible print partners

Contents

List of Abbreviations

ACA	Affordable Care Act
APA	American Psychological Association
BIP	batterer intervention program
BIRCWH	Building Interdisciplinary Research Careers in Women's Health
BRFP	Based Responsible Fatherhood Project
CBIM	Coaching Boys Into Men
CCI	Center for Court Innovation
CDC	Centers for Disease Control and Prevention
CLS	criminal legal system
COR	conservation of resources
CP	Circles of Peace
DRC	Democratic Republic of Congo
DVSD	Domestic Violence Safe Dialogue
EMPOWER	Enhancing and Making Programs and Outcomes Work to End Rape
EMR	electronic medical records
FGM	female genital mutilation
FP	family planning
GBV	gender-based violence
GTO	Getting to Outcomes
ICLI	Islamic Center of Long Island
ICT	information and communication technology
IPV	intimate partner violence
IVAWA	International Violence Against Women Act
JCAHO	Joint Commission on the Accreditation of Healthcare Organizations
KASAP	Kentucky Association of Sexual Assault Programs
LGBTQ	lesbian, gay, bisexual, transgender, and queer
LGBTQI	lesbian, gay, bisexual, transgender, queer, and intersex
MOVERS	Measure of Victim Empowerment Related to Safety
MSV	Men Stopping Violence
MVP	Mentors in Violence Prevention
NASMHPD	National Association of State Mental Health Program Directors

NAYA	Native American Youth and Family Center
NCADV	National Coalition Against Domestic Violence
NGO	nongovernmental organization
NIH	National Institutes of Health
NIJ	National Institute of Justice
NRCDV	National Resource Center on Domestic Violence
NSF	National Science Foundation
NYU	New York University
OWH	Office on Women's Health
PFP	Pigs for Peace
POL	popular opinion leaders
RC	reproductive coercion
RCT	randomized control trial
RESTORE	Responsibility and Equity for Sexual Transgressions Offering a Restorative Experience
RJ	restorative justice
RJC	restorative justice conferencing
RPE	Rape Prevention Education
RSVP	Resolve to Stop the Violence Project
RWAMREC	Rwanda Men's Resource Center
SCPT	State Core Planning Team
SDA	safety decision aid
SPT	State Prevention Team
STOP	StoryTelling and Organizing Project
SV	sexual violence
TDV	teen dating violence
TH	therapeutic horticulture
UN	United Nations
UNFPA	United Nations Population Fund
USPSTF	United States Preventive Services Task Force
VAWA	Violence Against Women Act
VOC	victim–offender conferencing
VOD	victim–offender dialog
VOM	victim–offender mediation
VOMA	Victim Offender Mediation Association
VVH	Victims' Voices Heard
WHO	World Health Organization
WIC	Women, Infants, and Children
WRC	White Ribbon Campaign
YSC	Youth Services Center

Notes on Contributors

Victoria L. Banyard is a Professor in the Psychology Department at the University of New Hampshire, NH, and member of the Prevention Innovations Research Center. Her research focuses on understanding the consequences and prevention of interpersonal violence, especially using the lens of resilience. She is the author of *Toward the next generation of bystander prevention of sexual and relationship violence* (Springer, 2015) and numerous journal articles and book chapters. She is on the editorial board of the journal *Psychology of Violence* and the Principal Investigator on numerous federal grants to evaluate sexual violence prevention program effectiveness.

Dr. Ann L. Coker has served as Endowed Chair in the Center for Research on Violence Against Women at the University of Kentucky, KY, since 2007. She also serves as faculty in the Department of Obstetrics and Gynecology at the College of Medicine, University of Kentucky. Her research as an epidemiologist has focused on the mental and physical health effects of intimate partner and sexual violence, primarily among women and girls. More recently, Dr. Coker has changed her research trajectory to identify and evaluate promising primary prevention interventions to reduce the frequency and impact of gender-based violence (GBV).

Rebecca M. Cudmore, PhD, earned her doctoral degree in criminology and justice policy from Northeastern University, MA. Her policy and research interests are in the area of violence and victimization, with a specific focus on sexual offending, intimate partner violence, human trafficking, and the relationship between victimization and delinquency.

Dr. Carlos A. Cuevas is an Associate Professor and Co-Director of the Violence and Justice Research Laboratory in the School of Criminology and Criminal Justice at Northeastern University, MA. He earned his PhD in clinical psychology from the California School of Professional Psychology at Alliant International University. Dr. Cuevas's research focuses on interpersonal violence, victimization, and trauma. His work examines the overlap between various forms of victimization, psychological distress, and service utilization, particularly among Latinos and other people of color, as well as factors that may impact the victimization–delinquency link. Dr. Cuevas is also a licensed psychologist, providing clinical services to victims of violence.

Shamita Das Dasgupta is a Co-Founder of Manavi, an organization in the US that focuses on violence against women in the South Asian community. She has taught at Rutgers University, NJ, and New York University Law School, NY. Her published books are: *The demon slayers and other stories: Bengali folktales* (Interlink Books, 1995), *A patchwork shawl: Chronicles of South Asian women in America* (Rutgers University Press, 1998), *Body evidence: Intimate violence against South Asian women in America* (Rutgers University Press, 2007), *Mothers for sale: Women in Kolkata's sex trade* (Dasgupta-Alliance, 2009), and *Globalization and transnational surrogacy in India: Outsourcing life* (Lexington Books, 2014).

Michele R. Decker, ScD, MPH, is an Associate Professor of Population, Family and Reproductive Health at the Johns Hopkins Bloomberg School of Public Health, where she also directs the Women's Health and Rights program in the Center for Public Health and Human Rights. Trained as a social epidemiologist and behavioral scientist, she brings over a decade of research and programmatic experience in GBV prevention and intervention, as well as its impact on sexual health and HIV risk behavior and infection. Her research spans both general populations and highly marginalized groups, including homeless, unstably housed, and runaway youth, and those involved in the sex trade and trafficking or sexual exploitation. She serves as an advisor to the World Health Organization (WHO), the United Nations Population Fund (UNFPA), the US Agency for International Development (USAID), Futures Without Violence, and the National Resource Center on Domestic Violence (NRCDV) on these topics.

Diane Fleet is a 20-year veteran of domestic violence advocacy and is currently serving as the Assistant Director of GreenHouse17, a domestic violence program in Central Kentucky, KY. In partnership with GreenHouse17 leadership and staff, Diane has implemented a trauma-informed, therapeutic horticulture program, which has received numerous awards and recognitions, most recently the Mary Byron Celebrating Solutions Award, the Kentucky Non-Profit Network

Innovative Non-Profit of 2013, and the Center for Non-Profit Excellence Pyramid Award for Social Innovation. GreenHouse17 was also a finalist in the Partnership for Freedom/Reimagine Opportunity Award. Diane co-presented at the 2015 World Shelter Conference in The Hague and the National Coalition Against Domestic Violence (NCADV) conference in 2016. She currently serves on the Board of Directors for Green Dot, Inc., a primary prevention program addressing power-based personal violence.

Diane R. Follingstad, PhD, is the Director and Endowed Chair in the Center for Research on Violence Against Women and a Professor at the University of Kentucky, KY. This follows her career as Distinguished Professor Emeritus in clinical and forensic psychology at the University of South Carolina, SC. She holds a diplomate in forensic psychology (American Board of Professional Psychology) and received Fellow status in the American Psychology-Law Society, a division of the American Psychological Association (APA). Her experience includes forensic expert, academician, researcher, administrator, professor and practicum supervisor, and practicing clinician. Dr. Follingstad's research has covered battered women, physical dating violence, measurement of psychological maltreatment, and factors impacting jury verdicts in battered women's cases.

Nancy Glass, PhD, MPH, RN, is a Professor and Associate Dean for Research at the Johns Hopkins School of Nursing and Associate Director of the Johns Hopkins Center for Global Health. Dr. Glass conducts community-based interventions with diverse populations across multiple domestic and global settings. She is the Principal Investigator of several multidisciplinary studies to test employment, economic empowerment, and safety interventions to improve the health of survivors of GBV and their families.

Leigh Goodmark is a Professor of Law at the University of Maryland Carey School of Law, MD. Professor Goodmark directs the Gender Violence Clinic, which provides direct representation in matters involving intimate partner abuse, sexual assault, and trafficking. Professor Goodmark's scholarship focuses on domestic violence. She is the Co-Editor of *Comparative perspectives on gender violence: Lessons from efforts worldwide* (Oxford University Press, 2015) and the author of *A troubled marriage: Domestic violence and the legal system* (New York University, 2012), which was named a *CHOICE* Outstanding

Academic Title of 2012. Professor Goodmark is a graduate of Yale University and Stanford Law School.

Lisa Y. Larance, MSW, LCSW, LMSW, is a practitioner–scholar whose work focuses on meeting the needs of women and their families. Ms. Larance is the Founder of two innovative community-based programs providing intervention, advocacy, and support for women who have used force in their relationships: Vista and RENEW. She is also the Co-Creator of the prison-based *Meridians Program for Incarcerated Women*.

Elizabeth Miller, MD, PhD, is a Professor in Pediatrics and Chief of the Division of Adolescent and Young Adult Medicine at the Children's Hospital of Pittsburgh, University of Pittsburgh Medical Center, and University of Pittsburgh School of Medicine, PA. Trained in internal medicine and pediatrics and medical anthropology, she has over a decade of practice and research experience in addressing interpersonal violence in clinical and community settings.

Susan L. Miller is a Professor in the Department of Sociology and Criminal Justice at the University of Delaware, DE. Her research interests include gendered violence, justice-involved women, victims' rights, IPV, gender, and criminal justice policy. She has published numerous articles about the intersection of victimization and offending among IPV survivors, including a book, *Victims as offenders: The paradox of women's use of violence in relationships* (Rutgers University Press, 2005). Her most recent book, *After the crime: The power of restorative justice dialogues between victims and violent offenders* (New York University Press, 2011), won the national 2012 Outstanding Book Award presented by the Academy of Criminal Justice Sciences.

Bethsaida Nieves is a PhD Candidate in the Department of Curriculum and Instruction at the University of Wisconsin–Madison. Her research interests include international and comparative education, and education reform policy for economic development. Her recent publications include "Imagined geographies and the construction of the *campesino* and *jíbaro* identities" in *Indigenous concepts of education: Toward elevating humanity for all learners* (Palgrave Macmillan, 2014); "Systems of reason(ing) in the idea of education reforms for economic development: The Puerto Rican context" in *Economics, aid and education: Implications for development* (Sense Publishers, 2013); and

"Rafael Cordero" in *Dictionary of Caribbean and Afro–Latin American biography* (Oxford University Press, 2016).

James Ptacek, PhD, has been working on issues of violence against women in the US for over 30 years. He has worked as a batterers' counselor and has conducted trainings on domestic violence intervention for hospital, mental health, and legal professionals. He has conducted research on men who batter, rape and battering on college campuses, and battered women's experiences with the courts. He is the Editor of *Restorative justice and violence against women* (Oxford University Press, 2010). Jim is a Professor of Sociology at Suffolk University, MA.

Eileen A. Recktenwald has been the Executive Director of the Kentucky Association of Sexual Assault Programs (KASAP)—the statewide coalition of Kentucky's 13 regional rape crisis centers located in its capital, Frankfort—since 2001. She is a graduate of the University of Maryland, MD, and the University of Kentucky, KY, where she earned her Master's degree in social work and received an honorary doctorate in humane letters. She was the first Director of a domestic violence shelter in the Appalachian region of Kentucky, and provided direct advocacy services there for 5 years. She also directed and provided advocacy services to child sexual assault victims at a Rape Crisis Center for 11 years. For the last 15 years, she has focused on the primary prevention of sexual violence, changing the social norms that encourage interpersonal violence, increasing the quality and accessibility of rape crisis services, and seeking justice for and giving sexual assault victims a voice in Kentucky.

Claire M. Renzetti, PhD, is the Judi Conway Patton Endowed Chair in the Center for Research on Violence Against Women, and Professor and Chair of the Sociology Department at the University of Kentucky, KY. She is Editor of the international, interdisciplinary journal, *Violence Against Women*, Co-Editor (with Jeffrey Edleson) of the Interpersonal Violence book series for Oxford University Press, and Editor of the Gender and Justice book series for University of California Press. She has authored or edited 24 books, as well as numerous book chapters and articles in professional journals. Much of her research has focused on the violent victimization experiences of socially and economically marginalized women—a serious public health problem in the US and globally. Her current research includes an evaluation of a horticultural therapy program at a shelter for battered women, studies examining the relationship between religiosity and IPV perpetration and victimization, and a study of potential jurors' prototypes of sex trafficking victims and perpetrators.

Richard M. Tolman, MSW, PhD, is the Sheldon D. Rose Collegiate Professor of Social Work at the University of Michigan, MI. His current work includes studying men as allies in violence prevention, and engaging expectant and new fathers to promote positive partnering and parenting and prevent abusive behavior.

Tova B. Walsh, PhD, MSW, is an Assistant Professor in the School of Social Work at the University of Wisconsin–Madison, where she is also affiliated with the Institute for Research on Poverty. She is currently a Scholar in the UW—Madison Building Interdisciplinary Research Careers in Women's Health (BIRCWH) Program, an institutional training grant funded by the National Institutes of Health (NIH). Her research, teaching, and practice experience reflect her commitment to working with vulnerable families to support emerging competencies in early parenthood, promote nurturing parent–child relationships, and prevent childhood exposure to violence.

Workshop participants

- Victoria L. Banyard, Department of Psychology, University of New Hampshire, NH
- Ann L. Coker, Department of Obstetrics and Gynecology, College of Medicine; Department of Epidemiology, College of Public Health; Center for Research on Violence Against Women, University of Kentucky, KY
- Carlos A. Cuevas, School of Criminology and Criminal Justice, Northeastern University, MA
- Shamita Das Dasgupta, Manavi, Inc., Montville, NJ
- Michele R. Decker, Johns Hopkins University Bloomberg School of Public Health, MD
- Jeffrey Edleson, School of Social Welfare, University of California, Berkeley, CA
- Diane Fleet, Greenhouse 17, Lexington, KY
- Diane Follingstad, Department of Psychiatry, College of Medicine; Center for Research on Violence Against Women, University of Kentucky, KY
- Nancy Glass, Johns Hopkins University School of Nursing, MD

- Leigh Goodmark, Francis King Carey School of Law, University of Maryland, MD
- Sherry Hamby, Department of Psychology, Sewanee: The University of the South, TN
- Lisa Y. Larance, Catholic Social Services of Washtenaw County, MI
- Elizabeth Miller, Division of Adolescent Medicine, Children's Hospital of Pittsburgh, PA
- Susan L. Miller, Department of Sociology and Criminal Justice, University of Delaware, DE
- Nia Parson, Department of Anthropology, Southern Methodist University, TX
- James Ptacek, Department of Sociology, Suffolk University, MA
- Eileen A. Recktenwald, Kentucky Association of Sexual Assault Programs, Frankfurt, KY
- Claire M. Renzetti, Department of Sociology, Center for Research on Violence Against Women, University of Kentucky, KY
- Beth Richie, Department of Criminal Justice, University of Illinois at Chicago, IL
- Richard M. Tolman, School of Social Work, University of Michigan, MI
- Tova B. Walsh, School of Medicine and Public Health, School of Social Work, University of Wisconsin–Madison, WI

Student associates

- Allison Adair, Department of Sociology, University of Kentucky, KY
- Jocelyn Anderson, Johns Hopkins University School of Nursing, MD
- Aneesa Baboolal, Department of Sociology and Criminal Justice, University of Delaware, DE
- Amy Bush, Department of Sociology, University of Kentucky, KY
- Rebecca M. Cudmore, School of Criminology and Criminal Justice, Northeastern University, MA
- Charvonne Holliday, Children's Hospital of Pittsburgh, PA
- Sarah Peitzmeier, Johns Hopkins University Bloomberg School of Public Health, MD
- Brianna VanArsdale, Department of Sociology and Criminal Justice, University of Delaware, DE

Preface

This book evolved from a workshop on preventing IPV that we organized and convened in May, 2014 in Arlington, Virginia. We were motivated by our observation that over the past four decades, the majority of resources to address IPV have been expended on providing services to victims and on criminal justice responses to increase perpetrator accountability. Although these foci are not unimportant, far less attention has been given to preventing IPV from occurring, despite mounting evidence that IPV is preventable. Over the course of two days, teams of researchers and practitioners from diverse backgrounds and fields explored the "state of the art" of IPV prevention. The discussion addressed several key questions:

- How should "success" in IPV prevention be defined and measured?
- What are the ongoing challenges to effective outreach, especially to underserved populations?
- Which prevention programs have been identified through rigorous empirical evaluation to hold significant promise in terms of positive outcomes?
- What are the most pressing priorities in terms of preventing IPV moving forward?

The chapters in this book represent workshop participants' answers to these questions. Each chapter examines critical issues in IPV prevention at the individual, community, and systems levels. The authors present an overview of the extant evidence from current evaluations of promising, innovative prevention programs, including those designed to meet the needs of underserved groups, in the US and throughout the world. In addition, the chapters present collaborative, interdisciplinary work to identify gaps in knowledge about IPV prevention, and to offer recommendations for future research on and prioritizing of prevention strategies. The workshop was funded by the Law and Social Sciences Program of the National Science Foundation (NSF; Award No. 1341983) in collaboration with the National Institute of Justice (NIJ).

We wish to take this opportunity to thank Dr. Marjorie Zatz, Program Director of the Law and Social Science Program at NSF at the time of the workshop; Dr. Zatz's successor, Dr. Helena Silverstein; and Dr. Bethany Backes, Social Science Analyst, Violence and Victimization Research Division at NIJ, for their support and advice during the planning and delivery of the workshop and with post-workshop activities. The opinions, conclusions, and recommendations expressed in this book are those of the editors and authors, and do not necessarily reflect the views of NSF, NIJ, or the US government.

We also thank Allison Adair and Amy Bush, graduate research assistants, for aiding in organizing the workshop, designing and maintaining the workshop website, and communicating with workshop participants and book contributors. We are grateful as well to Mary Boulton; Kyna Estes; Cherice Phelps; Kelley Salyers; Pamela Thompson; and Patsy Wood in the Office of Sponsored Research and the College of Arts and Sciences at the University of Kentucky, KY, for their assistance in preparing the grant application and administering the grant.

Finally, we thank the workshop participants—both those who contributed to this volume and those who could not due to other commitments—for their insight, collegiality, and passion for promoting IPV prevention.

ONE

Preventing Intimate Partner Violence: An Introduction

Claire M. Renzetti, Diane R. Follingstad, and
Ann L. Coker

Introduction

Intimate partner violence (IPV) includes any threatened or completed acts of physical, sexual, or psychological abuse committed by a spouse, ex-spouse, current or former boyfriend or girlfriend, or dating partner (Saltzman et al., 1999). This definition includes such behaviors as physical violence, rape, stalking, reproductive coercion, and coercive control (that is, the deliberate and systematic use of violence, intimidation, isolation, or control to undermine a partner's autonomy and to compel their obedience) (Stark, 2007). IPV is a form of gender-based violence in that the majority of victims are women, and there is widespread evidence that IPV affects a sizable number of women throughout the world. Although estimates of IPV rates vary depending on the sample studied and how questions are worded, commonly cited estimates in the US are that 12–25% of women are physically and/or sexually assaulted by an intimate partner each year (Black et al., 2011; Tjaden & Thoennes, 2000). Globally, it is estimated that nearly one third (30%) of women who have been in an intimate relationship have experienced some form of physical and/or sexual violence perpetrated by an intimate partner in their lifetime (World Health Organization, 2016). In some regions of the world, the percentages are even higher: 40.6% in Andean Latin America, 41.8% in West Sub-Saharan Africa,

41.7% in South Asia, and 65.6% in Central Sub-Saharan Africa (Devries et al., 2013).

That women are more likely to be IPV victims and men are more likely to be IPV perpetrators does not mean that men are never victimized by IPV. In the US, for example, it is estimated that 7.6–11.5% of men are physically and/or sexually assaulted by an intimate partner each year (Black et al., 2011; Tjaden & Thoennes, 2000). Most studies, however, show that there are important differences between IPV perpetrated by women and IPV perpetrated by men in heterosexual relationships. Research indicates, for example, that women's and men's motivations for using violence against an intimate partner differ. Men are more likely to use violence when they perceive themselves to be losing control of the relationship, or when they interpret their partner's words or behavior as challenges to their authority. In contrast, women are more likely to use violence—especially severe physical violence—in self-defense, when they believe they are in imminent danger of being attacked, or in retaliation for being attacked (Barnett et al., 1997; Dobash et al., 1998; Miller, 2001; Rajan & McCloskey, 2007). Men's IPV is also typically more severe; women are more likely to be injured when they are assaulted by their male intimate partners, and their injuries are more serious and more likely to require medical treatment or hospitalization (Hamberger & Guse, 2002; Menard et al., 2009; Tjaden & Thoennes, 2000). Men are also more likely than women to kill their intimate partners. In the US, about 39% of female homicide victims are killed by an intimate, whereas only 3% of male homicide victims are killed by an intimate (Catalano, 2013). Although many European countries do not disaggregate homicide statistics by victim–offender relationship, in countries for which such data are available, we see a similar pattern. In France, for instance, women are 85% of victims in homicides involving an intimate partner (Small Arms Survey, 2016). In the Netherlands, more than 50% of female homicide victims killed from 2011–15 were killed by a current or former intimate partner, whereas 30% of male homicide victims during the same period were killed by an acquaintance (Small Arms Survey, 2016). It is important to note that these countries have comparatively low violent death rates—yet the proportion of women and girls killed is above the global average (Small Arms Survey, 2016). These figures, however, are underestimates of IPV homicide in that they do not account for "collateral victims," including the partners' children or others close to the woman, such as her new partner if she has begun a new relationship (Hamby, 2018; Meyer & Post, 2013; Smith et al., 2014).

In addition to physical injuries—and, potentially, death—IPV victims suffer other serious health impacts, including elevated rates of chronic pain, irritable bowel syndrome, sexually transmitted infections, pregnancy complications and other gynecological problems, and depressed immune system functioning (Campbell, 2002). The psychological outcomes of IPV victimization include higher rates of depression, post-traumatic stress disorder (PTSD), eating and sleeping disorders, substance use, self-harm, and suicide (Black et al., 2011; Bonomi et al., 2007; Coker, 2007). The economic impacts of IPV on an individual level include job loss and increased risk of homelessness; on a societal level, it is estimated that IPV negatively affects a country's economy through such factors as medical expenses, legal system costs, missed work or school days, and reduced productivity (Duvvury et al., 2013).

Clearly, IPV is a significant and persistent public health problem throughout the world. But although it is a daunting problem, there is growing empirical evidence that IPV is preventable (WHO, 2014). The purpose of this book is to highlight prevention efforts that have been identified through rigorous evaluation to hold significant promise in terms of preventing IPV, and to explore how significant obstacles to prevention may be overcome. In addition, the authors discuss such provocative issues as how "success" with regard to IPV prevention should be defined and measured, and how successful outcomes may vary across different populations. To begin, however, we will present the prevention model that informed the development of subsequent chapters, and provide an overview of the topics the chapter authors address.

Prevention science

Prevention encompasses a range of activities—usually called *interventions*—that are designed to reduce risks or threats to health and wellbeing (Institute for Work and Health, 2015). A commonly used model in prevention science is the *stages* or *levels* of prevention model. In this model, there are three levels of prevention: primary, secondary, and tertiary.

The goal of *primary prevention* is to stop a problem from occurring—or, more modestly perhaps, to reduce the number of new incidents. Primary prevention requires knowledge of both the risk factors that contribute to the unhealthy or injurious behavior and the factors that protect against the unhealthy or injurious behavior. Primary prevention efforts therefore focus on eliminating or removing sources of risk, as well as promoting protective factors and widely educating or raising awareness about the threatening behavior. With regard to IPV, primary prevention efforts have largely focused on education and training campaigns. In this volume, Ann L. Coker, Victoria L. Banyard, and Eileen A. Recktenwald (Chapter 3) discuss one such educational and training effort—active bystander intervention programs—which are primary prevention programs designed specifically for a high-risk group—young women and men in high school and college.If a problem cannot be prevented, then the goal is to reduce its impact by identifying and responding to "early-stage" cases so they do not become more severe—known as *secondary prevention*—and providing services to those who have been affected to help them recover and to reduce the likelihood that the problem will persist or recur—known as *tertiary prevention*. Screening for exposure to the problem is one of the most commonly used secondary prevention strategies. In Chapter 5, Michele R. Decker, Elizabeth Miller, and Nancy Glass review the empirical evidence on screening for IPV in various venues, such as health care settings. Several other chapters—including those by Larance and Miller (Chapter 6) and Renzetti, Follingstad, and Fleet (Chapter 9)—examine a variety of programs intended as tertiary prevention.

The stages of prevention model has been critiqued as too rigid. Critics point out that, in practice, the boundaries between prevention levels are often blurred and are context-dependent. In other words, a single prevention program or strategy, such as screening, may be labeled by those who develop it as secondary prevention, but for some groups or in some circumstances it may be primary prevention. For instance, screening may identify women who are at risk for or who have experienced IPV, but simply being asked the screening questions may make some women aware of a problem they had not thought about before, motivating them to learn more about IPV and act to reduce risk factors in their own lives and those of others close to them.Another way to think about prevention is not in terms of stages, but rather in terms of *who* the prevention efforts are designed to affect. Prevention programs designed to reach everyone in a population, regardless of their level of risk, are considered *universal* prevention programs. *Selective* prevention programs target specific groups who have been identified as being at high risk of experiencing the harm or problem. *Indicated* prevention programs target individuals and groups who have already engaged in or experienced the problematic behavior. In Chapter 4, Tolman, Walsh, and Nieves discuss all three types of prevention strategies in terms of engaging men and boys in efforts to prevent IPV.

While both the *stages of prevention* and *targets of prevention* models offer useful typologies for categorizing various prevention strategies, they nevertheless conceptualize prevention largely on an individual—or, at best, a family—level. Efforts targeted at individuals or families—be they universal, selective, or indicated prevention efforts—tend to rely on educational tools (for example, brochures, videos, or public service announcements) with the goal of changing individual behavior. As Cohen and Swift (1999) point out, however, such an approach will have only limited success because most persistent, largescale problems are not solely due to individual behavior. Instead, a broader, multifaceted, but integrated approach is needed to optimize prevention. Cohen and Swift's (1999) prevention model, the *spectrum of prevention* (Figure 1), provides this comprehensive approach. Cohen developed the spectrum of prevention because he perceived that prevention practice is too often trivialized as simply re-education when, in fact, effective prevention for complex problems—such as IPV—requires an array of collaborative initiatives at multiple levels of social life: the individual, the community, and the society.

As we see in Figure 1, the spectrum of prevention is made up of six interrelated action levels. The first two are the most familiar to us, since they describe the most common types of prevention: strengthening individual knowledge and skills, and promoting community education. The third level of action, though, moves "beyond brochures" to educating providers—that is, those who hold positions in their fields of expertise that afford them opportunities to transmit information and skills and to motivate their clients, patients, and colleagues. In the case of IPV, this group includes health care professionals, social service workers, criminal justice personnel, victim advocates, and others who have contact with victims and/or abusers, as well as their family, friends, or co-workers.

The fourth action level of the spectrum—fostering coalitions and networks—recognizes that most complex problems are multidimensional, so that only addressing one or two dimensions will not likely resolve the problem: "Like a jigsaw puzzle, each piece is important, and only when put together does the picture become clear" (Cohen & Swift, 1999, p. 5). Moreover, agencies and groups that work together on a problem avoid duplicating effort and also utilize scarce resources more efficiently. The fifth and sixth action levels of the spectrum focus on organizational practices and public policy. Level 5 calls for an examination of organizational practices—for example, in the case of IPV, a careful analysis of how law enforcement and the courts have traditionally responded to victims and abusers—with the

Figure 1: The Spectrum of Prevention

Level 6: Influencing policy and legislation
Developing strategies to change laws and policies to influence outcomes
Example: Lobbying for legal system reforms that provide the option for alternatives to traditional criminal justice processing, such as restorative justice models

Level 5: Changing organizational practices
Adopting regulations and shaping norms to improve health and safety
Examples: Providing police officers, prosecutors, and judges with training on unconscious bias to reduce racial disparities in IPV arrests, prosecutions, and sentences; training police officers on how to identify the primary aggressor when responding to an IPV incident, so as to reduce dual arrests or the arrest of IPV victims who acted to defend themselves

Level 4: Fostering coalitions and networks
Bringing together groups and individuals for broader goals and greater impact
Example: Victim advocates, shelter staff, community leaders, law enforcement, health care providers, batterer treatment providers, and other stakeholder groups meet regularly to share information, provide one another with feedback about specific efforts, and collaborate on initiatives such as integrated services and public awareness campaigns

Level 3: Educating providers
Informing providers who will transmit skills and knowledge to others
Example: Training programs for various service providers (for instance, health care professionals, teachers, hair dressers) on how to recognize physical and psychological markers of potential IPV; how to broach the subject with a possible victim (such as a patient, student, parent, or client); and how to share helpful resources, thus increasing safety, reducing harm, and possibly preventing revictimization

Level 2: Promoting community education
Reaching groups of people with information and resources to promote health and safety
Example: Media campaigns (for instance, billboards, posters in grocery stores and public transport hubs, public service announcements on local television) to raise awareness of IPV and the resources available in the community to address it, with the goal of encouraging the public to recognize that IPV is a *community* issue, not just an *individual* issue, and therefore *all* community members have a responsibility to prevent it

Level 1: Strengthening individual knowledge and skills
Enhancing an individual's capability of preventing injury and promoting safety
Example: Teaching adolescents and young adults to recognize dating partners' controlling behaviors (for instance, telling them what to wear; monitoring their email, phones, and social media accounts) as warning signs of IPV, and teaching them skills for getting help, so they can increase their personal safety

Source: Reproduced from *Injury Prevention*, Cohen, L. & Swift, S. (1999), 5, 203–207, with permission from BMJ Publishing Group Ltd.

goal of identifying areas that require change in order to better promote prevention. But the model recognizes that sometimes organizational change is brought about only through legislative change, which is Level 6. In this volume, a variety of organizational and legislative changes regarding IPV prevention are analyzed and discussed (see Chapters 6, 7, and 8). Importantly, the spectrum of prevention emphasizes that changes at the organizational and policy levels are not conclusive or irrevocable. Rather, all changes must undergo continual evaluation to determine their prevention efficacy.

Organization of the book

This book incorporates elements of all three prevention models discussed here, examining IPV prevention efforts in terms of the stages of prevention and the targeted audiences these efforts were designed to influence. But perhaps more significantly, the chapters in this book, taken together, examine IPV prevention at all six action levels of the spectrum of prevention, and—through a collaboration of researchers, practitioners, and students—critically review the empirical evidence regarding effectiveness and identify gaps in knowledge with the ultimate goal of improving IPV prevention efficacy. As scholars of the battered women's movement have shown, until the 1960s and 1970s, IPV was viewed as a private issue that affected a small number of aberrant couples or families. Beginning in the 1960s and 1970s, feminist and civil rights activists successfully reframed IPV as a social problem and spearheaded numerous campaigns to raise public awareness, improve services for victims, and hold perpetrators accountable for their abusive behavior. But as mainstream feminism drew greater attention to the gendered nature of IPV—that is, that the vast majority of IPV victims are women and that men historically abused their intimate partners with impunity—the movement also came under increasing criticism from women of color, who argued that the emphasis on gender overlooks other forms of oppression, such as racism and social class inequality, which make some groups more vulnerable to all forms of violence (Ake & Arnold, 2018). The popular "universal-woman" argument—that is, that *all* women are at risk of becoming IPV victims—certainly contributed to mobilizing public support for victim services and legislative reforms, and to reducing the stigma associated with IPV victimization. But at the same time, this argument ignored intersectional inequalities of "race", ethnicity, social class, immigration status, age, sexual orientation, and ability, which affect not only victimization and perpetration risk, but also responses to both victims and perpetrators from the criminal justice system, social services, health care, and others (Durfee, 2018). Carlos A. Cuevas and Rebecca M. Cudmore examine these issues in Chapter 2, by discussing how various marginalized and underserved groups are differentially affected by IPV and the need for prevention efforts to recognize these differences and be designed in culturally responsive ways. Their focus is largely on "race", ethnicity, and immigration status—but as they point out, the principles of cultural competence in prevention can and should be extended to meet the unique needs of other marginalized communities. As noted earlier, one group at elevated risk for IPV is adolescents and young adults.

In Chapter 3, Ann L. Coker, Victoria L. Banyard, and Eileen A. Recktenwald discuss prevention strategies that were developed specifically for this population group. Coker and her colleagues review more than two decades of evaluation research on IPV and sexual violence prevention school- or campus-based programs in both high-income and low-to-middle-income countries. The evidence they examine shows that active bystanding interventions appear to have a significant impact on reducing IPV and sexual violence among adolescents and young adults—a promising outcome, indeed. They also provide a case study of a specific active bystander intervention program—Green Dot—which has been extensively evaluated in one US statewide randomized control trial. The authors emphasize the importance of a holistic approach to prevention programming that includes recognizing the links between IPV and other problems such as substance use, the need for prevention efforts to be continuous across developmental stages of youth into adulthood, and the importance of incorporating multiple significant others—for example, peers, parents, teachers, and coaches—into the prevention nexus.

Engaging multiple stakeholders in IPV prevention requires engaging men and boys. Just as the mainstream battered women's movement has been criticized for using the "universal-woman" argument to raise awareness of IPV and promote empathy for victims, it has also been criticized for implying—and, sometimes, explicitly stating—that *all* men are potential abusers. Although men are the majority of IPV perpetrators, most men do not perpetrate or condone IPV, and—as Richard M. Tolman, Tova B. Walsh, and Bethsaida Nieves argue in Chapter 4—men have a central and positive role to play in preventing IPV. Most IPV prevention programs for men have been at the tertiary stage in the form of batterer intervention programs (BIPs) mandated by the courts for men arrested for IPV. But Tolman and his colleagues focus on both primary and secondary prevention programs for men, looking at selected and universal efforts, as well as at strategies that cut across the prevention spectrum—from individual knowledge and skill building to community engagement and changing cultural norms. And significantly, these programs are not just *for* men and boys; many are developed and implemented *by* men and boys. Although few of these programs have yet to be rigorously evaluated, Tolman and his colleagues suggest the research questions that such evaluations should be designed to answer and the methods for undertaking this research. What is more certain, however, is the need for evidence-based strategies that directly engage men and boys in preventing IPV.

Chapter 5 focuses on what we identified earlier as the most common form of secondary prevention—screening—and more specifically, screening in health care settings. The efficacy of IPV screening in health care settings has been the subject of debate for well over a decade. Some researchers maintain that there is no unequivocal evidence to support universal IPV screening in health care settings (MacMillan et al., 2009), while others point to evidence that screening and brief interventions in health care settings result in increases in safety behaviors, which can reduce victimization (Macy et al., 2005). In the absence of any evidence that screening is harmful, and given the potential role health-providers might play in alleviating IPV, many observers argue that all female patients should receive information about IPV and victim services as a routine part of care. This would send the message that the physician's office or clinic is a safe place to discuss such problems, while also educating women about IPV and available assistance (Miller et al., 2018). In the US, routine IPV screening by health care providers along with brief counseling for those who screen positive have received increased attention in recent years—not only because many national medical organizations and agencies endorse these practices, but also because they are among the free preventive services mandated by the Affordable Care Act 2010. As Michele R. Decker, Elizabeth Miller, and Nancy Glass discuss in Chapter 5, there is still some resistance to universal screening and brief counseling interventions in clinical settings. Nevertheless, they present evidence collected through multiple methods on the efficacy of screening and clinical interventions, including data from interviews with IPV survivors. Decker and her colleagues also discuss several prevention efforts designed to overcome both clinicians' and patients' resistance to screening and disclosure, as well as using innovative technologies to improve survivors' access to health care and safety planning in especially difficult settings, such as refugee camps.

While health care has been the chief site for secondary prevention efforts, the criminal justice system has been at the center of tertiary prevention strategies, particularly in response to perpetration. Activists in the early battered women's movement documented how the police would frequently decline to arrest IPV perpetrators, treating IPV more as a nuisance than a serious crime. In the US, following the report of research findings that suggested arrest has a greater deterrent effect than counseling the perpetrator or having the perpetrator temporarily leave the premises (see Sherman & Berk, 1984), as well as several lawsuits against police departments for failing to protect IPV victims from their perpetrators (Ake & Arnold, 2018), standard responses to IPV calls by the police changed considerably. Most US jurisdictions enacted mandatory or preferred arrest policies for IPV cases, and states enacted laws permitting warrantless arrest for IPV misdemeanors. The Violence Against Women Act (VAWA) 1994 was the first federal law to recognize IPV as a crime, and provided substantial funding for improved and coordinated criminal justice responses to IPV (Ake & Arnold, 2018; Goodmark, 2012).

Although VAWA contained numerous provisions that expanded victim services and improved safety, its firm grounding on the premise that the most effective responses to IPV lie in the criminal justice system has also produced several unintended negative consequences. In Chapter 6, Lisa Y. Larance and Susan L. Miller discuss one of these consequences: the dramatic increase in arrests of women for IPV perpetration. As we noted previously, while men make up the majority of IPV perpetrators, some women do use force against their intimate partners—even though research indicates that they do so for different reasons to those of male perpetrators. Miller and Larance explore in greater detail women's motivations for using force in their intimate relationships, and challenge the appropriateness of criminalizing this behavior and of relying on criminal legal intervention for tertiary prevention. They suggest instead alternative prevention strategies that take into account the contextual factors that influence women's use of force against intimate partners.

Other researchers have pointed out that an emphasis on criminalizing IPV has had a disproportionately negative impact on communities of color, the poor, and immigrant communities, which are already subjected to over-policing and mass incarceration (Richie, 2012). Ironically, then, measures intended to increase victims' safety may make them more reluctant to call the police for help—particularly if they have personally had negative experiences with the police in the past, or they worry about how their partners will be treated if arrested (Richie, 2012). Consequently, some IPV researchers and advocates have called for alternatives to criminal legal responses to IPV. In Chapter 7, James Ptacek discusses the use of restorative justice as one potential alternative. As Ptacek notes, the empirical research evaluating restorative justice responses to IPV is limited; he draws on studies evaluating restorative justice applications to other types of offending in order to address questions regarding its prospects as a tertiary prevention strategy for IPV.

Leigh Goodmark continues this discussion in Chapter 8, arguing that the criminal legal system frequently fails to prevent IPV because it does not effectively control perpetrators' behavior or provide meaningful support to victims. She characterizes the criminal legal response as too narrow, and maintains that a broader conceptualization of justice—one that takes into account what justice actually means to IPV survivors—would likely produce more innovative responses to IPV, and therefore be more impactful in terms of prevention. Goodmark's argument, while provocative, needs to be tested empirically, particularly with regard to survivors' conceptualizations of and desires for justice.

Tertiary prevention strategies for women who have experienced IPV have taken many forms, including legal remedies such as civil protection orders and various types of counseling. Often these services are provided in a shelter setting. Domestic violence or battered women's shelters, first established in the early 1970s in England, Scotland, and the US, were designed to provide women fleeing abusive partners with safe, temporary housing. Over more than four decades, the services offered at shelters have expanded to include not only legal assistance and psychological counseling, but also (in some shelters) substance use treatment, help finding transitional or permanent housing, and job-seeking assistance. In Chapter 9, Claire M. Renzetti, Diane R. Follingstad, and Diane Fleet note that shelters are increasingly recognizing the need to offer residents programs that foster financial skills and economic empowerment, in light of research that shows financial instability and the threat or actual experience of poverty are among the factors that compel women to return to abusive partners. Renzetti and her colleagues discuss several economic empowerment programs that may improve not only financial, but also physical and mental health, outcomes for IPV survivors.

The book concludes with a discussion by Shamita Das Dasgupta (Chapter 10) on future directions for IPV prevention work and the research needed to further evaluate our prevention efforts. As Dasgupta argues, there is a need for sweeping, largescale cultural changes; smaller—but faster and more tangible—institutional changes that affect people's everyday lives; and changes in personal behavior. Dasgupta outlines the types of research needed to evaluate and support these various prevention efforts. She emphasizes, however, the imperative for researchers to include more people of color, immigrants, members of other marginalized groups, and people from the Global South in their study samples, so that the findings reflect the diverse attitudes and experiences of women and men throughout the world. She brings us full circle, in fact, with her wise counsel that prevention programming—regardless of its stage or level on the spectrum—must be context-specific and culturally sensitive.

References

Ake, J., & Arnold, G. (2018). A brief history of the anti-violence-against-women movements in the United States. In C.M. Renzetti, J.L. Edleson, & R.K. Bergen (Eds.), *Sourcebook on violence against women* (3rd Ed.) (pp. 3–25). Thousand Oaks, CA: Sage.

Barnett, O.W., Lee, C.Y., & Thelan, R. (1997). Gender differences in attributions of self defense and control in partner aggression. *Violence Against Women*, *3*(5), 462–481.

Black, M.C., Basile, K.C., Breiding, M.J., Smith, S.G., Walters, M.L., Merrick, M.T., et al. (2011). *The National Intimate Partner and Sexual Violence Survey (NISVS): 2010 summary report.* Atlanta, GA: National Center for Injury Prevention and Control, Centers for Disease Control and Prevention.

Bonomi, A.E., Anderson, M., Rivara, F.P., & Thompson, R.S. (2007). Health outcomes in women with physical and/or sexual intimate partner violence. *Journal of Women's Health*, *16*, 987–997.

Campbell, J.C. (2002). Health consequences of intimate partner violence. *The Lancet*, *359*(9314), 1331–1336.

Catalano, S. (2013). *Intimate partner violence: Attributes of victimization, 1993–2011.* Washington, DC: US Department of Justice, Bureau of Justice Statistics.

Cohen, L., & Swift, S. (1999). The spectrum of prevention: Developing a comprehensive approach to injury prevention. *Injury Prevention*, *5*, 203–207. Retrieved from: www.preventioninstitute.org.

Coker, A.L. (2007). Does physical intimate partner violence affect sexual health? A systematic review. *Trauma, Violence, & Abuse*, *8*, 148–177.

Devries, K.M., Mak, J.Y.T., Garcia-Moreno, C., Petzold, M., Child, J.C., Falder, G., et al. (2013). The global prevalence of intimate partner violence against women. *Science*, *340*, 1527–1528.

Dobash, R.P., Dobash, R.E., Cavanagh, K., & Lewis, R. (1998). Separate and intersection realities: A comparison of men's and women's accounts of violence against women. *Violence Against Women*, 4(4), 382–414.

Durfee, A. (2018). Intimate partner violence. In C.M. Renzetti, J.L. Edleson, & R.K. Bergen (Eds.), *Sourcebook on violence against women* (3rd Ed.) (pp. 109–134). Thousand Oaks, CA: Sage.

Duvvury, N., Callan, A., Carney, P., & Raghavendra, S. (2013). *Intimate partner violence: Economic costs and implications for growth and development*. The World Bank Group. Retrieved from: http://documents. worldbank.org/curated/en/412091468337843649/pdf/825320WP 0Intim00Box379862B00PUBLIC0.pdf.

Goodmark, L. (2012). *A troubled marriage: Domestic violence and the legal system*. New York: New York University Press.

Hamberger, L.K., & Guse, C.E.. (2002). Men's and women's use of intimate partner violence in clinical samples. *Violence Against Women*, 8(11), 1301–1331.

Hamby, S. (2018). Are women really as violent as men? The "gender symmetry" controversy. In C.M. Renzetti, J.L. Edleson, & R.K. Bergen (Eds.), *Sourcebook on violence against women* (3rd Ed.) (pp. 78–82). Thousand Oaks, CA: Sage.

Institute for Work and Health. (2015). *What do researchers mean by... primary, secondary and tertiary prevention?* Retrieved from: www.iwh. on.ca/wrmb/primary-secondary-and-tertiary-prevention.

MacMillan, H.L., Wathan, C.N., Jamieson, E., Boyle, M.H., Shannon, H.S., Ford-Gilboe, M., et al. (2009). Screening for intimate partner violence in health care settings: A randomized trial. *Journal of the American Medical Association, 302*, 493–501.

Macy, R.J., Nurius, P.S., Kernic, M.A., & Holt, V.L. (2005). Battered women's profiles associated with service help-seeking efforts: Illuminating opportunities for intervention. *Social Work Research, 29*(3), 137–150.

Menard, K.S., Anderson, A.L., & Godboldt, S.M. (2009). Gender differences in intimate partner recidivism: A 5-year follow-up. *Criminal Justice and Behavior, 36*(1), 61–76.

Meyer, E., & Post, L. (2013). Collateral intimate partner homicide. *SAGE Open, 3*(2). doi: 10.1177/2158244013484235.

Miller, E., Decker, M.R., & Glass, N. (2018). Innovative health care responses to violence against women. In C.M. Renzetti, J.L. Edleson, & R.K. Bergen (Eds.), *Sourcebook on violence against women* (3rd Ed.) (pp. 305–319). Thousand Oaks, CA: Sage.

Miller, S.L. (2001). The paradox of women arrested for domestic violence: Criminal justice professionals and service providers respond. *Violence Against Women, 7*(12), 1339–1376.

Rajan, M., & McCloskey, K.A. (2007). Victims of intimate partner violence: Arrest rates across recent studies. *Journal of Aggression, Maltreatment, & Trauma, 15*(3–4), 27–52.

Richie, B. (2012). *Arrested justice: Black women, violence, and America's prison nation.* New York: New York University Press.

Saltzman, L.E., Fanslow, J.E., McMahon, P.M., & Shelley, G.A. (1999). *Intimate partner violence surveillance: Uniform definitions and recommended data elements, version 1.0.* Atlanta, GA: Centers for Disease Control and Prevention.

Sherman, L.W., & Berk, R.A. (1984). The specific deterrent effects of arrest for domestic assault. *American Sociological Review, 49*(2), 261–272.

Small Arms Survey. (2016). *A gendered analysis of violent deaths.* Geneva, Switzerland: Small Arms Survey.

Smith, S. G., Fowler, K. A., & Niolon, P. H. (2014). Intimate partner homicide and corollary victims in 16 States: National Violent Death Reporting System, 2003–2009. *American Journal of Public Health, 104*(3), 461–466.

Stark, E.A. (2007). *Coercive control: How men entrap women in personal life.* New York: Oxford University Press.

Tjaden, P., & Thoennes, N. (2000). *Extent, nature, and consequences of intimate partner violence: Findings from the National Violence Against Women Survey.* Washington, DC: National Institute of Justice and Centers for Disease Control and Prevention.

World Health Organization (WHO). (2014). *Global status report on violence prevention, 2014.* Geneva, Switzerland: World Health Organization.

World Health Organization (WHO). (2016). *Fact sheet: Violence against women. Intimate partner violence.* Retrieved from: www.who.int/mediacentre/factsheets/fs239/en/.

TWO

Intimate Partner Violence Prevention Among Underserved and Understudied Groups: The Roles of Culture and Context

Carlos A. Cuevas and Rebecca M. Cudmore

Introduction

As the population of the US has grown and diversified over the past 20 years, cultural competency in violence prevention and service delivery has become increasingly vital. Census estimates suggest that the US population will be substantially more racially and ethnically diverse by 2060 (US Census Bureau, 2012). Specifically, the total minority population is projected to increase dramatically—from 37% in 2012 to 57% by 2060 (US Census Bureau, 2012). The US is projected to become a majority-minority country by 2043—meaning that, although non-Hispanic whites will still represent the largest group, no single group will make up the majority (US Census Bureau, 2012). It is thus problematic that mainstream prevention programs do not have a larger focus on cultural factors associated with the prevalence and consequences of intimate partner violence (IPV) within a growing population of people of color. In addition, many programs do not adapt their curricula to account for other aspects of culture, for example sexual orientation, gender identity, immigration status, age, or disability. It is no longer appropriate to assume that mainstream treatment and prevention work targeting the general population will be effective with increasingly diverse populations that have historically been understudied and are often underserved in the social services and prevention arenas.

Within the fields of mental health, trauma, and IPV, it is generally accepted that for interventions to be effective they must be specifically tailored to the needs, values, and experiences of the survivors they treat. There are many factors that can influence an individual's experience of IPV; these include perceptions of abuse, access to services, response to interventions, and perspectives and constraints on leaving a relationship. Specific cultural factors are also vital and include—but are not limited to—the role of family; language; faith; community; acculturation process; and gender roles. In order to provide effective prevention and reduce barriers, programs must recognize these factors and appropriately respond to them.

In recent years, violence research has begun to draw attention to underserved and understudied populations, such as people of color; lesbian, gay, bisexual, transgender, and queer (LGBTQ) individuals; the elderly; and disabled people. While there has been progress in this arena, continued efforts need to be made to highlight how different communities are affected by violence and what best methods can be used in prevention. This chapter will discuss how IPV prevention efforts can be adapted to recognize the experiences of underserved groups and develop culturally sensitive techniques and approaches. This chapter uses the traditional public health classification of prevention initiatives, which divides them into *primary*, *secondary*, and *tertiary* efforts (Caplan, 1964). In the context of IPV, *primary* prevention programs are long-ranging in scope and aim to change social norms about what kind of behavior is healthy in relationships (Mitchell & Anglin, 2009). *Secondary* prevention of IPV includes services and interventions to detect abuse, such as screening in the health care system. *Tertiary* prevention of IPV is an immediate response intended to prevent a severe outcome, and often includes protecting the safety needs of victims. Primary and secondary/tertiary prevention efforts will be explored in the context of how they can be tailored to account for the unique needs of diverse communities.

While the focus of this chapter will be on people of color, many of the prevention efforts highlighted can be customized to target other populations, including LGBTQ communities, the elderly, and disabled people. We will also note the importance of recognizing within-group heterogeneity in the process of modifying interventions to these individuals' unique needs. In addition, implications for international settings will be presented. Finally, the chapter will conclude with a discussion of future research directions and areas for growth within the field of violence prevention as it applies to people of color and other understudied populations.

Defining culture and cultural competency

One significant problem with much of the material on cultural competency is the dichotomous view of a culture that assumes an individual is either part of a particular culture or not (Warrier, 2009). This perspective ignores the complexities of culture and the reality that one can simultaneously inhabit certain elements of one or more cultural groups. Warrier (2009) thus suggests avoiding a "packaged picture" of culture and instead recognizing the dynamic nature of identities. A more appropriate conceptualization of culture requires recognizing that human identities include "race", ethnicity, gender, sexual orientation, immigration status, disability, age, and many other constructs. In addition, these constructs are interconnected and fluid, making them subject to change with the political and social structure. The starting point in prevention and treatment work with underserved groups is to assess how the individual interprets their culture, and then determining best practices (Warrier, 2009).

Although this chapter will review evaluations of prevention programs with specific cultural groups (usually based on racial or ethnic identity), it should not be assumed that these programs will generalize to all members of that particular racial or ethnic group. In addition, most evaluation literature is limited to Caucasian samples; when samples of people of color are included, other types of identity constructs—such as sexual orientation or disability—are not explored within the same study. Therefore, all research reviewed here should be considered a starting point for appreciating the differences among groups. Suggestions made here for culturally competent prevention work do not take a one-size-fits-all approach; instead, they encourage prevention programs to take a dynamic approach to working with underserved groups. This is not to say that adaptations to prevention efforts cannot be effective either with or for heterogeneous racial groups. Rather, it is to suggest that the nuance and diversity within groups needs to be considered in adaptation endeavors, so as to maximize the effectiveness of prevention approaches—without losing the ability to reach broader audiences.

Evaluating and adapting primary prevention efforts

Existing programs

The majority of current mainstream primary prevention efforts are school-based dating violence programs (Mitchell & Anglin, 2009). One prominent primary prevention program is Safe Dates, which aims to increase individuals' knowledge about dating violence by addressing gender roles and teaching conflict resolution (Foshee et al., 1996). Although there is strong evidence that Safe Dates is effective at changing attitudes about—and preventing—dating violence (Foshee et al., 2004), the program is limited in that it is normed on a primarily white population (Whitaker et al., 2006). Another school-based program is The Youth Relationships Project, an 18-session program that aims to prevent dating violence among adolescents. It focuses on positive alternatives to aggressive problem-solving styles and gender-based role expectations. Wolfe et al. (2003) conducted a rigorous evaluation of the program and found that, over the 2 years of the study, youth who participated were less abusive toward their significant others, and also reported less victimization by their partners. It should be noted that the majority of participants in the study (85%) were Caucasian.

Families for Safe Dates is an adaptation of Safe Dates that similarly recognizes the importance of involving families in preventing teen dating violence (Foshee et al., 2012). It aims to increase caregiver engagement in dating violence prevention efforts in order to reduce risk factors for teen dating violence. Foshee et al. (2012) conducted a randomized evaluation of the Families for Safe Dates program. Participants included randomly selected families that spoke English and had at least one 13- to 15-year-old living in the home. Roughly 80% of the study participants were Caucasian; the remaining participants were either Black or "other." Evaluation of the program showed that teens in the Families for Safe Dates treatment condition had a significantly lower rate of physical dating violence victimization between baseline and follow-up than those in the control group. In addition, the program was shown to be effective in promoting discussion about teen dating violence within the family context and decreasing teen acceptance of dating violence.

Bystander education and training programs are another form of primary prevention. These aim to change the social norms supporting partner violence and encourage potential bystanders to intervene with peers to prevent violence from occurring (Banyard, 2013; Centers for Disease Control and Prevention, 2016). Banyard (2011) indicates there are a number of interpersonal (for example, gender, personal beliefs, emotions) and contextual (for example, peer and family influences, characteristics of the situation) variables that impact an individual's decision to help in situations of abuse and violence. One study of barriers and facilitators of dating violence bystander action among high-school students found that bystanders who were able to relate to the victim (based either on their relationship to the victim or their personal experience with victimization) were more likely to intervene (Edwards et al., 2015). The authors therefore suggest that bystander prevention curricula must include material intended to increase victim empathy. Recent research suggests bystander programs significantly increase bystander interventions in situations of dating violence (Banyard et al., 2007; Miller et al., 2012; Moynihan et al., 2011; Moynihan et al., 2015). However, these studies have primarily included Caucasian samples, and none have analyzed the program's effectiveness in terms of "race" or ethnicity. An additional caveat is that most of these studies have evaluated specific programs (for example, Bringing in the Bystander) in randomized controlled trials. This leaves questions regarding the degree of generalizability of the findings and broader efficacy of the programs.

Two bystander-based prevention programs with promising evidence of effectiveness are Green Dot and Bringing in the Bystander (Centers for Disease Control and Prevention, 2016). Green Dot is designed to change social norms, increase positive bystander behavior, and reduce interpersonal violence (see also Chapter 3 in this book). Although the program was developed for college students, it has been adapted for high schools, communities, and military populations. The program curriculum focuses on two primary behaviors: reactive responses (for example, helping victims of sexual or dating violence), and proactive responses (for example, engaging safely with potential victims and offenders to reduce violence risk). One recent evaluation of the program utilized a stratified random sample of undergraduate students. The majority of participants in all conditions were Caucasian; 20–25% participants across conditions identifying as non-Caucasian. Results showed significantly lower violent victimization rates among students attending the campus with Green Dot than two comparison campuses (Coker et al., 2015). Analysis of the effectiveness of the program across racial groups was not conducted.

Bringing in the Bystander is a bystander prevention program for college students. It intends to teach the skills necessary for individuals to support victims of sexual violence, intervene in potentially violent situations, and speak out against language that perpetuates rape myths and sexism (Centers for Disease Control and Prevention, 2016). The program also aims to increase students' sense of responsibility for making change in their community related to sexual violence. Banyard et al. (2007) conducted an evaluation of the effectiveness of the Bringing in the Bystander program among undergraduate students. A little more than half of participants were female, and the majority (90.4%) were Caucasian. Participants were split into three groups: those who did not receive the intervention (control group), those who participated in the one-session prevention program, and those who participated in the three-session prevention program. The authors found that participants showed decreased acceptance of rape myths and increased knowledge of sexual violence over a 2-month follow-up period (Banyard et al., 2007). The study also found increased bystander efficacy, increased bystander behaviors, and increased prosocial bystander attitudes. In addition, those who participated in the longer intervention program (three sessions) displayed a greater increase in knowledge and positive bystander attitudes, as well as lower rape myth acceptance, than those in the shorter intervention program.

Several primary prevention efforts have been developed for, or evaluated specifically, with minority ethnic/racial groups. For instance, Weisz and Black (2001) evaluated a sexual assault and dating violence prevention program that targeted seventh-grade students at an urban school, the population of which was 99% African American. The program consisted of 12 sessions of 1.5 hours each over a 6-week period. Program sessions were primarily led by African American trainers and were separated by gender (with female groups led by female trainers and male groups led by male trainers). Group leaders developed the program to specifically address salient risk factors for low-income, inner-city, African American youth. The goals of the program included increased knowledge of adolescent dating violence and sexual assault, knowledge regarding available community resources, decreased tolerance for sexual and dating abuse, and increases in preventing or responding to sexual assault and dating violence. Findings from the evaluation revealed the program was effective at increasing knowledge and improving attitudes. The authors assert that cultural sensitivity contributed to the effectiveness of the program, as the material was designed to be culturally relevant and the program leaders were all either African American or experienced in working with African American adolescents. The authors also posit that program effectiveness may have been related to the positive relationships developed between youth and group leaders.

Belknap et al. (2013) conducted a pilot test of a theater prevention program with Mexican American youth. This program used two plays, performed for eighth-grade Latino students, to raise awareness of the dynamics and consequences of teen dating violence. The material for the plays was derived from prior qualitative studies regarding perceptions of dating relationships and violence among male and female Mexican American youth. The program aimed to increase participants' confidence and intention to resolve dating conflicts in a nonviolent manner. Findings from this study showed the theater program significantly decreased acceptance of teen dating violence, and increased participants' confidence in resolving conflicts nonviolently, as well as their intention to do so. Results also showed teens expressed a preference for approaching a same-gender parent or relative for help with teen dating violence. In addition, the theater intervention produced small but significant post-test results, mainly decreased acceptance of dating violence and increased intention to act—and confidence in acting—nonviolently.

Adapting primary prevention for underserved groups

Most primary prevention programs are based within the school and aim to engage adolescents. However, a number of other domains should also be included in primary prevention—particularly for underserved groups—including families, medical and health groups, and communities. In addition, a number of specific themes have emerged from work with underserved groups that may be relevant to incorporate into prevention programs.

Gender roles are important to assess in any culturally competent IPV prevention work. For instance, Latino youth have been shown to more strongly endorse traditional gender stereotypes (Black & Weisz, 2005; Ulloa et al., 2008). Latino cultures also promote male dominance (*machismo*) and female submission (*marianismo*) (Gonzalez-Guarda et al., 2013). Research consistently shows that, among Latinos, orientation toward Latino/a culture is associated with less gender egalitarianism (Ulloa et al., 2008). Therefore, youth from cultures that emphasize traditional gender roles might benefit from activities that result in female empowerment and encourage equality between the sexes (Black & Weisz, 2005). However, these programs have to be sensitive to findings suggesting that the risk of dating violence increases when transitions to egalitarian roles occur at different times between partners (Sanderson et al., 2004). Thus, female victims could actually be at *increased* risk for dating violence when they depart from the traditional female role within the home (Perilla et al., 1994). Prevention programs may benefit from helping victims bolster protective factors, such as family support, in order to mitigate this effect.

Prevention programs for males who hold traditional cultural values should be sensitive to these values, but emphasize the more respectful and less controlling behaviors of traditional male roles. In addition, mentoring programs can connect young men with male role models who display positive gender roles. Mentors can demonstrate that men do not lose respect by treating women as equals within a relationship.

Expectations from family members should also be considered when developing primary prevention programs. Youth with parents from other cultures can struggle to balance the pressure from parents not to date with the US media's sex-inundated images (Black & Weisz, 2005). Differences between youth and parents in levels of integration into US culture can also create potential discrepancies in expectations about dating. Attitudes and expectations about dating can carry over into adolescents' behaviors within intimate partner relationships. Therefore, these youths should be encouraged to discuss these challenges within prevention curricula (Williams et al., 2012). Parents can also be enlisted to help their children balance the challenges of conflicting cultural expectations about dating.

Evaluating and adapting secondary/tertiary prevention efforts

Existing programs

As with primary prevention programs, secondary/tertiary programs are available in schools. The Expect Respect program consists of support groups in the school environment for students who have already been involved in abusive dating relationships (victims and perpetrators), or have risk factors for dating violence (that is, a previous history of domestic violence or sexual abuse) (Ball et al., 2009). Support groups are provided separately for males and females, with same-gender leaders. The program curriculum spans 24 weeks and covers five units: developing group skills; choosing equality and respect; recognizing abusive behavior; learning skills for healthy relationships; and spreading the message against violence. One qualitative evaluation of the program found that youth reported learning new and healthy skills, increased knowledge about healthy relationships and warning signs of dating violence, and increased awareness of their own and others' abusive behaviors (Ball et al., 2009).

Another form of secondary/tertiary prevention includes screening procedures and interventions within the health care setting. Here, screening includes a clinician asking the patient several short, open-ended questions (sometimes as part of an assessment tool) in any setting in which health issues are addressed (for example, emergency departments; patient treatment centers; the offices of primary care and other health care practitioners) (de Boinville, 2013). The health care setting provides a unique opportunity for clinicians to assess for existing violence or risk of future violence. One reason for this is that clinicians typically meet with patients in a private, one-on-one setting, which gives patients the chance to disclose abuse without the perpetrator present (de Boinville, 2013). Screening and counseling for domestic violence was formally adopted in 1992 after the Joint Commission on the Accreditation of Healthcare Organizations (JCAHO) required emergency departments to have protocols in place for identifying and treating victims of domestic violence (JCAHO, 2009). Many health associations have since supported the adoption of screening protocols for domestic violence.

Over the years, however, there have been mixed findings about the effectiveness of such screening procedures, leading to medical groups making contradictory recommendations regarding their use. For instance, the 2004 United States Preventive Services Task Force (USPSTF) was unable to recommend routine screening procedures in medical settings, given insufficient evidence of their effectiveness (USPSTF, 2004). Since the publication of the USPSTF's findings in 2004, however, more studies have begun to examine the effectiveness of IPV screening efforts in medical settings. For instance, McCloskey et al. (2006) found that women who discussed IPV with a health care provider were more likely to utilize interventions and to leave the abusive relationship, and that exiting the abusive relationship was linked to improved physical health. In addition, other medical groups—such as the American College of Obstetricians and Gynecologists and the American Nursing Association—recommend routine screening among female patients for domestic violence (American College of Obstetricians and Gynecologists, 2007; Griffin & Koss, 2002). In 2012, the USPSTF updated its recommendation regarding the screening of women for IPV after reviewing studies published since its previous report in 2004 (Nelson et al., 2012). This review concluded that screening tools used in health care settings could accurately identify women experiencing IPV, and potentially reduce IPV and improve both physical and mental health outcomes (see also Chapter 5 in this book).

One of the most important secondary/tertiary prevention efforts has been the enactment of laws that criminalize the perpetration of IPV (Vera, 2013). Since the 1970s, the criminal justice system has become increasingly involved in preventing and criminalizing IPV (Indiana Coalition Against Domestic Violence, 2009). The primary focus of these efforts has been improving the legal response to IPV in order to protect victims and punish offenders (Fagan, 1996); this has included laws enabling IPV victims to place restraining orders on abusers, and incarceration of abusers. These criminal justice efforts can protect victims and communities from sources of further violence (Vera, 2013). McFarlane et al. (2004) found that female victims of IPV who applied and qualified for 2-year protection orders reported significantly lower levels of violence during the subsequent 18 months, whether or not they were actually granted the order of protection. The authors suggest that just the decision to reach out to authorities takes away the private nature of IPV and may contribute to its cessation. In addition, the application for a protective order may signify some measure of control in the victim's life and be a pronouncement that the victim will no longer tolerate the abuse (see also Chapter 7 and Chapter 8 in this book).

The emergence of domestic violence shelters in the 1970s is another example of tertiary IPV prevention. Given the increase in domestic violence services, there is surprisingly little research examining the impact of shelters on IPV, and existing research draws mixed conclusions. For instance, in a 1999 study, Dugan et al. found little evidence that domestic violence shelters affected female victimization rates. However, in a later study, they found that exposure reduction variables (such as domestic violence shelters) were linked to declines in intimate partner homicide (Dugan et al., 2001, 2003). Berk et al. (1986) collected data from female victims in Santa Barbara County, CA, in 1982 and 1983 to evaluate the impact of shelters on IPV. The results showed that, while the main effect of utilizing a shelter did not impact future victimizations, women who accessed shelters were at a lower risk of future victimization when they also engaged in other help-seeking behaviors (see Chapter 9 in this book).

There is a dearth of literature examining secondary/tertiary prevention programs for underserved populations. One study piloted a culturally specific risk-reduction intervention for Spanish-speaking Latinas with HIV, in response to the high overlap between HIV and IPV among Latinas (Davila et al., 2008). The intervention involved small-group discussions related to HIV and IPV decision making and skill building, with a focus on whether the participants were in "healthy and safe" relationships and whether they were keeping themselves "healthy and safe" (Davila et al., 2008, p. 221). The curriculum incorporated two relevant cultural concepts: *marianismo* (subordination of women) and *familismo* (the importance of family). Results from the pilot study showed a significant change in attitudes toward, and intention to perform, HIV-IPV risk reduction behaviors between pre-intervention and 1 month post-intervention. The authors suggest that, given the high prevalence and interrelatedness of HIV and IPV among women, HIV services should be expanded to include IPV education, screening, assessment, and referral to community resources.

Adapting secondary/tertiary prevention for underserved groups

Cultural traditions and values influence the ways in which victims respond to victimization, and can thus affect a victim's unique help-seeking profile (Sabina et al., 2012). While some research shows that people of color are less likely to disclose abuse to *formal* sources of support, other studies find that these groups tend to be less likely to disclose abuse to *informal* sources. This tells us that prevention efforts need to be sensitive to barriers to using both formal and informal resources, and how they can be used to diminish the risk of victimization. Specific cultural factors (such as level of integration into US culture) should therefore be considered to account for these differences.

For instance, in a national survey of Latino women living in the US, Sabina et al. (2012) found that victimized women with low levels of orientation to US culture (acculturation) were less likely to utilize formal help-seeking services (that is, police, courts, social service agencies, and medical care). The authors suggest that victimized Latinas with higher levels of acculturation are likely to have more knowledge of local legal, medical, and social services. This is also consistent with findings that traditional Latino culture emphasizes the importance of keeping personal problems within the family (Canive & Castillo, 1997; Fierros & Smith, 2006; Torres, 1998). In contrast, certain groups of people of color have shown lower rates of IPV disclosure to informal sources of support, such as family members or friends (Sylaska & Edwards, 2014). Low rates of disclosure to informal supports have been found among Latino women, Korean immigrant women, and African American women (Kim & Lee, 2011; Rizo & Macy, 2011). Therefore, secondary/tertiary efforts should be sensitive to the challenges of disclosure, and recognize that individuals from certain cultural groups may be more comfortable seeking help from alternative sources.

Having strong family expectations can be one specific challenge for victims of IPV disclosing abuse to their family, because it could be perceived as a source of shame (Gonzalez-Guarda et al., 2013). Different cultural groups also have unique expectations of privacy in their relationships, and may perceive IPV as a private matter between couples. For instance, in a qualitative study of African American youth's views of peer intervention in dating violence, Weisz and Black (2008) found that adolescents would be unlikely to intervene in a peer's abusive relationship because they view IPV as a private issue for that couple. These victims would likely have difficulty discussing IPV, and might perceive disclosure of abuse as a betrayal of the relationship. Although this may also be a challenge for white victims, there are particular concerns that are unique for African Americans; for instance, the authors suggest some African American IPV victims hesitate to report abuse because they believe it will reinforce negative stereotypes of their community.

It may be particularly difficult for some women to leave abusive relationships if they are from cultures in which being independent is not culturally accepted. It is thus important to develop and promote empowerment programs for underserved women that inform them of their rights and how to access services in the community (Gonzalez-Guarda et al., 2013). These programs should include lessons on finance and economics so that women can be financially independent, as perceived economic dependence is associated with a lower likelihood of leaving abusive relationships (Gonzalez-Guarda et al., 2013).

To make secondary/tertiary efforts more widely available to underserved groups, criminal justice agencies and community organizations that work with these populations should focus on making IPV prevention materials and resources available. This is particularly important for recent immigrants and those who do not speak English, who may not understand the nuances of the criminal justice system, how to disclose abuse, and what resources are available for assistance. One recent study found that Latino victims of teen dating violence indicated the primary reason for not seeking help was "not thinking of it" (Sabina et al., 2014), suggesting they did not think getting help was an option for what they were experiencing (although it was unclear if they had labeled the behavior as abusive). Therefore, agencies that do provide resources for victims of IPV should work on increasing knowledge about their services, particularly among underserved groups.

Programs and resources should also focus on schools, since they are a primary source of support for most children and adolescents. Schools can provide information to students about different avenues (both formal and informal) for disclosure and support. If students gain knowledge about the availability of support offered within the school, they may be more likely to formally disclose IPV. Students who do not feel comfortable seeking formal means of assistance may still benefit from encouragement to seek informal sources, such as friends and parents. However, school-based interventions should be seen as a starting point—not the sole source of prevention opportunities.

Training professionals who work with victims of IPV to be culturally competent is a complicated endeavor. As Warrier (2009) notes, "developing cultural competency work is not just about training. Training is the first component" (p. 83). Cultural competence is not developed through short, standardized presentations given to staff. Rather, staff develop cultural competency through practicing screening and intervening; examining personal and institutional bias; and understanding standardized best practices—in a way that also recognizes there is room for flexibility as practitioners encounter unique cultural practices. It is vital that those who provide secondary/tertiary prevention services attempt to understand the victim's own interpretation of their culture, rather than imposing a uniform version of it (Warrier, 2009).

Prevention research

Whitaker et al. (2006) conducted a systematic review of evaluation studies of IPV primary prevention programs published between 1990 and April 2003. Eight of the 11 studies reported the racial/ethnic makeup of their participants—six of which included primarily Caucasian participants and only two of which (Macgowan, 1997; Weisz & Black, 2001) included primarily people of color, mostly Black youth. Neither of the latter studies (Macgowan, 1997; Weisz & Black, 2001) were rated as having a high-quality design, based on various threats to validity (descriptions, sampling, measurement, analysis, interpretation of results). For instance, Weisz and Black (2001) evaluated a sexual assault and dating violence prevention program for urban youth. They used a quasi-experimental design, and the follow-up period was immediately after the intervention. Macgowan (1997) evaluated a

5-session relationship violence prevention program for middle-school youth. Although this study utilized a randomized experimental design, the follow-up period was short (one day after the intervention). Immediate follow-up periods are problematic because they do not allow sufficient time for participants to experience a significant change in attitudes or knowledge.

Murray and Graybeal (2007) conducted a similar review and identified only nine evaluation studies of IPV prevention since 1990—only one of which (McFarlane et al., 2000) was deemed methodologically acceptable (meeting at least 11 of the 15 methodological criteria) based on sampling procedures and study design. This study (McFarlane et al., 2000) examined pregnant Latina women. It found that victims who applied and qualified for a 2-year protection order reported significantly lower levels of violence during the 18-month follow-up period, regardless of whether the protection order was granted. As mentioned, Weisz and Black (2001) examined the impact of a sexual assault and dating violence prevention program among African American middle-school students. The results showed that the program was effective at increasing knowledge of and improving attitudes toward dating violence and sexual assault. However, Murray and Graybeal (2007) determined this study was only methodologically adequate[1], receiving a score of 10 out of 15 on the methodological criteria.

Results from these systematic reviews demonstrate the dearth of empirical research on IPV prevention more broadly, with even fewer studies examining IPV prevention programs for underserved populations. This signals the need for more rigorous evaluation of the impact of prevention programs, with particular attention to programs specifically designed for people of color. Evaluation studies of IPV prevention programs for underserved populations need to:

- Use representative sampling procedures and randomized group assignment;
- Be explicit about the criteria used to exclude participants from prevention programs;
- Utilize standardized, psychometrically sound assessment instruments;
- Employ assessment strategies that include multiple levels of variables, to avoid sole reliance on participant attitudes about violence behaviors; and
- Expand the scope of research studies to include societal-level variables that may be influenced by prevention programs (for

example, economic conditions, social norms, and oppression of groups of people) (Murray & Graybeal, 2007).

In addition to the challenges of conducting evaluation studies of mainstream IPV prevention programs, studies that recruit participants from underserved groups may have unique obstacles. For instance, women of color have been historically hesitant to participate in research (Keyzer et al., 2005; Umana-Taylor & Bamaca, 2004; Yanceya et al., 2006). In order to recruit people of color, researchers may need to spend more time discussing the purpose of the data and the steps that will be taken to protect confidentiality (Campbell & Adams, 2009). In addition, respected community leaders can help in recruiting participants and allaying fears regarding the study. Research shows that community leaders who have been involved in the study from the start are more likely to facilitate access to a difficult population (Israel et al., 2005; McIntyre, 2008; Viswanathan et al., 2004). Another method that has been particularly helpful in recruiting Latino populations is face-to-face strategies, personal networks, and snowball sampling (Keyzer et al., 2005; Klevens et al., 2007; Larkey et al., 2002; Lee et al., 1997; Lira et al., 1999; Umana-Taylor & Bamaca, 2004; Yancey et al., 2006).

Implications for international settings

Although this chapter focuses on IPV prevention among underserved and understudied groups in the US, its recommendations can be adapted for the broader international community. According to a World Health Organization (WHO) report, the majority of data on the effectiveness of primary prevention strategies for IPV comes from the US and other high-income countries (WHO/London School of Hygiene and Tropical Medicine, 2010). It is therefore essential for policy makers, practitioners, and other relevant stakeholders to adapt empirically based prevention programming to fit a range of settings, including nations with fewer resources.

Effective prevention programming in any setting should be based on research determining what unique cultural factors are predictive of IPV. Prevention programs should also focus on broader societal factors that influence IPV. Social norms may exist that promote IPV or uphold traditional gender roles that condone physical discipline within intimate partner relationships. Thus, implementing prevention programs may have limited impact without first addressing gender disparity. For instance, the WHO suggests creating national legislation and supportive policies that allow women equal rights within the political system, education, work, and social security.

In spite of the dearth of empirical evaluation of prevention strategies around the globe, there is evidence that school-based programs to prevent dating violence are effective in a variety of international settings (WHO/London School of Hygiene and Tropical Medicine, 2010). For instance, The Youth Relationship Project in Ontario, Canada aims to help 14–16-year-olds with histories of childhood maltreatment to develop non-abusive dating relationships (Wolfe et al., 2003). Results from a randomized controlled trial found that the program was effective in reducing incidents of physical and emotional abuse over a 16-month period. Although school-based programs are the only prevention programs the WHO considers to be effective in preventing IPV, these programs still require assessment in diverse settings, particularly settings with few resources and outside North America.

Conclusion

Individuals from underserved populations encounter a number of barriers to accessing IPV prevention programs. Information barriers, such as unfamiliarity with US culture, prevent some individuals from knowing what resources are available and how to access them. In addition, there are varying definitions of IPV across cultural groups. Some victims may not conceptualize the dynamics in their relationships as abusive, or understand that there are options for them to leave the relationship or find other ways to obtain personal safety (for example, protective orders or removal of the perpetrator). Relatedly, language barriers exist for non-English or limited-English speakers in the US; prevention efforts should therefore be accessible in a large variety of languages, especially in areas with large or growing non-English-speaking groups. Finally, social isolation can be a problem for individuals who have recently moved to the country and have limited social networks or informal support mechanisms. This can be a risk factor for getting involved in an abusive relationship, and a challenge for individuals attempting to leave an abusive relationship. People who leave a relationship also need to be assured that they will not face social isolation or lose their sense of cultural identity (Pennel & Kim, 2010).

A number of steps can be taken to overcome barriers to prevention programming in underserved communities. First, there should be increased collaboration between community groups representing underserved populations and those working in IPV prevention. One such model is the LA VIDA partnership—a collaboration of diverse organizations in Detroit, MI, that aims to assure the availability, accessibility, and utilization of culturally competent IPV prevention and support resources for Latino women and men in Southwest Detroit (Maciak et al., 1999). These organizations include Detroit community-based organizations, the Detroit Health Department, the University of Michigan, and the Centers for Disease Control and Prevention. LA VIDA utilizes a community-based approach that focuses on locally relevant and culturally competent approaches to IPV prevention within a particular minority ethnic community. LA VIDA ensures cultural competence by grounding its approach in the smallest unit of community identity—the local neighborhood, as opposed to the broader city- or county-wide community. This is in contrast to programs with a broader context, which may not represent the unique cultural needs of a particular community. The benefits of this approach are that it promotes local ownership of the problem and builds trust within the community, which in turn ensures strong and stable leadership from that community (Maciak et al., 1999).

Second, cultural competence should be required within prevention programs. As Warrier (2009) notes, cultural competency is more than merely a 1-to-2-hour standardized training. Rather, competency trainings must include real-life case studies, exercises that encourage critical thinking, and an assessment of the culture of the provider, intervention, or institution. All prevention and intervention work includes an intersection between the victim/client and the provider. Cultural competency trainings must therefore recognize the contribution the provider makes in that relationship, and the potential for bias they may bring to the therapeutic environment. To truly address the needs of the victim/client, providers should engage in continuous self-assessment and education where necessary.

Third, prevention efforts should incorporate relevant examples and case scenarios in their curricula so that participants are able to relate to the material (Williams et al., 2012). Although it is not possible to represent every cultural group, there needs to be more diverse representation. For instance, it should not be assumed that Latinos will readily relate to programs that use scenarios that portray Caucasian partnerships or are devoid of culturally salient components. If individuals fail to relate to the material, they may, in turn, feel their experience is undervalued because it is not recognized.

As discussed earlier, IPV prevention programs must not take a static view of culture; instead, they should recognize the heterogeneity of various groups and the fluid nature of cultural adaptation. All IPV prevention efforts should recognize multifaceted identities and be flexible in adapting programs to meet the needs of the individuals and communities they aim to serve. As the population of the US continues to grow and diversify, IPV prevention programs will need to adapt to meet the needs of this changing population.

Note

1. "Acceptable" was deemed the best, and "unacceptable" the worst. "Adequate" was in the middle.

References

American College of Obstetricians and Gynecologists. (2007). *Guidelines for women's health care: A resource manual* (3rd Ed.). Washington, DC: American College of Obstetricians and Gynecologists.

Ball, B., Kerig, P.K., & Rosenbluth, B. (2009). "Like a family but better because you can actually trust each other": The Expect Respect dating violence prevention program for at-risk youth. *Health Promotion Practice, 10*, 45S–58S. doi: 10.1177/1524839908322115.

Banyard, V.L. (2011). Who will help prevent sexual violence: Creating an ecological model of bystander intervention. *Psychology of Violence, 1*(3), 216–229.

Banyard, V.L. (2013). Go big or go home: Reaching for a more integrated view of violence prevention. *Psychology of Violence, 3*(2), 115–120. doi: 10.1037/a0032289.

Banyard, V.L., Moynihan, M.M., & Plante, E.G. (2007). Sexual violence prevention through bystander education: An experimental evaluation. *Journal of Community Psychology, 35*(4), 463-481. doi: 10.1002/jcop.20159.

Belknap, R.A., Haglund, K., Felzer, H., Pruszynski, J., & Schneider, J. (2013). A theater intervention to prevent teen dating violence for Mexican-American middle school students. *Journal of Adolescent Health, 53*(1), 62–67. doi: 10.1016/j.jadohealth.2013.02.006.

Berk, R.A., Newton, P.J., & Berk, S.F. (1986). What a difference a day makes: An empirical study of the impact of shelters for battered women. *Journal of Marriage and Family, 48*, 481–490.

Black, B.M., & Weisz, A.N. (2005). Dating violence: A qualitative analysis of Mexican American youths' views. *Journal of Ethnic & Cultural Diversity in Social Work, 13*(3), 69–90.

Campbell, R., & Adams, A.E. (2009). Why do rape survivors volunteer for face-to-face interviews? A meta-study of victims' reasons for and concerns about research participation. *Journal of Interpersonal Violence, 24*, 395–405.

Canive, J.M., & Castillo, D.T. (1997). Hispanic veterans diagnosed with PTSD: Assessment and treatment issues. *NC–PTSD Clinical Quarterly*, *71*, 12–14.

Caplan, G. (1964). *Principles of prevention psychiatry*. Oxford: Basic Books.

Centers for Disease Control and Prevention. (2016). *Sexual violence: Prevention strategies*. Retrieved from: www.cdc.gov/ violenceprevention/sexualviolence/prevention.html.

Coker, A.L., Fisher, B.S., Bush, H.M., Swan, S.C., Williams, C.M., Clear, E.R., & DeGue, S. (2015). Evaluation of the Green Dot Bystander Intervention to reduce interpersonal violence among college students across three campuses. *Violence Against Women*, *21*, 1507–1527. doi: 10.1177/1077801214545284.

Davila, Y.R., Bonilla, E., Gonzalez-Ramirez, D., Grinslade, S., & Villarruel, A.M. (2008). Pilot testing HIV and intimate partner violence prevention modules among Spanish-speaking Latinas. *JANAC: Journal of the Association of Nurses in AIDS Care*, *19*, 219–224.

de Boinville, M. (2013). *Screening for domestic violence in health care settings*. Washington, DC: Office of the Assistant Secretary for Planning and Evaluation.

Dugan, L., Nagin, D.S., & Rosenfeld, R. (1999). Explaining the decline in intimate partner homicide: The effects of changing domesticity, women's status, and domestic violence resources. *Homicide Studies*, *3*, 187–214.

Dugan, L., Nagin, D.S., & Rosenfeld, R. (2001). *Exposure reduction of backlash? The effects of domestic violence resources on intimate partner homicide, final report*. Washington, DC: US Department of Justice, National Institute of Justice.

Dugan, L., Nagin, D.S., & Rosenfeld, R. (2003). Exposure reduction or retaliation? The effects of domestic violence resources on intimate-partner homicide. *Law and Society Review*, *37*, 169–198.

Edwards, K.M., Rodenhizer-Stampfli, K.A., & Eckstein, R.P. (2015). Bystander action in situations of dating and sexual aggression: A mixed methodological study of high school youth. *Journal of Youth and Adolescence*, *44*, 2321–2336. doi: 10.1007/s10964-015-0307-z.

Fagan, J. (1996). *The criminalization of domestic violence: Promises and limits*. Washington, DC: US Department of Justice, National Institute of Justice.

Fierros, M., & Smith, C. (2006). The relevance of Hispanic culture to the treatment of a patient with posttraumatic stress disorder. *Psychiatry*, *3*, 49–56.

Foshee, V.A., Bauman, K.E., Ennett, S.T., Linder, G.F., Benefield, T., & Suchindran, C. (2004). Assessing the long-term effects of the Safe Dates Program and a booster in preventing and reducing adolescent dating violence victimization and perpetration. *American Journal of Public Health*, *94*, 619–624.

Foshee, V.A., Linder, G.F., Bauman, K.E., Langwick, S.A., & Arriaga, X.B. (1996). The Safe Dates Project: Theoretical basis, evaluation design, and selected baseline findings. *American Journal of Preventive Medicine*, *12.5*, 39–47.

Foshee, V.A., McNaughton Reyes, H.L., Ennett, S.T., Cance, J.D., Bauman, K.E., & Bowling, J.M. (2012). Assessing the effects of Families for Safe Dates, a family-based teen dating abuse prevention program. *Journal of Adolescent Health*, *51*, 349–356. doi: 10.1016/j.jadohealth.2011.12.029.

Gonzalez-Guarda, R.M., Cummings, A.M., Becerra, M., Fernandez, M.C., & Mesa, I. (2013). Needs and preferences for the prevention of intimate partner violence among Hispanics: A community's perspective. *Journal of Primary Prevention*, *34*, 221–235. doi: 10.1007/s10935-013-0312-5.

Griffin, M.P., & Koss, M.P. (2002). Clinical screening and intervention in cases of partner violence. *Online Journal of Issues in Nursing*, 7, 28–39.

Indiana Coalition Against Domestic Violence. (2009). *History of battered women's movement*. Retrieved from: www.icadvinc.org/what-is-domestic-violence/history-of-battered-womens-movement/.

Israel, B., Eng, E., Schulz, A.J., Parker, E.A., & Satcher, D. (2005). *Methods in community-based participatory research for health*. San Francisco, CA: Jossey-Bass.

JCAHO (Joint Commission on Accreditation of Healthcare Organizations) (2009). *Accreditation participation requirements*. Retrieved from: http://canainc.org/compendium/pdfs/D%201.%20JC%20Standards%202010.pdf.

Keyzer, J., Melnikow, J., Kuppermann, M., Birch, S., Kuenneth, C., Nuovo, J. et al. (2005). Recruitment strategies for minority participation: Challenges and cost lessons from the POWER interview. *Ethnicity & Disease*, *15*, 395–406.

Kim, J.Y., & Lee, J.H. (2011). Factors influencing help-seeking behavior among battered Korean women in intimate relationships. *Journal of Interpersonal Violence*, *26*, 2991–3012.

Klevens, J., Shelley, G., Clavel-Arcas, C., Barney, D.D., Tobar, C., Duran, E.S. et al. (2007). Latinos' perspectives and experiences with intimate partner violence. *Violence Against Women*, *13*, 141–158.

Larkey, L., Staten, L., Ritenbaugh, C., Hall, R., Buller, D., Bassford, T., & Altimari, B. (2002). Recruitment of Hispanic women to the Women's Health Initiative: The case of Embajado-ras in Arizona. *Controlled Clinical Trials*, *23*, 289–298.

Lee, R., McGinnis, K., Sallis, J., Castro, C., Chen, A., & Hickman, S. (1997). Active vs. passive methods of recruiting ethnic minority women to a health promotion program. *Annals of Behavioral Medicine*, *19*, 378–384.

Lira, L.R., Koss, M.P., & Russo, N.F. (1999). Mexican American women's definitions of rape and sexual abuse. *Hispanic Journal of Behavioral Sciences*, *21*, 236–265.

Macgowan, M.J. (1997). An evaluation of a dating violence prevention program for middle school students. *Violence and Victims*, *12*, 223–235.

Maciak, B.J., Guzman, R., Santiago, A., Villialobos, G., & Israel, B.A. (1999). Establishing LA VIDA: A community-based partnership to prevent intimate violence against Latino women. *Health Education & Behavior*, *26*, 821–840. doi: 10.1177/109019819902600606.

McCloskey, L.A., Lichter, E., Williams, C., Gerber, M., Wittenberg, E., & Ganz, M. (2006). Assessing intimate partner violence in health care settings leads to women's receipt of interventions and improved health. *Public Health Reports*, *121*, 436–444.

McFarlane, J., Malecha, A., Gist, J., Watson, K., Hall, I., & Smith, S. (2004). Protection orders and intimate partner violence: An 18-month study of 150 black, Hispanic, and white women. *American Journal of Public Health*, *94*, 613–618.

McFarlane, J., Soeken, K., & Wiist, W. (2000). An evaluation of interventions to decrease intimate partner violence to pregnant women. *Public Health Nursing, 17,* 443–451.

McIntyre, A. (2008). *Participatory action research*. Thousand Oaks, CA: Sage.

Miller, E., Tancredi, D.J., McCauley, H.L., Decker, M.R., Virata, M.C., Anderson, H.A. et al. (2012). "Coaching boys into men": A cluster-randomized controlled trial of a dating violence prevention program. *Journal of Adolescent Health*, *51*(5), 431–438. doi: 10.1016/j.jadohealth.2012.01.018.

Mitchell, C., & Anglin, D. (Eds.). (2009). *Intimate partner violence: A health-based perspective*. New York: Oxford University Press.

Moynihan, M.M., Banyard, V.L., Arnold, J.S., Eckstein, R.P., & Stapleton, J.G. (2011). Sisterhood may be powerful for reducing sexual and intimate partner violence: An evaluation of the Bringing in the Bystander in-person program with sorority members. *Violence Against Women*, *17*, 703–719. doi: 10.1177/1077801211409726.

Moynihan, M.M., Banyard, V.L., Cares, A.C., Potter, S.J., Williams, L.M., & Stapleton, J.G. (2015). Encouraging responses in sexual and relationship violence prevention: What program effects remain 1 year later? *Journal of Interpersonal Violence*, *30*, 110–132. doi: 10.1177/0886260514532719.

Murray, C.E., & Graybeal, J. (2007). Methodological review of intimate partner violence prevention research. *Journal of Interpersonal Violence*, *22*, 1250–1269. doi: 10.1177/0886260507304293.

Nelson, H.D., Bougatsos, C., & Blazina, I. (2012). Screening women for intimate partner violence: A systematic review to update the 2004 US Preventive Services Task Force recommendation. *Annals of Internal Medicine*, *156*, 796–808.

Pennel, J., & Kim, M. (2010). Opening conversations across cultural, gender, and generational divides: Family and community engagement to stop violence against women and children. In J. Ptacek (Ed.), *Restorative justice and violence against women* (pp. 177–192). New York: Oxford University Press.

Perilla, J.L., Bakerman, R., & Norris, F.H. (1994). Culture and domestic violence: The ecology of abused Latinas. *Violence and Victims*, *9*, 325–339.

Rizo, C.F., & Macy, R.J. (2011). Help seeking and barriers of Hispanic partner violence survivors: A systematic review of the literature. *Aggression and Violent Behavior*, *16*, 250–264.

Sabina, C., Cuevas, C.A., & Rodriguez, R.M. (2014). Who to turn to? Help-seeking in response to teen dating violence among Latinos. *Psychology of Violence*, *4*(3), 348–362.

Sabina, C., Cuevas, C.A., & Schally, J.L. (2012). The cultural influences on help-seeking among a national sample of victimized Latino women. *American Journal of Community Psychology*, *49*, 347–363. doi: 10.1007/s10464-011-9462-x.

Sanderson, M., Coker, A.L., Roberts, R.E., Tortolero, S.R., & Reininger, B.M. (2004). Acculturation, ethnic identity, and dating violence among Latino ninth-grade students. *Preventive Medicine: An International Journal Devoted to Practice and Theory*, *39*, 373–383.

Sylaska, K.M., & Edwards, K.M. (2014). Disclosure of intimate partner violence to informal social support network members: A review of the literature. *Trauma, Violence, & Abuse*, *15*, 3–21. doi: 10.1177/1524838013496335.

Torres, S. (1998). Intervening with battered Hispanic pregnant women. In J. Campbell (Ed.), *Empowering survivors of abuse: Health care for battered women and their children* (pp. 259–270). Thousand Oaks, CA: Sage.

Ulloa, E.C., Jaycox, L.H., Skinner, S.K., & Orsburn, M.M. (2008). Attitudes about violence and dating among Latino/a boys and girls. *Journal of Ethnic & Cultural Diversity in Social Work: Innovation in Theory, Research & Practice*, *17*, 157–176.

Umana-Taylor, A.J., & Bamaca, M. (2004). Conducting focus groups with Latino populations: Lessons from the field. *Family Relations*, *53*, 261–272.

US Census Bureau. (2012). US Census Bureau projections show a slower growing, older, more diverse nation a half century from now [Press release]. Retrieved from: www.census.gov/newsroom/releases/archives/population/cb12-243.html.

USPSTF (United States Preventive Services Task Force) (2004). Screening for family and intimate partner violence: Recommendation statement. *Annals of Family Medicine*, *2*, 156–160. doi: 10.1370/afm.128.

Vera, E.M. (2013). *The Oxford handbook of prevention in counseling psychology*. New York: Oxford University Press.

Viswanathan, M., Ammerman, A., Eng, E., Gartlehner, G., Lohr, K.N., Griffith, D. et al. (2004). *Community-based participatory research: Assessing the evidence. Summary, evidence/technology assessment: Number 99. AHRQ Publication Number 04–E022–1, August 2004*. Rockville, MD: Agency for Healthcare Research and Quality.

Warrier, S. (2009). Culture and cultural competency in addressing intimate partner violence. In C. Mitchell & D. Anglin (Eds.), *Intimate partner violence: A health-based perspective* (pp. 79–85). Oxford: Oxford University Press.

Weisz, A.N., & Black, B M. (2001). Evaluating a sexual assault and dating violence prevention program for urban youths. *Social Work Research*, *25*, 89–100.

Weisz, A.N., & Black, B.M. (2008). Peer intervention in dating violence: Beliefs of African-American middle school adolescents. *Journal of Ethnic & Cultural Diversity in Social Work*, *17*, 177–196.

Whitaker, D.J., Morrison, S., Lindquist, C., Hawkins, S.R., O'Neil, J.A., Nesius, A. M. et al. (2006). A critical reivew of interventions for the primary prevention of perpetration of partner violence. *Aggression and Violent Behavior*, *11*, 151–166. doi: 10.1016/j.avb.2005.07.007.

WHO (World Health Organization)/London School of Hygiene and Tropical Medicine. (2010). *Preventing intimate partner and sexual violence against women: Taking action and generating evidence*. Geneva: WHO.

Williams, L.R., Adams, H.L., & Altamirano, B.N. (2012). Mexican American adolescents' perceptions of dating violence programs: Recommendations for effective program design and implementation. *Qualitative Social Work*, *11*, 395–411. doi: 10.1177/1473325012438633.

Wolfe, D.A., Wekerle, C., Scott, K., Straatman, A.-L., Grasley, C., & Reitzel-Jaffe, D. (2003). Dating violence prevention with at-risk youth: A controlled outcome evaluation. *Journal of Consulting and Clinical Psychology*, *71*, 279–291.

Yancey, A., Ortega, A., & Kumanyika, S. (2006). Effective recruitment and retention of minority research participants. *Annual Review of Public Health*, *27*, 1–28.

THREE

Primary Intimate Partner Violence Prevention Programs for Adolescents and Young Adults

Ann L. Coker, Victoria L. Banyard, and
Eileen A. Recktenwald

Introduction

Several recent publications related to violence prevention have highlighted the importance of creating connections across silos in this work. Hamby and Grych (2013) describe empirical support for a *web of violence*, characterized by research showing that different forms of violence co-occur and many forms of violence share common risk and protective factors. Shared risk and protective factors across multiple violence forms could more comprehensively be addressed via common prevention strategies. The Centers for Disease Control and Prevention (CDC) publication, *Connecting the dots*, highlights how prevention efforts need to be more comprehensive—looking beyond single forms of violence and including the array of common risk and protective factors (Wilkins et al., 2014). Banyard (2013) and Hamby et al. (2016) expand notions of connecting the dots by highlighting ways in which violence prevention can benefit from making linkages across developmental moments in the lifespan, across researcher and practitioner silos of expertise, and across topic areas in health promotion (for example, considering the prevention of risky health behaviors in conjunction with violence prevention).

In this chapter, we will provide an overview of how "best" and "promising" practices for intimate partner violence (IPV) (dating violence) and sexual violence (SV) among adolescent and young adults exemplify elements of a "connecting the dots" approach, and suggest directions for future research and practice to further such an agenda. As an illustration of both the potential and challenges of this work, we provide a case example of one statewide initiative that aimed to put some of these key elements into practice. We pay particular attention to school settings, as they have powerful potential as contexts where such connected work can take place. What "dots" do we need to connect? The following are key components of a more comprehensive and connected approach to dating violence and sexual assault prevention:

- Creating prevention curricula that address more than one form of violence (DeGue et al., 2013; Hamby & Grych, 2013; Wilkins, 2014). This can be accomplished via curricula and tools that discuss more than one form of violence at a time, or by creating sequential and connected curricula that address different forms of violence.
- Creating links between prevention efforts across time and development (Banyard, 2013). We know that prevention efforts in schools go beyond academics by attending to aspects of social and emotional development; these efforts are widespread and effective in increasing prosocial behavior change for all ages, from elementary through high school (Durlak et al., 2011). We also know that exposure to prevention programing among youth is widespread (Finkelhor et al., 2014). To date, however, most prevention curricula focus on one age group or one school setting; little explicit connection is made between efforts in elementary, middle, or high school, or between high school and college campuses.
- Creating links across professional silos. Making linkages between researchers and practitioners, and across school and college settings and community-based centers for violence prevention, is essential. This is exemplified by growing discussions of "team science" approaches to solving complex problems in science; that is, using diverse teams from different disciplines and discussions of collaborative approaches to violence-specific research (Cheruvelil et al., 2014; Mulford & Blachman-Demner, 2013).
- Creating links beyond intimate partner violence topics to examine the intersection between intimate partner violence prevention and the prevention of other health problems. As described by Lippy

and DeGue (2016), college-based opportunities to prevent both sexual assaults and alcohol abuse among college students may be particularly appropriate and cost-effective prevention interventions, because sexual assaults and alcohol use or abuse frequently co-occur and both have negative impacts for students' academic success and their mental and physical health.

- Connecting across different relationships in a child or teen's social ecology. Prevention that has an impact consists of programs with elements that engage parents (Finkelhor et al., 2014; Foshee, et al., 2012) and the school building (Taylor et al., 2013). Both Finkelhor et al. (2014) and Foshee et al. (2012) observed additional impact for prevention programming that involves both students and parents or guardians; future prevention programming may likewise benefit from involving important others as part of students' social ecology. The recommendation for including a school's physical environment stems from findings reported by Taylor et al. (2013) in which a significant reduction in violence was observed with the intervention component of building-based restraining orders, reinforced by higher levels of faculty/security presence in safe/unsafe "hot spots" (as mapped by students relative to the control condition).

Creating connections in schools: Overview of programs with demonstrated efficacy to reduce IPV in adolescents

As Finkelhor et al. (2014) observed, exposure to violence prevention in educational settings may be relatively high; in a national survey, 55% of students reported receiving violence prevention programming in schools in the past year. Thus, while violence messaging may be high, the question remains: are implemented programs actually effective in reducing violence? This chapter reviews the evidence of program efficacy for sexual violence (SV) and IPV prevention, as well as to explore the challenges to implementing and adopting programs focusing on the primary prevention of sexual and dating violence, with a particular focus on school settings.Researchers at the CDC maintain a Violence Prevention Evidence Base tool (see www.preventviolence. info/evidence_base.aspx), which identifies published studies that have directly measured the effectiveness of interventions to prevent violence. From this tool, the following studies were identified as school-based programs, evaluated using rigorous analytic designs, and found to have efficacy to reduce IPV:

- Safe Dates (Foshee et al., 1998; 2004; 2005);
- Shifting Boundaries (Taylor et al., 2011; 2013);
- Fourth R: Strategies for Healthy Youth Relationships (Wolfe et al., 2003; 2009);
- Coaching Boys Into Men (Miller et al., 2012; 2013; 2014).

In different ways, these programs begin to exemplify a "connecting the dots" approach (Wilkins et al., 2014). In summarizing the small number of studies, and to use a rigorous analytic design when evaluating the effectiveness of violence prevention programming, we chose to report the available measures of effect and associated p value provided by authors. This means that effect sizes across studies cannot be easily compared because studies differed in the sample sizes and measures of effect used.

Safe Dates

Safe Dates is a middle-school curriculum consisting of 10 teacher-administered sessions of 45 minutes each, a student-led theater production, and a poster contest (Foshee et al., 2004). It includes parent education and some community-based capacity building. This program was evaluated using a randomized intervention design. Eighth-grade students who participated in Safe Dates had lower rates of physical and sexual dating violence perpetration at follow-up relative to students randomized to the control condition (Foshee et al., 2004). Additionally, significant program effects were found at all four follow-up periods on psychological, moderate physical, and sexual dating violence perpetration, and moderate physical dating violence victimization, while marginal effects were found on sexual victimization.

Safe Dates has also been adapted for implementation as a family-based teen dating abuse prevention program; 324 primary caregivers and teens (ages 13–15) were recruited into this US-based nationwide randomized intervention trial and completed follow-up interviews. The program had efficacy to reduce the onset of physical dating abuse victimization (p=.04); 3% (n=3) of teens in the treatment condition became victims of physical dating violence relative to 11% (n=14) of those in the control condition (Foshee et al., 2012). Safe Dates has additionally been adapted for adolescents exposed to domestic violence (Foshee et al., 2012).

Based on the established efficacy of Safe Dates, the Division of Violence Prevention at the CDC has recently embarked on a new initiative directed at teens and their families in approximately 45 schools in urban communities—Dating Matters: Strategies to Promote Healthy Teen Relationships (Tharp, 2012). Safe Dates was included as standard practice for this intervention trial of Dating Matters (available at www. vetoviolence.org). As described by Niolon et al. (2016), this multisite longitudinal cluster randomized controlled trial is being conducted through health department partnering with local middle schools in urban communities. Schools were randomized to Dating Matters, comprehensive violence prevention, or a "standard of care" intervention (based on Safe Dates). Teens are being recruited and followed through age 17 to determine the longer-term relative efficacy of Dating Matters on dating violence victimization and perpetration. At the time of going to press, findings had not yet been reported. These programs, then, "connect the dots" across several different types of interpersonal violence and involve both youth and their parents in complementary prevention training.

Teen Choices

Although Teen Choices was not included in the CDC Violence Prevention Evidence Base tool, this web-based intervention deserves mention here for its potential reach and feasibility. Teen Choices provides another example of a high-school-based dating violence intervention with the important "connecting the dots" innovations of providing web-based training in the form of a brief (3-session) multimedia (text, images, audio, and video) intervention, which is individually-tailored to students based on their teen dating violence (TDV) risk and their current dating status (Levesque, 2007). Thus, this program takes a developmental perspective by individually tailoring messages based on both adolescents' current dating status and prior TDV experience. In their recently completed cluster randomized trial of 20 high schools randomized to Teen Choices or a comparison condition, Levesque et al. (2016) observed significantly reduced odds of emotional and physical TDV victimization and perpetration over study follow-up at 6 and 12 months. Further, this intervention had efficacy for those with and without a past history of TDV. The efficacy of using web-based programs to reduce TDV in high-school settings may be particularly important, because schools are increasingly pressured to focus on raising academic achievement scores. This pressure then results in less class time for providing "non-academic" training, regardless of the intervention benefit.

The Fourth R: Strategies for Healthy Youth Relationships

While the first randomized intervention trial conducted on The Fourth R: Strategies for Healthy Youth Relationships (Wolfe et al., 2003) was not school-based, this work deserves mention here. This trial focused on dating violence prevention among at-risk youth, defined as those with histories of child maltreatment. In this community-based randomized intervention trial, 158 teenagers aged 14–16 were randomly assigned to a no-treatment control group or a preventive intervention group based on *The Fourth R*'s curriculum. This intervention consisted of education about healthy and abusive relationships, conflict resolution and communication skills, and social action activities. Over time, there was a significant reduction in physical dating violence perpetration (β_{TIME} -.008; $p<.01$) and emotional abuse (β_{TIME} -.006; $p<.05$) (Wolfe et al., 2003).

More recently, Wolfe and colleagues conducted a cluster randomized trial in which 1,722 students aged 14–15 from 20 public Canadian schools were recruited and randomized into either the control condition (without training or materials) or a 21-lesson healthy relationship curriculum delivered by teachers in ninth-grade health classes (Wolfe et al., 2009). Dating violence prevention was integrated with core lessons about healthy relationships, sexual health, and substance use prevention, using interactive exercises. All participants (52.8% of whom were female) were asked to self-report use of dating violence over the prior year. When participants were followed for 2.5 years, those in the control versus intervention condition had higher physical dating violence perpetration rates (9.8% versus 7.4%; $p=.05$), and the effect was greater for boys than girls. This program makes links across key issues in health promotion and violence prevention, in that interpersonal violence prevention is addressed in conjunction with addressing key issues of sexual health and substance use.

Shifting Boundaries

Shifting Boundaries is a middle-school (sixth to seventh grades) program with a classroom-based curriculum and school-building-based components (Taylor et al., 2013). The classroom intervention included a 6-session curriculum emphasizing the laws and consequences for perpetrators of dating violence and sexual harassment, gender roles, and healthy relationships, while the building-based intervention included "building-based restraining orders, higher levels of faculty/security presence in safe/unsafe 'hot spots' mapped by students, and posters to increase violence awareness and reporting" (Taylor et al., 2013, p. 64).

A large multilevel, experimental, randomized intervention trial was conducted among 30 public middle schools in New York City to evaluate the classroom-based and building-based components of the program alone or in combination relative to a no-treatment control condition. Over 2,500 students from 117 sixth- and seventh-grade classes were randomized to receive one of four conditions in this trial. Students were surveyed at baseline and up to 6-months post-intervention. The frequency and prevalence of peer or dating partner SV victimization and perpetration were lower in the building-only ($p<.05$) and the combined classroom and building groups ($p<.01$) relative to the control condition, yet the dating violence frequency did not differ between the classroom-only and control conditions. Shifting Boundaries appears to be particularly effective for reducing peer violence rather than dating violence perpetration; in this way, it provides an example of prevention work that seeks to address multiple forms of violence (Taylor et al., 2013). This program exemplifies using prevention tools that connect across the community ecology to involve teachers and policy change, rather than just education of individual students.

Coaching Boys Into Men (CBIM)

CBIM is a curriculum-based dating violence prevention program designed specifically for student athletes and administered by athletic coaches (see curriculum: www.coachescorner.org/). Miller et al. (2012) evaluated the application of this curriculum using a cluster randomized trial in 16 New York City public high schools (as the unit of cluster randomization), recruiting 1,513 male athletes in grades 9–11 and surveying them over time. At 3-month follow-up, no significant differences in any "abusive behavior" perpetration were observed in the intervention versus control condition; however, those in the intervention arm did report greater intention to intervene with peers (to engage in positive bystander behaviors) and greater recognition of abusive behaviors. At 12-month follow-up (Miller et al., 2013), perpetration of dating violence was significantly lower among male athletes in the CBIM intervention relative to those in the control condition (intervention effect of -0.15; $p<.05$). The intervention was also associated with a reduction of negative bystander behaviors (such as laughing or going along with peers' abusive behaviors). This program, like Shifting Boundaries, capitalizes on making connections across community relationships by involving coaches as trainers, teachers, and role models for youth. CBIM has now been implemented and evaluated as effective in changing violence rates with cricket team members in India (Miller et al., 2014; see also Chapter 4 in this book).

Global Programs with Evidence of IPV or SV Prevention Potential

Lundgren and Amin (2015) provided a review of effective adolescent sexual and partner violence prevention approaches using a global focus. Two studies, set in low- or middle-income countries and using experimental evaluation designs, deserve mention here.

No Means No Worldwide (Sinclair et al., 2013) is a standardized 6-week self-defense program that was evaluated using a non-randomized census-based longitudinal design. Female students from 10 participating high schools in Nairobi, Kenya, were recruited and followed for 10 months by condition: No Means No Worldwide in eight intervention schools (n=402), and a life-skills class in two control schools (n=120). Over follow-up, the incidence of sexual assault decreased significantly ($p < .001$)—from 24.6% to 9.2% in the intervention condition—while the incidence rates in the control condition did not change (24.2% to 23.1%; $p=.10$). The intervention training appeared to be the mechanism for this reduction in sexual assaults, given that more than half of those in the intervention reported using self-defense skills to avert a sexual assault after the training.

Findings reported by Senn and Forrest (2015) from their rigorously evaluated randomized clinical trial of Enhanced Assess, Acknowledge, Act Sexual Assault Resistance, set in three Canadian universities, provide additional support for feminist-based self-defense as an effective primary prevention tool. Self-defense rape resistance risk-reduction efforts are "connecting the dots" in prevention by capitalizing on protective factors that can be disseminated in diverse cultures and community contexts.

The second global study to highlight, Stepping Stones, was conducted not in an educational setting but in 70 villages in the Eastern Cape province of South Africa. This cluster randomized controlled trial evaluated Stepping Stones, a 50-hour program aimed at improving sexual health by using "participatory learning approaches to build knowledge, risk awareness, and communication skills and to stimulate critical reflection" (Jewkes et al., 2008, p. 391). The majority of the 1,360 men and 1,416 women (aged 15–26) recruited into this study were currently attending school. The 70 villages were randomized to receive either Stepping Stones or a 3-hour intervention on HIV and safer sex (control condition). While the intervention aimed to reduce HIV incidence, researchers found a significant reduction in young men reporting perpetration of IPV across the 2-year follow-up (Jewkes et al., 2008). This study further exemplifies "connecting the dots" by combining shared risk and protective factors across not only violence forms but also related health outcomes (for example, sexually transmitted infection and forms of IPV).

Summary of secondary school sexual or partner violence prevention programing

A number of themes can be identified across the programs highlighted in the previous section. All addressed school-aged students, and all involved multipronged or multisession efforts. All used some sort of interconnected approach (involving either connecting teens to parents/family or coaches, schoolwide interventions, or connecting dating violence prevention messages to other health promotion and prevention messages that teens receive). The potential for such interconnections is perhaps more easily done in secondary school settings, where students have more contact with teachers and parents, spend more time in classrooms where prevention messages can be delivered, and spend time in school buildings that are more geographically bounded for schoolwide interventions than other settings (such as communities or college campuses). Other educational settings (college campuses in particular) have made many efforts to prevent IPV and sexual assault, but their rigorous evaluation—see, for example, reviews by Anderson and Whiston (2005), and Casey and Lindhorst (2009) —and use of more comprehensive strategies like the aforementioned programs have trailed behind, and college settings are not highlighted in the CDC review.

Bystander interventions as a point of connection for prevention programming

While not yet fully an evidence-based practice for primary prevention of violence, another set of prevention programs exemplifies the potential for creating connections thematically across prevention efforts—bystander interventions. The CDC highlighted bystander interventions as "promising" for college-based programs. Such interventions attempt to involve all members of a community to change a culture that may silently support the use of violence. The community may be defined as a college campus, a middle or high school, a sports team, or a fraternity or sorority. Because bystander interventions approach participants not as potential victims or perpetrators but as potential allies, both defensiveness and victim-blaming attitudes are reduced (Banyard et al., 2004; Berkowitz, 2002). Bystander violence prevention programs share a common philosophy that all members of the community have a role in shifting social norms to prevent violence. The ultimate goal is to educate the community to recognize situations that promote violence and to safely and effectively intervene (Moynihan & Banyard, 2008).

From a "connecting the dots" perspective, bystander actions have already been used in other public health areas—such as drunk-driving campaigns (Potter, 2016) —and thus can connect our violence work to other health initiatives. Further, bystander actions can be applied to a variety of forms of violence, including bullying, IPV, and sexual assault. Bystander intervention research has also considered connections across layers of the social ecology for prevention work. For example, McMahon (2015a) provided a comprehensive research agenda, outlining key areas of campus environments and their potential influences on prevention intervention. Through her review of the bystander behavior literature, McMahon identified several themes affecting bystander (helping) behaviors toward violence prevention: social norms; sense of community; prosocial modeling; policies and accountability cues; and physical environment. The influence of campus physical environment on either violence rates or bystander intervention effectiveness was highlighted as one of the least researched areas, which may have great importance for campuses and their host communities. Concrete examples of a campus's physical environment that may affect either a lack of bystander behaviors (due to increased apathy) or increased violence include a greater proximity or density of bars, liquor stores, or "gentlemen's clubs." Thus, a focus on bystander action may also help expand prevention lenses beyond individuals.

Mentors in Violence Prevention (MVP)

MVP was one of the earliest bystander programs; it targeted student athletes and leaders, and has been widely adopted on college campuses. MVP initially focused on men to encourage leadership on issues of gender violence, bullying, and school violence (Katz, 1995), but now includes training for men and women in different age groups and social settings.

Banyard et al. (2007) provided the first empirical evidence of the effectiveness of a bystander approach in a study of college students attending a rural public college campus in the northeast of the US. Participation in a bystander intervention focusing on SV improved students' attitudes around rape myths, as well as increasing their bystander efficacy and expressed intent to take action to help others before, during, or after there was risk for an assault. Researchers found preliminary evidence that students who received the bystander training engaged in a greater variety of bystander actions post-training than those in the control group. These results have been supported by additional studies using select groups of students (leaders, athletes, fraternity and sorority members) and in a multicampus study (Banyard et al., 2009; Cares et al., 2015; Moynihan et al., 2015).

The Men's Project

A novel program designed by Gidycz et al. (2011) provided early evidence of bystander program efficacy to reduce sexual aggression among college men. This program included The Men's Project (Berkowitz, 2002) as part of the Ohio University's Community Programming Initiative, which included a risk-reduction program for women. Students in first-year residence halls were randomly assigned to the treatment or control groups. College men and women in the treatment groups were invited to participate in either prevention or risk-reduction programs. A total of 635 college students were recruited over two years (56% response rate), and surveys were administered before the intervention and at 4 and 7 months after the intervention. At 4-month follow-up, men receiving bystander training reported lower sexually aggressive behaviors (1.5%) relative to men in the control group (6.7%; $p<.05$), though no differences in aggressive behaviors were noted at 7-month follow-up. This research provided the first direct evidence for the efficacy of bystander training to reduce self-reported sexual aggression over time among men attending college.

Green Dot

The Green Dot program, designed by Dr. Dorothy Edwards (see www.livethegreendot.com), also uses a bystander-based approach to address interpersonal or "power-based" violence by seeking to change social norms through increasing positive bystander behaviors. This program differs from other bystander programming in that it adds targeted selection and bystander training of "popular opinion leaders" (POLs), also known as "early adopters." These students are selected as POLs because of their influence in their own communities and their ability and potential to diffuse the bystander training rapidly throughout their spheres of influence.

Prior research indicated that college students who received intensive Green Dot bystander training and were recruited as POLs on their campus had lower SV acceptance scores and more positive or proactive bystander behaviors than students on the same campus who did not receive the training (Coker et al., 2011). Furthermore, two recent studies provide data to suggest that violence rates are lower on the campus with Green Dot training than similarly sized public universities with no bystander program (Coker et al., 2015; 2016). For the academic year 2009–10, students attending the Green Dot campus (n=2,768) had lower rates of unwanted sexual victimization, stalking, sexual harassment, and psychological dating violence victimization and perpetration than students attending the comparison campuses (n=4,258) (Coker et al., 2015). When freshmen on these same three college campuses were surveyed over 4 years (2010–13), specific rates of interpersonal violence perpetration were 21% lower on the intervention versus comparison campuses ($p<.01$). Similarly, rates of violence were lower on the intervention campus ($p<0.01$) for unwanted sexual victimization, sexual harassment, stalking, and psychological dating violence victimization and perpetration (Coker et al., 2016).

Green Dot is an example of using prevention tools that connect across related forms of violence. Palm Reed et al. (2015) also provided experimental data indicating program efficacy across two forms of violence. Following students over time, they found that bystander programs focusing on both sexual assault and dating violence increased bystander efficacy relative to traditional psychoeducation programs.

Peer-facilitated bystander training

The influence of peers in risk-taking behaviors—including violence—has been well described (Schwartz & DeKeseredy, 2008). Acknowledging this influence, Elias-Lambert and Black (2015) evaluated the effectiveness of a peer-facilitated bystander training to reduce SV. A quasi-experimental design with pre-, post- and follow-up surveys was used among two groups of university males at low and high risk of sexually coercive behaviors. When compared with controls, those receiving peer-facilitated bystander training had significant reductions in both rape myth acceptance and self-reported sexually coercive behaviors. This was particularly the case among high risk (fraternity) men. Again using the peer impact theme, Senn and Forrest (2015) found peer educators to be effective in delivering bystander sexual assault prevention programming. Using a quasi-experimental design with online surveying over three time points up to 4 months, the peer training increased bystander efficacy, intentions, and proactive bystander behaviors in both male and female college students. Prevention researchers have also advocated involving adolescents with researchers and practitioners in all phases of violence prevention programming, including development, implementation, and evaluation (Edwards et al., 2016).

New methods for delivering bystander training

Bystander interventions are now taking place on campuses using a variety of methods. Both the iScream theater at Rutgers University, NJ (McMahon et al., 2015b) and InterACT at the University of California, CA (Ahrens et al., 2011) use interactive theater to model prosocial bystander actions to prevent sexual assault. Kleinsasser et al. (2015) described a successful online intervention focused on bystander action. Using a randomized controlled trial, Salazar et al. (2014) provided evidence indicating effectiveness of the online bystander-based training *RealConsent*, relative to a web-based general health promotion program to reduce SV perpetration and change SV-supporting knowledge and attitudes. Campuses have also successfully used social marketing campaigns that promote social norms and positive bystander actions (Potter et al., 2011).

To summarize the findings considered so far, much of the strongest evidence base for sexual assault and IPV prevention comes from secondary schools, while the majority of evaluation studies of bystander interventions have been on college campuses. Programs like Safe Dates showcase the need for multipronged efforts that extend over time and involve not only classroom curricula for students but also training for parents. Classroom-based training models (CBTM) show ways to leverage out-of-school time to train and engage key role models to promote prevention and Shifting Boundaries reminds us that we need to look beyond training individuals toward changing school and community policies in order to promote the actions we wish to see and deliver change through innovative methods such as theater, online programs, or social marketing campaigns. Research on college campuses shows the promise of bystander interventions and to transmit messages to students beyond in-person workshops.

What is needed next is an integration of these lessons across different types of educational settings to create an interconnected prevention agenda (Banyard, 2013; 2014). For example, bystander work to prevent SV and IPV—which has mostly taken place on college campuses—is now being brought to high schools, where programs like MVP and CBTM are working successfully with boys and also, in the case of MVP, with girls (Katz et al., 2011). This work is connecting with bullying prevention, which was centered in elementary and middle school settings, and has used a bystander approach for many years (Polanin et al., 2012). Lessons from secondary schools regarding the need to attend to the social ecology of students—to engage not only individuals but also mentors, coaches, parents, and schools themselves—should be brought to college campuses (McMahon, 2015a).

The goal of such an interconnected prevention agenda focuses on bridging knowledge and practices across educational settings, from elementary school through college. Differences in developmental stages over this wide age range would require adaptations of prevention programming to best fit the specific age of those trained. Based on foundational work by Hamby and Grych (2013), who discussed the ways in which violence prevention itself is overly siloed and could benefit from better integration across types of violence addressed, the agenda we describe here seeks to link prevention efforts in schools across time. If preventionists who work in school settings could better connect their work—building on a set of mutually reinforcing messages across educational contexts—we might be more successful in achieving the prevention of SV and IPV at all ages, which has eluded us so far. One way to describe such an agenda is through a case study that illustrates many of the features of a "connecting the dots" approach—the use of prevention tools that connect across forms of violence, involve more than individuals, connect across educational settings, and are grounded in researcher–practitioner collaborations. In the next section we present a case example of Green Dot, as adapted from the original design for a college campus to a high school setting. The project involved a collaboration between prevention specialists (working in community agencies that work across the lifespan in a variety of educational settings) and researchers (interested in documenting the program's effectiveness). The elements of an interconnected agenda highlighted in this case study are:

- Adapting prior Green Dot training designed for college settings with direct involvement with the developer (Dr. Dorothy Edwards) ("developmentally informed").
- Involving a multidisciplinary team of practitioners (rape crisis center educators and our state Department of Public Health); school administrators and staff; the Green Dot developer and training team; and a diverse university-based research team ("breaking down silos").
- Tailoring Green Dot training to address co-occurring forms of interpersonal violence experienced or used by adolescents, and measuring these outcomes in the evaluation ("co-occurrence of violence forms").

A case study of implementing and evaluating a statewide bystander program intervention

In 1995, with the first passage of the Violence Against Women Act (VAWA), funds were set aside to address awareness education regarding the scope of SV—a problem that had, until then, only been discussed in whispers. Previously, all federal sexual assault funding had been earmarked for victim assistance. These new funds were titled Rape Prevention Education (RPE) funds. For 10 years, Kentucky's regional rape crisis centers used these funds to engage middle and high schools, working hard to develop relationships, presenting wherever and whenever the schools asked, and focusing on where the highest risk for victimization existed and where dating behavior was beginning. Practitioners in Kentucky's rape crisis centers were coming to understand that potential victims were at greater risk from persons known to them than strangers. Awareness was intended to reduce the risk of sexual victimization, place the onus of protection on the potential victim, and even teach children how to avoid becoming a victim (during curricula such as Stranger Danger and Good Touch Bad Touch).

In 2005, with the third reauthorization of VAWA, the allowable uses of RPE funds changed from awareness to primary prevention. Concurrently, oversight of the funds moved from the Department of Justice to the CDC. In every state, the funding was now disseminated by departments for public health, providing opportunities to connect violence prevention with other public health issues. SV was newly identified as a public health issue to those providing victim assistance, with the message that it was possible to prevent SV before it happened. CDC required those receiving RPE funds to focus efforts on primary prevention of SV. This required a significant shift in thinking, actions, training, and ultimately reorganization of Kentucky's service delivery system to continue to provide sexual assault services (tertiary prevention), while adding staff with a different skillset to provide primary prevention. While rape crisis centers were unsure how to prevent SV—since there were no proven prevention strategies—they knew that during their 40-year engagement in the antiviolence movement the number of men, women, and children SV victims had steadily risen. The centers were unsure whether this was due to violence increasing or awareness efforts resulting in more disclosure and help-seeking. Regardless, if there was even a chance of reducing the number of victims, they were strongly motivated to develop statewide primary prevention program capacity. Historically, each of the 13 rape crisis centers had independently developed awareness education programs, borrowing from "programs in a box" and producing presentations intended to be age-appropriate and informative, yet not too explicit. Many schools would not allow the word "rape" to be used in the classroom, so educators became very creative and innovative to get their point across. Since no single program was being used statewide, presentations were not evaluated, and success was measured anecdotally by the number of students who disclosed abuse to the presenter.

In 2005 there was some discussion with CDC regarding RPE funds becoming competitive and funds only being awarded to states running primary prevention programs. While centers knew that awareness was an important part of primary prevention, they also knew they could not compete with other states because they were not the experts in this form of prevention. They had neither the language nor the public health lens to see sexual assault as preventable. Many of these experts were getting ready to retire, having delivered services for at least 25 years yet never witnessing a decrease in the number of victims or need for services that they hoped would be their legacy. They decided to group together, direct all RPE funds to just one project, and implement this project statewide— "connecting the dots" across one state—with the intention of becoming a primary prevention programming network in partnership with other public health practitioners.

These advocates began by making connections between research and practice, health promotion and practice, and across school settings. From 2005–08, using special grant funds from the CDC, the Kentucky Association of Sexual Assault Programs (KASAP)—a coalition of 13 rape crisis centers and the Cabinet for Health and Family Services—conducted the Enhancing and Making Programs and Outcomes Work to End Rape (EMPOWER) Project, intending to develop prevention capacity and find an effective strategy that could be implemented statewide. After drafting and discarding 11 lists of candidates to sit on a State Prevention Team (SPT), they invited professionals who were in positions of authority to create social change and who had a working knowledge of primary prevention in other fields, such as HIV, tobacco, and safety (seat belts, infant car seats, and so on). This involved "connecting the dots" across different issues in health prevention to pool best practices and lessons learned. Using a framework introduced to the SPT, by CDC's Injury Prevention branch, participating in an EMPOWER project called Getting to Outcomes (GTO)—originally designed for substance abuse prevention (Wandersman et al., 2004)—and employing the Empowerment Evaluation principles (Fetterman, 1994), the SPT designed a 14-goal Statewide Plan to Prevent the Perpetration of Sexual Violence.

Connections were then made across school settings. One of the goals discussed in the GTO process was testing the effectiveness of the Green Dot strategy. As mentioned earlier, this program was originally developed to promote bystander action among college students. However, the SPT was interested in applying it to high-school students: an at-risk population with whom the centers already enjoyed a good relationship. Green Dot was chosen following a review of six different curricula because it was the most in line with Nation et al.'s (2003) principles of prevention. Furthermore, the SPT was aware that Green Dot had produced some promising evidence indicating behavior change, and that direct access would be available to its developer for adaptation and curriculum consultation. Green Dot was also already in use at the University of Kentucky; its use in high schools could thus potentially help to "connect the dots" between high school and college prevention messages, since many state students who attend college attend the University of Kentucky. The SPT also sought to create connections between research and practice; rape crisis centers sought assistance from researchers at the University of Kentucky to develop a research design and apply for evaluation funding.

Twenty-six public high schools were recruited into the trial, randomized into the Green Dot intervention or control conditions (see Cook-Craig et al., 2014, for details). All schools signed memoranda of agreement to be randomized into the intervention or control condition, remain in the 5-year trial, and allow researchers to anonymously survey all consenting students each Spring, from 2010 to 2014. Green Dot was implemented in two phases: 1) persuasive speeches, and 2) peer opinion leader selected intensive bystander training. Rape crisis center staff were rigorously trained and their ability to provide the curriculum as the developer intended was monitored, using audio recordings with individual feedback provided by research staff throughout the trial. Prior to Green Dot implementation, rates of SV perpetration did not differ in the intervention and control schools, yet by Spring 2012 (when both phases of Green Dot were fully implemented) violence frequency scores began to change. After adjusting for sociodemographic differences across the schools, rates were significantly lower in the Green Dot intervention high schools by 2013, while violence rates increased slightly in the control schools (Coker et al., 2015).

These successes in "connecting the dots" could not have been achieved without a few crucial pieces of a rather intricate puzzle. First, the project was implemented by two separate and necessary teams, comprised of many people who communicated often, sometimes crossed over, and had very specific and defined roles. One team—"Team Green Dot"—consisted of the UK researchers, project managers, biostatisticians and funders; the other team—the State Core Planning Team (SCPT, pronounced "skipit") — consisted of the Executive Director of KASAP; the RPE Coordinator; the Empowerment Evaluator and co-PI on the research team (the cross over); a KASAP Board member, who chaired the implementation committee of rape crisis center educators; and a "coach."

Second, although the curriculum and data collection were well defined, the actual implementation of the project had to be processed over and over again. For this, the SCPT used the implementation drivers developed by Fixsen et al. (2005), which led to the hiring of the aforementioned coach. The coach—who was also trained in the Green Dot strategy—was able to provide constant feedback on the supports needed to help the educators maintain their relationships with the schools, as well as to monitor quality control while honoring the confidentiality of individual educators. The other crucial piece was the development of a training plan to address educator turnover. For the very first time, the rape crisis centers shared staff. If a center in one region lost an educator, an educator from another region would assist until another was hired and trained. Both of these steps were vital to adhering to the fidelity of the curricula, and cannot be overstated.

Briefly, the lessons learned from this multisite and multidisciplinary implementation and research team are as follows. Successful program development and implementation requires time, commitment, and coordination—from planning to evaluation. From idea inception to Green Dot selection and commencing educator training took at least 5 years. Recruiting the research team to write the evaluation funding grant took approximately 18 months. When funded, the research and implementation teams through KASAP met approximately monthly throughout the evaluation.

From the perspective of high-school administrators, there were challenges and important opportunities associated with participation in this trial. Of the 26 high schools beginning the trial, only two dropped out. These included one intervention school in the last year, and one control school in the second year (for which a replacement school was recruited). Researchers provided individual presentations of findings to all school principals, as well as findings in other formats: infographic, video, PowerPoint presentation, and one-page executive summary. Principals and staff thus had the information to make informed decisions regarding whether to continue (for intervention schools) or adopt (for control schools) the Green Dot program after the trial. KASAP negotiated with Green Dot's developer to provide the program at no cost to the high school if they opted to continue or adopt the program. From early follow-up data with these schools and rape crisis educators, 10 of the 13 intervention schools (77%) and 7 of the 13 control schools (54%) opted to receive Green Dot after the trial.

Davidov et al. (under review; 2016) conducted qualitative research to better understand these adoption patterns, given that Green Dot was very successful in reducing SV perpetration and victimization as well as related forms of interpersonal violence, such as sexual harassment, stalking, and dating violence (Coker et al., 2015). From in-depth interviews with rape crisis educators (described herein as "implementers" to distinguish from school staff, described as "educators"), Davidov et al. identified three factors that influenced continuation of this intervention:

- The schools' participation in the research process as an intervention or control site;

- Competing academic priorities for schools, balanced against recognizing violence as a problem for students in the school;
- Building relationships and gaining implementers' buy-in, with school administrators and staff.

Implementers clearly identified the challenges schools face in responding to state and local pressures to improve students' academic performance. Many perceived that school administrators did not view violence as a problem for their schools, and would not adopt the program despite low cost or effectiveness. An important "connect the dots" aspect of the Green Dot intervention is that those implementing it were trained as both rape crisis advocates and Green Dot prevention educators in schools. This dual training is unique, and potentially important for implementation in secondary schools. With their rape crisis training, educators could appropriately respond to students who disclosed experiencing SV, dating violence, or witnessing parental IPV. Because outcomes research requires asking about violence experienced, the team identified students in need of counseling and advocacy services during and after the surveying and intervention training. Asking the question is itself a form of secondary prevention or screening, which is appropriate in a community setting—*if* there are appropriate sources of counseling and referrals. These dually trained rape crisis educators, then, provided both primary and secondary prevention interventions; using these educators "connects the dots" by coordinating community agencies' resources and by connecting peers, schools, and community members with needed resources.

A further benefit to schools of dually trained educators is that they reduce the burden on teachers and the costs of training. The majority of school-based interventions are provided by trained school staff—primarily teachers—requiring time for teachers to receive and then implement the training. Busy teachers already have many responsibilities; the additional training and associated responsibilities are potentially burdensome, and both an opportunity cost and a direct cost to schools. Dual-trained staff at the crisis center also provided a clear connection between school-based and other community work relating to violence prevention and response. Youth Services Center (YSC) staff located within each school were key players. They were funded as part of Kentucky's education reform efforts to reduce or remove barriers to educational attainment for struggling students. YSC staff assisted Green Dot educators to access the schools; in turn, the educators could refer students in need to advocacy and/or therapy services.

In this trial, all Green Dot intensive training occurred during class time to allow all students the opportunity to participate. This approach met with push back from schools. Prevention intervention staff will need to consider means to provide effective training outside of class time, or perhaps electronically. As reviewed earlier, such efforts are underway. It is important to acknowledge here that schools do have an incentive to select the least expensive and shortest curriculum available, and this may not be the most efficacious program available.

One last attribute of the Green Dot approach deserves a brief mention. Because a POL approach was used to select and train students, only a small proportion (13–15%) of students were trained. If the intervention reduces violence, then this approach may be particularly cost-effective because only a fraction of students (one in seven) need be trained to see a school-level reduction in violence.

Next steps for researchers and prevention practitioners

This case study can provide a platform for progress for researchers and practitioners, including:

- Determining how interventions were actually implemented and whether the implementation attributes are associated with hypothesized outcomes. Here, outcome measures of program effectiveness included reducing violence used and experienced, changing norms supporting violence, and increasing positive or prosocial bystander behaviors. Examples of these implementation attributes (Durlak, 2015) include the fidelity with which educators provided the developer-approved Green Dot curriculum to students, the training quality, school-level dose, whether and how the curriculum was adapted by educators, and the degree of training diffusion (beyond those receiving training in the intervention and control schools) over time. This case study is an attempt to connect our violence prevention work with implementation science (Noonan et al., 2009).
- When evaluating intervention efficacy based on implementation attributes, we have observed that our unit of analyses differs for bystander-based programs. This observation has potential relevance for cluster-based bystander research. Bystander-based programs are hypothesized to change individual-level norms—and potentially individuals' actual prosocial bystander behaviors—if the individual

has the opportunity to engage another in violence prevention. For social norms and bystander behaviors evaluation, then, the unit of analysis is the individual trained. For the outcomes of interpersonal violence used or experienced, it is at the community (here, school) level that researchers may be most likely to observe an effect of the intervention over time and with intervention implementation. The nature of bystander interventions is that of interrupting potentially violent behaviors of others. Thus, the individual receiving training may or may not experience a reduction in their individual violence experience. This "diffusion" of intervention effect and its impact on analysis strategies should be carefully considered and justified, as it differs from standard individualized randomized controlled trial (RCT) protocols.

- When deciding to adopt a new prevention program, schools balance not only the program effectiveness but also the program cost. Based on RCT evaluation data (Coker et al., 2015), the number of violent events "prevented" by the program can be estimated, as well as the time to observe prevention effects. KASAP has data to additionally estimate the cost of intervention implementation (Bush et al., 2016). With these combined data sources, the cost per violent event prevented will be estimated.

A sobering thought, for both researchers and practitioners, is that conducting the implementation and evaluation research to identify an evidence base of effective prevention interventions is just the beginning of translational work toward primary violence prevention. Fortunately, the field of translation science—which combines elements of program implementation, dissemination, adoption, and sustainability—has matured, and can provide a systematic way forward. Toward "connecting the dots" for policy efforts, Herrenkohl et al. (2015) provide goals for prevention efforts from child abuse prevention that have direct relevance for interpersonal violence prevention in educational settings:

- Raise awareness (and community support or readiness to act) to promote safe and healthy relationships and environments;
- Collect and use data to inform actions;
- Create the context for healthy relationships through changing social norms supporting violence and through evidence-based programs;
- Create the context for healthy relationships through continuing advocacy for policy change (political support and prioritization).

These goals describe actions that communities of researchers, practitioners, and policy makers are encouraged to engage in toward the ultimate goal of primary prevention of SV and IPV. Meeting them is challenging because the process is iterative, requiring a prospective (long-term) approach and coordination across many stakeholders, advocates, and other community members. The following list, posed as joint questions for researcher–practitioner teams, provides targets for translating research into practice after evidence-based programs have been identified:

• Would a combination of programs be more effective? For example, that of combined different bystander programs with individual protection programming (Gidycz et al., 2011; Senn et al., 2015; Sinclair et al., 2013)? If so, for which groups?
• What is the minimum effective dose to see prevention efficacy?
• What evidence-based strategies work best to address multiple forms of violence?
• What evidence-based strategies work best at what developmental moments?
• What evidence-based strategies are more acceptable or sustainable in secondary and college or university settings?
• How can we find ways to partner across school settings so that curricula clearly build on each other and are coordinated?
• What are the best protective factors to build at each developmental moment and how do we sequence prevention work so that it is appropriate for each developmental stage but also builds on previous efforts (Hamby & Grych, 2013)?
• What capacities are needed to create connected relationships across educational, health, and practitioner agencies to build on successes for interpersonal violence prevention?
• How can other service providers become involved in primary prevention actions? For example, what roles do health care providers have in schools or clinics to reinforce violence prevention messaging or coordinate violence "screening" with therapeutic prevention interventions (Foshee et al., 2012; Wolfe et al., 2003; 2009)?
• What policies might effectively support primary prevention efforts? (See Klevens et al. [2015] for an exploration of policies that potentially impact on child abuse prevention, and Sumner et al. [2015] for interpersonal violence prevention policy efforts.)

Conclusion

Schools are a logical context for violence prevention efforts focused on the most at-risk age group (16–24). However, this age group also includes high schools and college campuses. While we have some evidence for programs that work for high-school students, more research is needed to establish strategies that reduce violence perpetration on college campuses. Improving on our past efforts will require a series of strategies to "connect the dots" from high school to college, to connect prevention work that addresses specific forms of violence, and to integrate violence prevention into other aspects of positive development and health curricula in school.

To actualize such an agenda, we need strong researcher–practitioner collaborations and multidisciplinary research teams to create, implement, and maintain prevention programming that engages adults and students in changing violence risk. Prevention programs need to intentionally contain mutually reinforcing messages across different developmental stages, while engaging both students and those adults who are important in students' lives (such as parents or teachers). In this chapter, we summarized key studies related to the evidence base for IPV prevention in schools and provided key questions for next steps in research and practice. A case example of one researcher–practitioner collaboration that used many facets of the "connecting the dots" approach was provided to illustrate strengths and challenges of this agenda.

References

Ahrens, C.E., Rich, M.D., & Ullman, J.B. (2011). Rehearsing for real life: The impact of the InterACT sexual assault prevention program on self-reported likelihood of engaging in bystander intervention. *Violence Against Women, 17*(6), 760–776. doi: 10.1177/1077801211410212.

Anderson, L.A., & Whiston, S.C. (2005). Sexual assault education programs: A meta-analytic examination of their effectiveness. *Psychology of Women Quarterly, 29*(4), 374–388. doi: 10.1111/j.1471-6402.2005.00237.

Banyard V.L. (2013). Go big or go home: Reaching for a more integrated view of violence prevention. *Psychology of Violence,* 3(2),115–120. doi: 10.1037/a0032289.

Banyard, V.L. (2014). Improving college campus based prevention of violence against women: A strategic plan for research built on multipronged practices and policies. *Trauma, Violence, & Abuse, 15*(4), 339–351. doi: 10.1177/1524838014521027.

Banyard, V.L., Moynihan, M.M., & Crossman, M.T. (2009). Reducing sexual violence on campus: The role of student leaders as empowered bystanders. *Journal of College Student Development, 50*(4), 446–457.

Banyard, V.L., Plante, E.G., & Moynihan, M.M. (2004). Bystander education: Bringing a broader community perspective to sexual violence prevention. *Journal of Community Psychology, 32*(1), 61–79. doi: 10.1002/jcop.10078.

Banyard, V.L., Plante, E.G., & Moynihan, M.M. (2007). Sexual violence prevention through bystander education: An experimental evaluation. *Journal of Community Psychology, 35*(4), 463-481.

Berkowitz, A.D. (2002). Fostering men's responsibility for preventing sexual assault. In P.A. Schewe (Ed.), *Preventing violence in relationships: Interventions across the life span* (pp. 163–196). Washington, DC: American Psychological Association.

Bush, J., Bush, H.M., Coker, A.L., Brancato, C.J., Clear, E.R., Recktenwald, E. (2016). Total and marginal cost analysis for a high school based bystander intervention. *Journal of School Violence*, online ahead of print. doi: 1080/15388220.20161275656.

Cares, A.C., Banyard, V.L., Moynihan, M.M., Williams, L.M., Potter, S.J., & Stapleton, J.G. (2015). Changing attitudes about being a bystander to violence: Translating an in-person sexual violence prevention program to a new campus. *Violence Against Women, 21*(2), 165–187. doi: 10.1177/1077801214564681.

Casey, E.A., & Lindhorst, T.P. (2009). Toward a multilevel, ecological approach to the primary prevention of sexual assault: Prevention in peer and community contexts. *Trauma, Violence, & Abuse, 10*(2), 91–114. doi: 10.1177/1524838009334129.

Cheruvelil, K.S., Soranno, P.A., Weathers, K.C., Hanson, P.C., Goring, S.J., Filstrup, C.T., & Read, E.K. (2014). Creating and maintaining high-performing collaborative research teams: The importance of diversity and interpersonal skills. *Frontiers in Ecology and the Environment, 12*(1), 31–38.

Coker, A.L., Bush, H.M., Fisher, B.S., Swan, S.C., Williams, C.M., Clear, E.R., & DeGue, S. (2016). Multiyear three campus evaluation of *Green Dot* bystander intervention to reduce interpersonal violence among college freshmen. *American Journal of Preventive Medicine, 50*(3), 295–302. doi: 10.1016/j.amepre.2015.08.034.

Coker, A.L., Cook-Craig, P.G., & Bush, H. (2015). *Green Dot across the bluegrass: Final report to the Centers for Disease Control and Prevention National Center for Injury Prevention and Control*, U01CE001675. Atlanta, GA: Centers for Disease Control and Prevention.

Coker, A.L., Cook-Craig, P.G., Williams, C.M., Fisher, B.S., Clear, E.R., Garcia, L.S., & Hegge, L.M. (2011). Evaluation of *Green Dot*: An active bystander intervention to reduce sexual violence on college campuses. *Violence Against Women, 17*(6), 777–796. doi: 10.1177/1077801211410264.

Coker, A.L., Fisher, B.S., Bush, H.M., Swan, S.C., Williams, C.W., Clear, E.R., & DeGue, S. (2015). Evaluation of the *Green Dot* bystander intervention to reduce interpersonal violence among college students across three campuses. *Violence Against Women, 21*(12), 1507–1527. doi: 10.1177/1077801214545284.

Cook-Craig, P.G., Coker, A.L., Clear, E.R., Garcia, L.S., Bush, H.M., Brancato, C.J., & Fisher, B.S. (2014). Challenge and opportunity in evaluating a diffusion-based active bystanding prevention program: *Green Dot* in high schools. *Violence Against Women, 20*(10), 1179–1202. doi: 10.1177/1077801214551288.

Davidov, D.M., Hill, K., Bush, H.M., & Coker, A.L. (Under review; 2016). Factors influencing adoption of the *Green Dot* primary prevention violence program: A qualitative descriptive study of implementers' perspectives.

DeGue, S., Massetti, G.M., Holt, M.K., Tharp, A.T., Valle, L.A., & Matjasko, J.L. (2013). Identifying links between sexual violence and youth violence perpetration: New opportunities for sexual violence prevention. *Psychology of Violence, 3*(2), 140–156. doi: 10.1037/a00298084..,–d: .

Durlak, J.A., Weissberg, R.P., Dvmnicki, A.B., Taylor, R.D., & Schiellinger, K.B. (2011). The impact of enhancing students' social and emotional learning: A meta-analysis of school-based universal interventions. *Child Development, 82*(1), 405–432.

Edwards, K.M., Jones, L.M., Mitchell, K.J., Hagler, M.A., & Roberts, L.T. (2016). Building on youth's strengths: A call to include adolescents in developing, implementing, and evaluating violence prevention programs. *Psychology of Violence, 6*(1),15–21. doi: 10.1037/vio0000022.

Elias-Lambert, N., & Black, B.M. (2015). Bystander sexual violence prevention program: Outcomes for high and low-risk university men. *Journal of Interpersonal Violence*. pii: 0886260515584346 (Epub ahead of print).

Fetterman, D.M. (1994). Empowerment evaluation. *American Journal of Evaluation, 15*, 1-15. doi: 10.1177/109821409401500101.

Finkelhor, D., Vanderminden, J., Turner, H., Shattuck, A., & Hamby S. (2014). Youth exposure to violence prevention programs in a national sample. *Child Abuse & Neglect, 38*, 677–686.

Fixsen, D.L., Naoom, S.F., Blasé, K.A., Friedman, R.M., & Wallace, F. (2005). *Implementation research: A synthesis of the literature*. Tampa, FL: University of South Florida.

Florida Mental Health Institute (FMHI), The National Implementation Research Network (FMHI Publication #231). Retrieved from: http://ctndisseminationlibrary.org/PDF/nirnmonograph.pdf.

Foshee, V., Bauman, K., Arriaga, X., Helms, R., Koch, G., & Linder, G. (1998). An evaluation of *Safe Dates*, an adolescent dating violence prevention program. *American Journal of Public Health*, *88*, 45–50.

Foshee, V., Bauman, K., Ennett, S., Linder, G., Benefield, T., & Suchindran, C. (2004). Assessing the long-term effects of the *Safe Dates* program and a booster in preventing and reducing adolescent dating violence victimization and perpetration. *American Journal of Public Health*, *94*(4), 619–624.

Foshee, V., Bauman, K., Ennett, S.T., Suchindran, C., Benefield, T., & Linder, G. (2005). Assessing the effects of the dating violence prevention program *Safe Dates* using random coefficient regression modeling. *Prevention Science*, *6*(3), 245–258.

Foshee, V., McNaughton Reyes, H.L., Ennett, S.T., Cance, J.D., Bauman, K.E., & Bowling, J.M. (2012). Assessing the effects of families for *Safe Dates*, a family-based teen dating abuse prevention program. *Journal of Adolescent Health*, *51*, 349–356.

Gidycz, C.A., Orchowski, L.M., & Berkowitz, A.D. (2011). Preventing sexual aggression among college men: An evaluation of a social norms and bystander intervention program. *Violence Against Women*, *17*(6), 720–742. doi: 10.1177/1077801211409727.

Hamby, S., & Grych, J. (2013). *The web of violence: Exploring connections among different forms of interpersonal violence and abuse*. Dordrecht, The Netherlands: Springer.

Hamby, S.L., Weber, M.C., Grych, J., & Banyard, V. (2016). What difference do bystanders make? The association of bystander involvement with victim outcomes in a community sample. *Psychology of Violence*, *6*(1), 91-102.

Herrenkohl, T.I., Higgins, D.J., Merrick, M.T., & Leeb, R.T. (2015). Positioning a public health framework at the intersection of child maltreatment and intimate partner violence. *Child Abuse & Neglect*, *48*, 22–28. doi: 10.1016/j.chiabu.2015.04.013.

Jewkes, R., Nduna, M., Levin, J., & Jama, N. (2008). Impact of Stepping Stones on incidence of HIV and HSV–2 and sexual behaviour in rural South Africa: Cluster randomised controlled trial. *British Medical Journal*, *337*(7666), 391–395. doi: 10.1136/bmj.a506.

Katz, J. (1995). Reconstructing masculinity in the locker room: The Mentors in Violence prevention project. *Harvard Educational Review*, *65*(2), 163–175.

Katz, J., Heisterkamp, H.A., & Fleming, W.M. (2011). The social justice roots of the Mentors in Violence prevention model and its application in a high school setting. *Violence Against Women*, *17*(6), 684–702.

Kleinsasser, A., Jouriles, E.N., McDonald, R., & Rosenfield, D. (2015). An online bystander intervention program for the prevention of sexual violence. *Psychology of Violence*, *5*(3), 227–235. doi: 10.1037/a0037393.

Klevens, J., Barnett, S.B.L., Florence, C., & Moore, D. (2015). Exploring policies for the reduction of child physical abuse and neglect. *Child Abuse & Neglect*, *40*, 1–11. doi: 10.1016/j.chiabu.2014.07.013.

Levesque D.A. (2007). *A stage-based expert system for teen dating violence prevention: Final report to the Center for Injury Prevention and Control from grant R43CE000499*. Atlanta, GA: Centers for Disease Control and Prevention.

Levesque, D.A., Johnson, J.L., Welch, C.A., Prochaska, J.M., & Paiva, A.L. (2016). Teen dating violence prevention: Cluster-randomized trial of Teen Choices, an online, stage-based program for healthy, nonviolent relationships. *Psychology of Violence*, *6*(3), 421–432. doi: 10.1037/vio0000022.

Lippy, C., & DeGue, S. (2016). Exploring alcohol policy approaches to prevention of sexual violence perpetration. *Trauma, Violence, & Abuse*, *17*(1), 26–42. doi: 10.1177/1524838014557291.

Lundgren, R., Amin, A. (2015). Addressing intimate partner violence and sexual violence among adolescents: Emerging evidence of effectiveness. *Journal of Adolescent Health,* 56(1 Suppl), S42 –50. doi: 10.1016/j.jadohealth.2014.08.012.

McMahon, S. (2015a). Call for research on bystander intervention to prevent sexual violence: The role of campus environments. *American Journal of Community Psychology*, 55, 472–489. doi 10.1007/s10464-015-9724-0.

McMahon, S., Winter, S.M., Palmer, J.E., Postmus, J.L., Peterson, N. A., Zucker, S. & Koenick, R. (2015b). A randomized controlled trial of a multi-dose bystander intervention program using peer education theater. *Health Education Research*, *30*(4), 554–568. doi: 10.1093/her/cyv022.

Miller, E., Tancredi, D.J., McCauley, H.L., Decker, M.R., Virata, M.C.D., Anderson, H.A., & Silverman, J.G. (2012). "Coaching Boys Into Men": A cluster-randomized controlled trial of a dating violence prevention program. *Journal of Adolescent Health*, *51*, 431–438. doi: 10.1016/j.jadohealth.2012.01.018.

Miller, E., Tancredi, D.J., MacCauley, H.L., Decker, M.R., Virata, M.C.D., Anderson, H.A. et al. (2013). One-year follow-up of a coach-delivered dating violence prevention program: A clustered randomized controlled trial. *American Journal of Preventive Medicine*, *45*(1), 108–112. doi: 10.1016/j.amepre.2013.03.007.

Miller, E., Das, M., Tancredi, D.J., McCauley, H.L., Virata, M.C.D., & Nettiksimmons, J, et al. (2014). Evaluation of a gender-based violence prevention program for student athletes in Mumbai, India. *Journal of Interpersonal Violence*, *29*(4), 758-778.

Moynihan, M.M., & Banyard, V.L. (2008). Community responsibility for preventing sexual violence: A pilot with campus Greeks and intercollegiate athletes. *Journal of Prevention and Intervention in the Community*, *36*, 23–28.

Moynihan, M.M., Banyard, V.L., Cares, A.C., Potter, S.J., Williams, L.M., & Stapleton, J.G. (2015). Encouraging responses in sexual and relationship violence prevention: What program effects remain 1 year later? *Journal of Interpersonal Violence*, *30*(1), 110–132. doi: 10.1177/0886260514532719.

Mulford, C.F., & Blachman-Demner, D.R. (2013). Teen dating violence: Building a research program through collaborative insights. *Violence Against Women*, *19*(6), 756–770.

Nation, M., Crusto, C., Wandersman, A., Kumpfer, G.L., Seybolt, D., Morrissey-Kane, E., & Davino, K. (2003). What works in prevention: Principles of effective prevention programs. *American Psychologist*, *58*(6–7), 449–456.

Niolon, P.H., Taylor, B.G., Latzman, N.E., Viviolo-Kantor, A.M., Valle, L.A., & Tharp, A.T. (2016). Lessons learned in evaluating a multisite, comprehensive teen dating violence prevention strategy: Design and challenges of the evaluation of Dating Matters: Strategies to promote healthy teen relationships. *Psychology of Violence*, *6*(3), 452–458. doi: 10.1037/vio0000043.

Noonan, R.K., Emshoff, J. G., Mooss, A., Armstrong, M., Weinberg, J., & Ball, B. (2009). Adoption, adaptation, and fidelity of implementation of sexual violence prevention programs. *Health Promotion Practice Supplement*, *10*(1), 59S–70S. doi: 10.1177/1524839908329374.

Palm Reed, K.M., Hines, D.A., Armstrong, J.L., & Cameron, A.Y. (2015). Experimental evaluation of a bystander prevention program for sexual assault and dating violence. *Psychology of Violence*, *5*(1), 95–105. doi: 10.1037/a0037557.

Polanin J.R., Espelage, D.L., & Pigott, T. D. (2012). A meta-analysis of school-based bullying prevention programs' effects on bystander intervention behavior. *School Psychology Review*, *41*(1), 47–65.

Potter, S.J. (2016). Reducing sexual assault on campus: Lessons from the movement to prevent drunk driving. *American Journal of Public Health, 106*(5), 822-829.

Potter, S.J., Moynihan, M.M., & Stapleton, J.G. (2011). Using social self-identification in social marketing materials aimed at reducing violence against women on campus. *Journal of Interpersonal Violence*, *26*(5), 971–990. doi: 10.1177/0886260510365870.

Salazar, L.F., Vivolo-Kantor, A., Hardin, J., & Berkowitz, A. (2014). A web-based sexual violence bystander intervention for male college students: Randomized controlled trial. *Journal of Medical Internet Research*, *16*(9), e203. doi: 10.2196/jmir.3426.

Schwartz, M.D., & DeKeseredy, W.S. (2008). Interpersonal violence against women: The role of men. *Journal of Contemporary Criminal Justice*, *24*(2), 178–185.

Sinclair, J., Sinclair, L., Otieno, E., Muling, M., Kapphahn, C., & Golden, N.H. (2013). A self-defense program reduces the incidence of sexual assault in Kenyan adolescent girls. *Journal of Adolescent Health*, *53*(3), 374–380. doi: 10.1016/j.jadohealth.2013.04.008.

Senn, C.Y., & Forrest, A. (2015). "And then one night when I went to class…": The impact of sexual assault bystander intervention workshops incorporated in academic courses. *Psychology of Violence*. doi: 10.1037/a0039660 (Epub ahead of print).

Sumner, S.S.A., Mercy, J.A., Dahlberg, L.L., Hillis, S.D., Klevens, J., & Houry, D. (2015). Violence in the United States: Status, challenges and opportunities. *Journal of the American Medical Association, 314*(5), 478–488. doi:10.1001/jama.2015.8371.

Taylor, B.G., Stein, N., Mumford, E., & Woods, D. (2013). Shifting Boundaries: An experimental evaluation of a dating violence prevention program in middle schools. *Prevention Science, 14*, 64-76.

Tharp, A.T. (2012). Dating Matters™: The next generation of teen dating violence prevention. *Prevention Science,13*, 398–401. doi: 10.1007/s11121-012-0307-0.

Wandersman, A., Keener, D.C., Snell-Johns, J., Miller, R.L., Flaspohler, P., Livet-Dye, M., et al. (2004). Empowerment evaluation: Principles and action. In LA. Jason, C.B. Keys, Y, Suarez-Balcazar, R.R. Taylor, & M.I. Davis (Eds.), *Participatory community research: Theories and methods in action* (pp. 139-156). Washington, DC: American Psychological Association.

Wilkins, N., Tsao, B., Hertz, M., Davis, R., & Klevens, J. (2014). *Connecting the dots: An overview of the links among multiple forms of violence*. Atlanta, GA: National Center for Injury Prevention and Control, Centers for Disease Control and Prevention.

Wolfe, D.A., Wekerle, C., Scott, K., Straatman, A.L., Grasley, C., & Reitzel-Jaffe, D. (2003). Dating violence prevention with at-risk youth: A controlled outcome evaluation. *Journal of Consulting and Clinical Psychology, 71*, 279–291.

Wolfe, D.A., Crooks, C., Jaffe, P., Chiodo, D., Hughes, R., Ellis, W., et al. (2009). A school-based program to prevent adolescent dating violence: A cluster randomized trial. *Archives of Pediatric & Adolescent Medicine, 163*, 692–699.

FOUR

Engaging Men and Boys in Preventing Gender-based Violence

Richard M. Tolman, Tova B. Walsh, and Bethsaida Nieves

Introduction

This chapter focuses on efforts to engage men and boys in preventing gender-based violence (GBV). We examine violence prevention efforts at the individual, family, community, and global levels. We highlight a range of innovative approaches from around the world, including restorative justice practices, online programs, culturally focused counseling, working with fathers and their children to recognize and prevent intergenerational violence, enhancing men's capacity to support their pregnant partners, and involving men as allies in the effort to prevent violence against women. We review the growing but still limited body of research on efforts to engage men and boys in preventing GBV, and we offer recommendations for future research directions.

Why engage men and boys in preventing GBV?

Worldwide, male violence against women is a pervasive problem. Women are substantially more likely to be killed by their spouse or adult son or sexually assaulted by someone they know than by strangers (Minerson et al., 2011). While constructions of male identity and masculinity play a crucial role in shaping some men's perpetration of violence, most men do not use or condone violence. Recently, efforts to prevent violence against women have begun to emphasize that men have a significant and positive role to play in helping to end men's violence (Minerson et al., 2011; Pease, 2008, p. 6; WHO, 2002). Minerson et al. (2011), for example, argue that gender inequality disadvantaging women and patriarchal power imbalances are the root cause of GBV, and therefore must be addressed as part of the solution (p. 2). Focusing on effective and positive program practices that educate, support, and help men and boys to develop healthy relationships, Minerson et al. (2011) consider GBV prevention efforts potentially transformative for both men and women.

Jewkes et al. (2015) also point out that social values and gender norms influence how men define themselves and their roles in social and intimate relationships (p. 1581). Involving men and boys in violence prevention programs with women and girls provides the opportunity to work on multiple levels to address social norms and change behaviors. Casey and Tolman et al. (2016) found that men who are motivated to engage in GBV prevention efforts are so motivated because they have a commitment to social justice, feel empathy toward survivors, or have multiple precipitants of antiviolence involvement (p. 16). These motivators also serve as leverage for becoming allies to women in a shared effort of advocacy and gender justice. When men learn about how women they know have survived violence, learn about violence in their communities, or have a personal experience with violence, they tend to be more receptive to violence prevention efforts.

We want to note that this chapter focuses specifically on engaging men and boys in preventing violence against women, first defined in the United Nations (UN) Declaration on the Elimination of Violence against Women as: "Any act of gender-based violence that results in, or is likely to result in, physical, sexual or psychological harm or suffering to women, including threats of such acts, coercion or arbitrary deprivations of liberty, whether occurring in public or in private life" (General Assembly, 1993). Men's violence against women is distinct from women's violence against men or violence in same-sex relationships in that it is fostered by power inequalities based on traditional gender roles. We acknowledge the diversity of contexts within which violence occurs, and we aim to highlight prevention efforts that are informed by an understanding of gender and focus on engaging men and boys to reduce GBV.

Promise and tensions

Engaging men in GBV prevention efforts holds great promise and has its tensions. The promise of these efforts lies in leveraging a vast and largely untapped resource for ending violence, including strategic leveraging of male power and privilege. There is growing evidence of programs' impact on attitudes and behavior toward women, and potential for broad social change across related health and equity issues. Overall, these programs can be an important component of larger efforts of mobilizing communities against violence. Despite the emergence and preliminary evidence of promising and innovative prevention programming, rigorous evaluation of these efforts has only recently begun. There are other tensions as well.

The involvement of men in prevention efforts is not without controversy. The possibility that efforts aimed at men could gain disproportionate prominence, thus underscoring men's position of privilege, is a notable concern. The promise of men's engagement efforts, however, includes the hope that men's involvement can leverage male power and privilege toward the goal of ending violence against women. Since most men do not accept or use violence against women, men might be a resource if they can be mobilized in positive and effective ways to join the struggle to end violence (Hart Research Associates, Inc., 2007; Minerson et al., 2011; Pease, 2008; WHO, 2002). Inviting men to join efforts to end GBV also invites concerns that women's leadership and stewardship of GBV efforts could be supplanted or diminished by men's participation. Moreover, resource competition could lead to a diminishment of funding and energy directed toward victim services and prevention efforts directed toward women (Pease, 2008). Other tensions include a proliferation and fragmentation of programs, limited (but emerging) evaluations of effectiveness, and a risk of "men's engagement" becoming an end in itself.

Prevention strategies

A comprehensive approach to ending men's violence against women requires a prevention perspective as well as a multistrategy focus. Many GBV prevention models focus on efforts at multiple levels of the human ecology (Heise, 1998; Tolman et al., 2010). One comprehensive conceptual model, the spectrum of prevention (Cohen & Swift, 1999), identifies six levels for strategy development and multiple levels of intervention:

1. Strengthening individual knowledge and skills in order to prevent injury or disease;
2. Promoting community education as a way to share information across groups to improve health;
3. Educating providers so they are up to date on the information they share with others;
4. Fostering coalitions and networks to secure expanded partnerships and ensure greater success;
5. Changing organizational practices by examining, evaluating, and changing institutional regulations and norms;
6. Influencing policy and legislation by amending existing policies, creating new policies, and improving how policies are enforced (Cohen and Swift, 1999, p. 2; see also Chapter 1 in this book).

Throughout our examination of efforts to engage men and boys in GBV prevention, we make reference to efforts at various levels of this spectrum.

When and where to engage?

Prevention strategies include *indicated*, *selective*, and *universal*[1]. *Indicated* strategies focus on boys or men who have already acted abusively or aggressively. *Selective* strategies target men or boys who are at greater risk for violence against women. *Universal* strategies are aimed at intervening with men and boys regardless of their risk for violence against women (Chamberlain, 2008).

Wells et al. (2013) identified multiple promising entry points for engaging men in GBV. These include engaging fathers in prevention; focusing on men's health and prevention; considering the roles of sports and recreation, the workplace, and peer relationships in prevention; and including men as allies in prevention (Wells et al., 2013). Researchers and practitioners are increasingly cognizant that engaging boys and men strategically across the life course is essential to GBV prevention efforts. For example, key developmental periods for targeted outreach efforts include the transition to parenthood (during a partner's pregnancy); when men become parents and caregivers; during school age and adolescent years; and during college years. Promising settings for efforts to engage men and boys include K-12 schools, colleges, sports, faith communities, and the military (Baobaid & Hamed, 2010; Crooks et al., 2007; DeKeseredy, Schwartz & Alvi, 2000). We will offer a more detailed discussion of three critical windows: the transition to parenthood, as parents and caregivers, and K-12 school and college settings.

Engaging men at the transition to parenthood

Engaging expectant and new fathers in prevention efforts is important for several reasons. Annually in the US, 324,000 women experience GBV during pregnancy (de Moseson, 2004). The range of prevalence of GBV during pregnancy is much wider in the Global South (3.8% to 31.7%) than in the Global North (3.4% to 11%), which is much closer to findings from North America (Campbell et al., 2004). Risks associated with men's abusive behavior during pregnancy include low birth weight (Rosen, Seng & Tolman, 2007; Sharps, 2007); premature labor (Cokkinides et al.,1999; El Kady et al., 2005; Fernandez & Krueger, 1999); miscarriage (Morland et al, 2008; Rachana et al. 2002); fetal trauma (Connolly et al., 1997; Berrios & Grady, 1991); and postpartum maternal depression (Blabey, et al., 2009). These risks demonstrate that pregnancy is a critical time for prevention efforts. On the other hand, fathers' support during pregnancy may also help to prevent negative birth outcomes (Marsiglio, 2008).

Childhood exposure to GBV increases the likelihood of being in an abusive relationship later in life (Osofsky et al., 2000; Smith & Farrington, 2004). Given the strength of childhood exposure to violence as a predictor for future violence perpetration (Ehrensaft et al., 2003; Whitefield et al., 2003), selective prevention efforts— that is, efforts aimed at those who have identifiable risk factors for GBV—should be targeted to this group. For example, men who have been exposed to violence during their childhood might benefit from prevention efforts when their partners are pregnant. This is a time when men may be more focused on their success as a parent and partner, which may encourage them to become more involved with their partner's prenatal care, labor, and/or delivery. Screening for traumatic childhood experiences might be effective in identifying men who could benefit from education and support to prevent abusive behavior toward their partners or children. One practice example in England, The Family Nurse Partnership, offers home visiting services to vulnerable teenage first-time mothers. The male partners of the teenage mothers who participated in this program were young, poor, unemployed, and did not have involved fathers during their own childhoods. They saw their engagement in The Family Nurse Partnership as helping them learn how to support their pregnant partners (Ferguson & Gates, 2015). While unexamined in terms of impact on prevention of abuse toward their partners during or after pregnancy, this type of program provides an example of how men might be engaged at this critical transition. As noted earlier, positive support by fathers during pregnancy has been associated with better birth outcomes.

Another study also provides some potential entry points for engaging expectant fathers in prevention programming. Walsh et al. (2014) conducted semistructured interviews with 22 fathers after ultrasound, analyzed data using principles of grounded theory, and built a conceptual model of how fathers experience ultrasound. Results suggest that ultrasound attendance contributes to paternal feelings of connection to the unborn baby and motivation to change behavior. Implications include fathers being more open to preventive interventions at this time; a consideration of how prenatal care providers perceive and interact with fathers; a conceptualization of preventive intervention efforts from a positive, empowering perspective that can build on fathers' strengths; and a focus on the relationships that fathers have with both the baby-to-be and their partner. Using nationally representative survey data, Walsh et al. (in press) found a substantial proportion of US fathers were present at prenatal ultrasounds, including low-income and non-cohabiting fathers. Prenatal ultrasounds may be a unique opportunity during pregnancy for programs to connect with a broad cross-section of fathers and engage them in needed services. Florsheim et al. (2011) evaluated the Young Parenthood Program, which aims to support violence prevention and positive communication between pregnant adolescents and their partners.

Couples that participated in the Young Parenthood Program were significantly less likely to have experienced violence 3 months after their baby's birth, but the strength of this finding diminished by 18 months after the baby's birth. This raises issues about the maintenance of these changes. A limitation of this study was that partner violence was measured at the couple level, thus not clearly identifying if reduced levels of violence were due to a change in behavior by male or female partners, or both.

Engaging men as parents and caregivers

When considering efforts to engage men as fathers, it is crucial to remember that most men who become fathers want to be good fathers. An enhanced understanding of the important role that fathers play in the development and lives of their children can lead fathers to reassess a variety of choices and behaviors. Therefore, education and support for men as fathers from a strengths-based perspective can empower men in their roles as parent and partner, which can help to create and strengthen positive relationships.

Sociodemographic factors that increase risk for both GBV and child maltreatment include fathers' age, employment status, and financial provision for the family (Guterman & Lee, 2005). Paternal psychosocial factors that increase the risks include substance abuse, a father's own childhood experiences of maltreatment, and the nature of the father's relationship with the mother (Guterman & Lee, 2005). Key parenting risk factors affecting child maltreatment include parental stress, irritability, and feelings of being ineffective as parents (Haskett et al., 2006). Fathers influence the risks for child maltreatment directly through their own perpetration of abusive behaviors, and indirectly through their influence on mothers' abusive behaviors (Dubowitz, 2006).

Protective factors for both GBV and child maltreatment include positive father involvement—often defined and measured in terms of three dimensions: direct interaction between a father and child (for example, playing, caretaking); accessibility, or how available a father is to his child when needed; and responsibility, or managing and providing resources for a child (for example, attending doctor's appointments, contributing to family income, paying child support). Involvement is associated with better developmental outcomes for children (Marsiglio et al., 2000), decreased likelihood that a child will experience maltreatment (Dubowitz et al., 2000), and lower levels of family conflict and violence (Barker & Verani, 2008; Pruett, 2000; Shapiro et al., 2011). A greater engagement in caring for their children is associated also with an increase in men's emotional wellbeing and capacity to express emotions and experience empathy (Allen & Daly, 2007; Horn et al., 1999). In addition, studies show that fathers' support for mothers can impact maternal wellbeing and caregiving. For example, mothers who feel supported are more sensitive to their children's cues (Crnic et al., 1983).

While abuse in one generation confers risk in the next, nurturing parenting may also be transmitted intergenerationally. For example, sons of involved and nurturing fathers are less likely to become violent in their intimate partner relationships as men (Barker & Verani, 2008; Foumbi & Lovich, 1997; Horn, 1999; Shapiro et al., 2011). Moreover, sons of nurturing fathers are likely to be more nurturing and gender equitable as fathers themselves, and daughters of nurturing fathers are more likely to value equitable partner relationships (Allen & Daly, 2007; Greene & Moore, 2000).

The MenCare+ initiative is one prominent example of work being done at the universal prevention level to engage men as caregivers. MenCare+ has worked with public health service providers in Brazil, South Africa, Rwanda, and Indonesia, among others, to engage expectant fathers in maternal and child health education programs that also address partner violence (Levtov et al., 2015). In January 2016, the first outcomes report from the MenCare+ initiative was published. The report covered program data for the past 3 years of the program based in Western Cape, South Africa. Overall, pre- and post-program participation questionnaires indicated that 27.5% of program participants increased from moderate support to high support for gender equitable attitudes, whereas 64% entered the program with a high level of support for gender equity (Olivier et al., 2016). According to the report, "After attending the MenCare+ sessions the men were of the opinion that to be a young man was to be responsible, supportive to your partner and community, and a role model to other young boys and men in their community" (Olivier et al., 2016, p. 7). Other attitudinal shifts after participating in the program include increased use of contraceptives and health care services, as well as increased communication with partners about family planning. Moreover, program participants increased their presence at their partners' prenatal care and delivery.

At the level of indicated prevention, men who perpetrate violence against women may also be fathers who plan to be actively involved in their children's upbringing (Bancroft et al., 2012; Edleson & Williams, 2007). Research shows that more than 60% of men who have been arrested for violence against their partners are fathers (Rothman et al., 2007). Moreover, studies suggest that both partnered and non-partnered abusive fathers spend similar amounts of time with their children (Fox & Benson, 2004). Intervention efforts overlap at this stage of parenting because they have the potential to help fathers after violence has occurred (indicated prevention), as well as to stop the intergenerational transmission of violence with children before they develop aggressive behaviors (selective prevention).

Models of intervention for fathers who batter their partners consider the act of fathering as end in itself, or as an entry point to changing violent behaviors (Perel & Peled, 2008). Intervention programs vary in their approach. Although not mutually exclusive, some intervention programs focus on helping men develop positive parenting relationships with their partners, while others focus on strengthening fathers' ability to build a positive relationship with their child (Arean & Davis, 2007; Donovan & Vlais, 2005; Stover & Morgos, 2013). Limited but growing evidence suggests that established batterer intervention group programs that include a parenting component can be effective. Interventions that address fathering, partner violence, and concurrent challenges such as comorbid substance abuse appear to be the most likely to succeed.

One of the best-documented programs is the Caring Dads program (Scott et al., 2006; http://caringdads.org/). Caring Dads uses a range of techniques, including motivational interviewing, psychoeducation, cognitive behavioral techniques, confrontation, and "shame work." The program seeks to address four goals:

1. Engaging men to examine their fathering by developing trust and motivation;
2. Increasing awareness and application of child-centered fathering;
3. Increasing awareness of, and responsibility for, abusive and neglectful fathering and violence against women;
4. Rebuilding children's trust in men's fathering and planning for the future.

Significant changes were observed in fathers' over-reactivity to children's misbehavior and respect for their partner's judgment, suggesting the potential of the Caring Dads program to promote change in parenting and co-parenting. The Caring Dads program has undergone two recent peer-reviewed evaluations by Scott and colleagues. Scott and Crooks (2007) evaluated 34 fathers before and after their participation in the program; they expressed an increased understanding of how to use their interpersonal skills. Scott and Lishak (2012) also evaluated 98 fathers before and after their participation in the program and found that fathers interacted more positively with their children and were better able to co-parent.

The aforementioned father-focused interventions only engage fathers. Stover (2013) presents a promising case study of Fathers for Change, which focuses on fathering throughout the course of substance use and domestic violence treatment. Stover (2015) found that Fathers for Change program participants decreased intimate partner violence (IPV), and increased positive child–father relationships. In Australia, the Dads on Board program engages fathers with a history of violence against women, and who have completed a behavior change program along with their infant/toddler (Bunston, 2013). Although more extensive evaluations are needed to assess the short- and long-term impact of program participation, preliminary results are promising.

Indicated intervention strategies that focus on men who have already committed violence can be complemented by selective intervention strategies that engage men who exhibit higher risk of committing violence against women. Men who have a higher risk include those who have experienced or witnessed abuse in their families, those with a criminal history, unemployed men, adolescent fathers, and expectant or new fathers. In this section, we focus on selective prevention strategies targeted toward at-risk individuals. We note, however, that very little research has been done in this particular area, and the programs we present are examples of the type of practice that might be considered.

The Baltimore Responsible Fatherhood Project (BRFP) teaches low-income non-custodial fathers how to develop and maintain healthy parenting and relationship skills, while also providing them with career development skills (Center for Urban Families, 2009). Some fathers in the program who have survived multiple stressors may also demonstrate a number of factors that predict a high possibility of violence against women. BRFP leaders identify violence when it has occurred, and advise men to seek help for their abusive behavior. BRFP also has a cooperative relationship with a batterer intervention program (BIP) at House of Ruth—a domestic violence center—in order to provide cross-training and service referrals.

Dads to Kids (Dad2K), an adaptation of the evidence-based SafeCare program, targets at-risk fathers (Self-Brown et al., 2015). The SafeCare program focused on building positive parenting skills and preventing family violence. The Dad2K program combines traditional home visits with innovative technology approaches to help fathers learn how to develop positive interactions with their children. By watching online videos that model specific approaches to parenting during the home visit, fathers can ask the home visitor for guidance with developing their parenting skills. Pilot data collected from four fathers suggests that the technology-enhanced program is useful and can improve father–child interactions.

The Men Stopping Violence (MSV) program in Atlanta, GA (Douglas et al., 2008), has numerous interlocking programs across multiple levels of prevention. Men involved in the MSV's BIP are asked to bring men from their workplace, peer group, or family to witness the work they are doing in the program. As the community witnesses begin to understand the participant's experiences and commitment to change, they can turn into sources of accountability, support, and sustained change for the men in the program. By the same token, community witnesses experiencing similar challenges may decide to change their own behavior and expand their efforts to end violence against women. MSV engages men and their families in a number of other programs, including the Community Restoration Program, which began as a follow-up program for men who had completed the MSV 24-week BIP (Douglas et al., 2008). The Community Restoration Program evolved into a form of restorative justice in which men participated in community projects, outreach, and advocacy. The dual focus on helping men maintain their non-abusive behaviors and sustain community change makes this program both an indicated and universal prevention effort. MSV also has a universal prevention effort called Because We Have Daughters. Through father–daughter activities and discussions, the Because We Have Daughters program teaches fathers how to be a positive influence in their daughters' lives, helps them become more aware of violence against women on a global scale, and encourages them to join local and community efforts in preventing violence against women.

Engaging men and boys in K-12 and college settings

Engaging men and boys in K-12 and college settings provides an opportunity to discuss peer culture and peer pressure, and to promote positive and healthy social norms during a formative period. As Casey et al. (2013) point out, "ending gender-based violence requires full community participation—and particularly the increased participation of men" (p. 229). Educational programs at schools and colleges can help men and boys understand how male privilege influences social and gender norms, how to deconstruct those narratives and power differentials, and how to advocate for gender equity.

Six promising programs exemplifying universal and selective prevention strategies in K-12 settings that focus on engaging boys and men are Mentors in Violence Prevention; the Youth Relationship Program; Relationships Without Fear; Coaching Boys Into Men; the Safe Dates Project; and the Fourth R (see also Chapter 4 in this book). The Mentors in Violence Prevention (MVP) program was developed by

Jackson Katz in 1993, and was designed to train male college and high school student athletes and other student leaders to use their status to speak out against rape, battering, sexual harassment, gay bashing, and all forms of sexist abuse. A component for female students was added in the second year with a similar approach of training female student athletes and others to be leaders. MVP focuses on young men not as potential perpetrators, but rather as empowered bystanders who can confront abusive peers and support abused ones. Moreover, MVP views young women not as victims or potential targets of harassment, rape and abuse, but rather as empowered bystanders who are similarly equipped to support abused peers and confront abusive ones. MVP's positive approach of shifting from perpetrators to empowered bystanders reduces men's defensiveness around these challenging issues and allows the emergence of more proactive and preventive responses. Furthermore, this positive approach has increased the numbers of women and men willing to become involved.

Selective prevention strategies such as the Youth Relationship Program have been implemented in schools. The Youth Relationship Program is designed for high-school students who have witnessed abuse, have a history of child maltreatment, or have experienced trauma in their families (Wolfe et al., 2003). The psychoeducational program was designed to help 14–16-year-olds recognize and prevent abuse in a dating relationship. A comparison of 96 teens that received the intervention (18 two-hour sessions) with a control group of 62 teens suggested that the intervention was effective at reducing physical and emotional abuse against a dating partner over the 2 years of the study.

Applied across a population, even an intervention that generates modest effects can have a widespread impact. Universal prevention efforts can include education and media programs, and often involve changing social norms, behaviors, and policies that directly and indirectly contribute to men's violence against women. As such, universal prevention is intrinsically part of a broad-based, long-term agenda. One approach to universal prevention in a school setting is the Coaching Boys Into Men (CMIB) program, which is a national prevention program developed by Futures Without Violence. The program's objective is to engage the key people in a boy's immediate environment and teach him how to relate to women and girls in respectful, nonviolent ways. CBIM is a multilevel campaign, which uses public service announcements to promote the idea that men have a responsibility to teach boys that violence against women is unacceptable. The program's curriculum is presented as a "playbook" and is used to help coaches find teachable moments for leading team discussions about nonviolence, respect for women, and deconstructing antiquated notions of masculinity. There is also a weekly curriculum available in the Coaches' Training Kit, which encourages coaches to get involved in community outreach efforts. Moreover, coaches have access to online program materials and teaching tips from fellow coaches. In a cluster randomized trial involving over 2,000 high school athletes from 16 high schools, athletes who participated in the program reported greater intentions to intervene and higher levels of actual, positive bystander intervention than athletes in the control group (Miller et al., 2012). There was no significant difference, however, between intervention and control athletes in gender equitable attitudes or violence perpetration (Miller et al., 2012). In an adaptation of the intervention implemented with cricket coaches in Mumbai, India, athletes on teams with intervention-trained coaches showed significant changes in gender attitudes compared to non-intervention-coached teams (Miller et al., 2014). Marginally significant changes in negative bystander behaviors were also demonstrated by the intervention-coached athletes. Taken together, these rigorous and well-conducted evaluations demonstrate the difficulty in bringing about behavior change. Attitude change does not necessarily translate into behavior. At this early stage of development in the field, however, even the marginal results hold some promise for evolving prevention efforts.

One approach to preventing the onset of men's violence against women is universal prevention efforts to teach men how to build positive communication and conflict resolution skills. Several studies demonstrate the efficacy of school-based programs to prevent dating violence (for example, Foshee et al., 1998; Jaffe et al., 1992; Weisz & Black, 2001; Wolfe et al., 2009). For example, a study of the Safe Dates Project used a randomized controlled trial to test the effects of a school-based intervention. Participants reported significantly less physical and sexual dating violence than the control group, and these results were maintained up to 4 years after the end of the study (Foshee et al., 2004). The Fourth R program is another example of a school-based universal prevention effort that targets dating and peer violence. In a randomized controlled trial involving over 1,700 ninth-grade students in 20 schools, participants reported less physical dating violence and better relationship skills than students in the control group (Wolfe et al., 2009). Program strategies were still effective at a 2.5-year post-intervention follow-up.

Outside of school settings, there is little research on universal programs to prevent men's violence against women. The few non-school-based programs tend to focus on a couple's major life transitions, which also coincide with moments of heightened stress. Marriage, pregnancy, and the birth of a child may increase the risk for violence against women.

Several longitudinal studies have found that early conduct disorder and the use of generalized violence predicts dating violence perpetration, thus suggesting that prevention and intervention in the area of conduct problems can also prevent dating violence (Brendgen et al., 2001; Ehrensaft et al., 2003; Lavoie et al., 2002; Magdol et al., 1998). Although, as mentioned, there have been some promising studies of dating violence prevention, a Cochrane Collaboration meta-analysis (Fellmeth et al., 2013) examined 38 rigorous studies and concluded: "The results showed no convincing evidence that the programs decreased relationship violence, or that they improved participants' attitudes, behaviors and skills related to relationship violence" (p. 4). Given this meta-analysis, we may infer that while several programs have demonstrated significant results for dating violence prevention, we cannot yet conclude that overall such efforts result in positive change. We clearly need continued efforts to translate attitude change and skill acquisition into real and lasting GBV behavioral changes.

Global efforts to engage men and boys in preventing GBV

On a global level, institutions and organizations have begun to involve men as key allies in their efforts toward ending GBV. This shift in beliefs and practices espouses the hope that men can play an important role in prevention efforts. Led by international programs and alliances such as the White Ribbon Campaign (WRC) and MenEngage, the number of culturally specific programs and global campaigns that engage men and boys in preventing GBV continues to expand and gain momentum. These programs work to change gender norms and unequal power relationships by helping men and boys to develop healthy masculinities. Working at multiple levels, these programs promote change and support at the individual, community, institutional, societal, and global levels. Here, we highlight some of these efforts.

Pledge-based campaigns have been some of the most prominent and successfully disseminated strategies for involving men as allies. Among the international organizations leading efforts to engage men and boys in preventing GBV is Canada's WRC (www.whiteribbon.ca). The WRC was created as a response to the December 6th Montreal Massacre, in which 14 women were killed. Since its founding in

1991, the WRC has established itself in more than 60 countries and has partnered with numerous governmental and nongovernmental organizations (NGOs), including the UN, to "never commit, condone, or remain silent about violence against women" (Minerson et al., 2011, p. 2). The WRC efforts seek not only to decrease men's willingness to engage in abusive behavior, but also to increase their willingness to challenge other men whose behavior is abusive (for example, telling a friend who has committed abuse that his behavior is unacceptable and helping him get assistance), or whose behavior contributes to or condones violence against women (for example, confronting someone who tells a sexist joke).

In 2014, the UN launched its HeForShe campaign (UN Women, 2014). HeForShe is "a solidarity movement for gender equality developed by UN Women to engage men and boys as advocates and agents of change for the achievement of gender equality and women's rights" (UNiTE to End Violence Against Women, 2015). The HeForShe campaign encourages male allies to speak out and take action against the inequalities that women and girls experience, including GBV, and includes the pledge: "I am one of billions of men who believe equality for women is a basic human right that benefits us all. And I commit to taking action against gender discrimination and violence in order to build a more just and equal world." As of the writing of this chapter, almost 1,000,000 men had signed the online pledge (www.heforshe.org).

Efforts to engage men as allies have emphasized the need for coalition building with other violence prevention fields, such as child abuse and community violence, as well as organizations addressing related social and health issues, such as HIV and poverty. When framed with these two key objectives, there is a growing global alliance of organizations dedicated to involving men in achieving gender equality. In 2004, MenEngage was formed when an international coalition of NGOs and UN agencies joined forces to prevent GBV. Comprised of partner organizations in Africa, Asia, Europe, North America, and South America, the MenEngage alliance shares information, conducts joint training activities, and participates in local and global advocacy (Minerson et al., 2011, p. 5). After its 2009 Global Symposium on Engaging Men and Boys in Gender Equality, MenEngage members created the Rio Declaration, which called for gender equality and ending GBV (Minerson et al., 2011, p. 6). The Declaration and Call to Action from the 2nd International MenEngage conference held in Delhi in 2014 included a broad conceptualization of gender equality work that can be built across issues:

> Priorities for specific policy areas and actions for engaging men and boys in gender justice work include: GBV; violence against women; violence against girls, boys, and trans children; violence among men and boys; violence in armed conflict; violence against human rights defenders; caregiving and fatherhood; gender and the global political economy; sexual and reproductive health and rights; sexual and gender diversities and sexual rights (LGBTQI); men's and boys' gender vulnerabilities and health needs; sexual exploitation; HIV and AIDS; youth and adolescents; the education sector; work with religious and other leaders; environment and sustainability; and strengthening the evidence base. (MenEngage, 2014)

As these efforts continue, it is clear that work focused on men who batter is an important, but relatively small, part of the developing global effort to address men's violence toward women. This broader focus—envisioned perhaps in the early days of the battered women's movement, and consistent with the pro-feminist principles of many of the male allies who began work with batterers—is now becoming a robust and identifiable global movement.

Insituto Promundo (2012) published a report detailing research on prevention programs in a number of different settings around the world, and demonstrating the presence and potential of efforts to engage men in GBV prevention in widely diverse contexts. The programs included a community-based intervention in India, a sport-based intervention in Brazil, a health-sector-based intervention in Chile, and a workplace intervention in Rwanda. Data collected showed these programs had the ability to impact violence-related outcomes. For example, in Rio de Janeiro, sports-based dialogs in low-income communities were accompanied by community-wide campaigns that included newsletters distributed at marches and a samba song played at soccer matches that addressed GBV. A total of 129 football players who participated in the program were compared with 132 who did not. While there were large decreases in men's self-reported violence against women, there was not a significant difference between the intervention and control groups. This project shows how programming can be creatively delivered to the spaces that men inhabit and value. It also offers a model of work that addresses multiple levels of prevention, including both direct dialogs with targeted individuals and community-level media. Going forward, however, rigorous evaluation efforts demonstrating positive impact on behavior will be needed to justify investment in such efforts.

Working in collaboration with Instituto Promundo, CulturaSaldud in Chile held workshops hosted by health professionals to teach men about different types of violence, including violence within families, IPV, assault, and sexual abuse. Men participating in the health-based intervention in Chile also expressed changing attitudes about behaviors. According to the Insituto Promundo (2012), "93.4% of the surveyed participants reported that they were more knowledgeable about types of violence" (p. 35). Moreover, "81% of the youth reported that the intervention gave them more tools to solve problems without resorting to violence" (p. 35). Instituto Promundo's work has also expanded to Rwanda, where it hosted GBV prevention trainings with the Rwanda Men's Resource Center (RWAMREC) (http://rwamrec.org) at local coffee cooperatives. Although impact results were not assessed for this program, coffee cooperatives proved to be a low-cost method for disseminating GBV prevention training to large groups of participants (Instituto Promundo, 2012, p. 40). While such evaluation yields useful information on the feasibility of reaching participants, we cannot draw any conclusions about the effectiveness of such approaches.

The Stepping Stones training workshops began in Uganda in 1993, and have since expanded globally (see also Chapter 3 in this book). This program uses culturally relevant training materials and critical literacy methods of instruction to guide participants in self-reflective discussions and analyses. For example, the program includes training workshops about "gender, HIV, communication and relationship skills" (Stepping Stones, 2015; www.steppingstonesfeedback.org). By using films, age-appropriate manuals, role-playing, and drawing, the Stepping Stones workshops help to foster a safe space for dialog and action (Casey et al., 2016b; Stepping Stones, 2015). Jewkes et al. (2014) conducted a study of two programs—Stepping Stones and Creating Futures—in two urban areas of South Africa. Using an interrupted time-series method, results indicated that the intervention increased gender equitable attitudes for both men and women, and women reported experiencing less sexual and/or physical IPV.

The Male Norms Initiative began in 2008 in Ethiopia, Namibia, and Tanzania as an effort to address GBV prevention and HIV/AIDS (PATH, 2016). Working with several local and global partners, the Male Norms Initiative sought to help men reconceptualize how they thought about and interacted with women and girls, as well as how they understood and internalized gender norms. In conjunction with changing attitudes and behaviors toward women, the program also advocated for HIV/AIDS prevention, care, and support. Pulerwitz et al. (2010) evaluated three sites in Ethiopia. Program participants at one site were part of both community engagement and group education initiatives, while participants at the second site were part of only the community engagement activities, and participants at the third site received a delayed intervention (p. 7). Post-intervention results indicate that men who participated in both community and group activities had more positive views toward gender equity, were more likely to openly talk about HIV prevention, and significantly reduced IPV. Those participating in the community engagement activities displayed more positive attitudes toward women and gender equitable norms (p. 27); however, program staff at this site expressed a greater need for resources and time to extend the program (p. 28). Overall, Pulerwitz et al. (2010) conclude that combined interventions had the greatest impact on program participants' views about gender equity, gender norms, and sexual health.

Efforts have begun to document the global scope and nature of IPV prevention work involving men. Kimball et al. (2013) conducted an online survey of organizations worldwide that identified as providing primary prevention services to men in an effort to prevent violence against women. The 165 organizations that participated in the survey came from every region of the world; North American countries were overrepresented, in part because the survey was only offered in English. Kimball et al. (2013) reported that only about 20% of the programs worked exclusively in domestic violence prevention aimed at involving men. Of those organizations that engaged in other efforts, the top three categories of activity were domestic violence service provision, social services, and sexual violence prevention, demonstrating that multilevel work is a common feature of efforts to end men's violence against women. About half of the organizations allocated 25% or less of their resources to primary prevention efforts directed toward men's involvement. It appears, therefore, that this work often takes place in organizations that have substantial involvement at other levels or toward other issues.

Casey et al. (2013) detailed some of the challenges and opportunities that arise in efforts to engage men at the community level. Among them was the challenge of dealing with male privilege when the focus of work is to challenge traditional definitions of masculinity that entail power and authority over women. Interviewees reported that a focus on privilege could be off-putting to some men, making it difficult to initially engage them and sustain their involvement. Interviewees further noted that homophobia, transphobia, and men's assumptions that anti-violence programs are inherently anti-male constitute related challenges. Carlson et al. (2015) detail some of the strategies programs use to address these difficulties, including personal invitations to men and boys to get involved; focusing on relationships, including fatherhood; avoiding blaming and accusatory language; and being hopeful about the potential for men and boys to change and to be partners in addressing violence. Finally, echoing the Kimball et al. (2013) survey results, Storer et al. (2016) found the accounts of program representatives showed that frontline prevention work challenges rigid distinctions between levels of prevention. For example, for programs engaged in work with individual perpetrators of violence, program representatives still considered their work as prevention because they were engaged in healing that could both prevent subsequent abuse by those men and decrease the chance of intergenerational transmission of violence. Program activities varied across the spectrum of prevention efforts.

Future directions for research

Research on engaging men and boys in preventing GBV is in its early stages. Primary prevention strategies that focus on engaging boys and men are largely new and relatively small in scope (Wells et al., 2013). There is a limited evidence base to date, and most efforts have not yet been subjected to rigorous evaluations. Although many promising practices have begun to collect participant and provider feedback and conduct informal evaluations, few have used experimental designs (Flood, 2011). Prominent strategies in the growing body of research on efforts to engage men and boys include engaging men as leaders and role models, and working with men and boys to promote positive constructs of masculinity—particularly with men who have the potential to influence other men's and boys' attitudes and behaviors (Campbell et al., 2010). Efforts also include teaching men how to be engaged as bystanders, who act to both prevent and address violence within their environments (Crooks et al., 2007).

We assert that research and prevention efforts need to address all forms of abuse and assess change in attitudes as well as behaviors. The existing evidence base has gaps in the areas of physical and sexual violence prevention. Some areas for future work may include pre- and post-surveys focusing on long-term attitudes and large samples in specific settings (for example, on one campus), which may render evidence for scalability and feasibility of promising practices in diverse settings. In addition, research on the cumulative effects of exposure to multiple prevention programs and campaigns, and on integrated approaches to preventing multiple forms of family, peer, and/or community violence, could help to expand our understanding of effective GBV prevention efforts. Lastly, research on integrated approaches to engaging men in efforts to prevent violence and simultaneously prevent other adverse outcomes (for example, substance abuse, risky sexual behavior) could also be of use in understanding best practices and outcomes.

In the area of engaging men as fathers, Labarre et al. (2016) address the significance of supporting fathers who are committed to improving their lives and creating stronger bonds with their children. The authors argue that part of this support system includes how researchers conduct their studies and gather data on the effectiveness of IPV prevention programs. Although evaluation methods and standards for determining the success of IPV prevention programs are still being created for the field (p. 21), Labarre et al. (2016) offer some direction for future researchers. For example, they problematize the validity of self-reported data (p. 20) and how researchers define "success" (p. 21), and call for researchers to include more rigorous protocols—such as psychosocial factors of the participants—when determining the success of an IPV prevention program (p. 21). They also suggest that researchers compare participant data between men who do and do not have children, the different types of programs that fathers attend (p. 20), and the overall behavioral changes for fathers, children, and mothers participating in the IPV prevention programs (p. 21). Furthermore, Labarre et al. (2016) suggest that researchers include data that describe how fathers are exhibiting healthy fathering skills (p. 22). According to the authors, this dual goal of violence cessation and improved parenting skills is key to supporting and helping fathers and their families (p. 22).

When examining the current state of research on gender transformative approaches to engaging men in GBV prevention, Casey and Tolman et al. (2016) point out that researchers could benefit from understanding how culturally specific notions of masculinities affect men's decisions to become part of GBV prevention efforts. Casey et al. (2013) also point out that research is needed with men who do not engage in GBV prevention programs. Having a deeper understanding of the disconnect between advocacy efforts and a lack of social change can help researchers create more culturally specific prevention models and help local and regional leaders build more sustainable cross-organizational coalitions. Moreover, understanding the risk factors for men's perpetration can help researchers understand men's lived experiences. Finally, Jewkes et al. (2015) emphasize the need for researchers to work with both men and women to understand the complex relationships between power and privilege in allyship efforts (Casey et al., 2016a; 2016b; Jewkes et al., 2015).

Banyard (2014) also suggests methodological improvements, noting that future GBV prevention research could include evaluating dose effects; testing moderator variables beyond gender; unpacking elements of prevention tools that are more important for creating change; using research to help integrate theories on which prevention is based; partnering with practitioners for evaluation; translating research programs to new communities; and developing new behavioral outcome measures. We also believe that future research on GBV prevention efforts may help to expand the field by considering the following:

- Longitudinal work to assess possible intergenerational impacts of GBV prevention efforts;
- Conducting more research on the effects of GBV prevention programs that include intergenerational impacts among other prevention and/or behavior-change goals;
- Increasing attention to what works, for whom, under what circumstances.

This may include a consideration of which programs can be successfully replicated in diverse settings, an evaluation of what kinds of modifications are necessary or acceptable, and a study of what kinds of programs can support the effective dissemination of local, regional, national and international efforts, with clear guidance regarding important components of prevention programs and areas for adaptation.

Conclusion

The proliferation and diversity of strategies for engaging men in preventing GBV has provided new understandings of how men can challenge hegemonic ideals of privilege and power, and how men as fathers, caregivers, and role models can help challenge and change gender norms and inequalities. Engaging men and boys can help facilitate introspection and reflection, interrupt the intergenerational transmission of GBV, and change social norms at multiple levels. For example, these programs can change attitudes and beliefs about sexuality, marriage, fatherhood, masculinity, feminism, and family relationships. Engaging men as allies and including men in the problem-solving process increases the potential for sustained individual, systemic, and societal changes. By taking advantage of windows of opportunity presented by critical development periods and developing tailored interventions consistent with the culture of settings including schools, the military, and so on, women and men of various ages can be involved in changing how gender norms are reproduced across the life course. Recognizing the rich innovation occurring globally, we emphasize the importance of promoting the crossnational dissemination of best practices and data evaluation methods, and sharing lessons learned.

Note

1. Preventive measures are often classified into *primary* (prevention of a condition from occurring), *secondary* (screening of those at risk with a view of early detection and prevention of a condition), and *tertiary* (efforts to prevent relapse or complications of a condition). These roughly correspond to the classifications we use: *Universal* strategies target all in the population—including those who may not be at risk or have previous GBV perpetration or exposure—hence, primary. *Selected* prevention is similar to secondary prevention, as individuals are selected for prevention efforts based on risk factors. *Tertiary* conforms to indicated prevention, as the targets of prevention efforts are those who have already perpetrated or been victimized by GBV.

References

Allen, S.M., & Daly, K.J. (2007). *The effects of father involvement: An updated research summary of the evidence.* Guelph, ON, Canada: Centre for Families, Work & Well-Being, University of Guelph.

Arean, J.D., & Davis, L. (2007). Working with fathers in batterer intervention programs: Lessons from the Fathering After Violence Initiative. In J.L. Edleson & O.J. Williams (Eds.), *Parenting by men who batter* (pp. 118–130). New York: Oxford University Press.

Bancroft, L., Silverman, J.G., & Ritchie, D. (2012). *The batterer as parent: Addressing the impact of domestic violence on family dynamics* (2nd Ed.). Thousand Oaks, CA: Sage.

Banyard, V.L. (2014). Improving college campus-based prevention of violence against women: A strategic plan for research built on multipronged practices and policies. *Trauma, Violence, & Abuse, 15*(2), 1–13.

Barker, G., & Verani, F. (2008). *Men's participation as fathers in the Latin American and Caribbean region: A critical literature review with policy considerations.* Rio de Janeiro: Instituto Promundo and Save the Children.

Berrios, D.C., & Grady, D. (1991). Domestic violence: Risk factors and outcomes. *Western Journal of Medicine, 155*(2), 133.

Blabey, M.H., Locke, E.R., Goldsmith, Y.W., & Perham-Hester, K.A. (2009). Experience of a controlling or threatening partner among mothers with persistent symptoms of depression. *American Journal of Obstetrics and Gynecology, 201*(2), 173–e1.

Brendgen, M., Vitaro, R., Tremblay, R.E., & Lavoie, F. (2001). Reactive and proactive aggression: Predictions to physical violence in different contexts and moderating effects of parental monitoring and caregiving behavior. *Journal of Abnormal Child Psychology, 29*(4), 293–304.

Bunston, W. (2013). "What about the fathers?" Bringing "Dads on Board" with their infants and toddlers following violence. *Journal of Family Studies, 19*, 70–79.

Campbell, J., Garcia-Moreno, C., & Sharps, P. (2004). Abuse during pregnancy in industrialized and developing countries. *Violence Against Women, 10*(7), 770–789.

Campbell, M., Neil, J.A., Jaffe, P.G., & Kelly, T. (2010). Engaging abusive men in seeking community intervention: A critical research & practice priority. *Journal of Family Violence, 25*(4), 413–422.

Carlson, J., Casey, E., Edleson, J.L., Tolman, R.M., Walsh, T.B., & Kimball, E. (2015). Strategies to engage men and boys in violence prevention: A global organizational perspective. *Violence Against Women, 21*(11), 1406-1425.

Casey, E., Carlson, J., Two Bulls, S., & Yager, A. (2016a). Gender transformative approaches to engaging men in gender-based violence prevention: A review and conceptual model. *Trauma, Violence, & Abuse*. doi: 10.1177/1524838016650191.

Casey, E.A., Tolman, R.M., Carlson, J., Allen, C.T., & Storer, H.L. (2016b). What motivates men's involvement in gender-based violence prevention? Latent class profiles and correlates in an international sample of men. *Men and Masculinities*. doi: 10.1177/1097184X16634801.

Center for Urban Families. (2009). Baltimore Responsible Father Project. Retrieved from: www.cfuf.org/Baltimore-Responsible-Fatherhood-Project/.

Chamberlain, L. (2008, March). *A prevention primer for domestic violence: Terminology, tools, and the public health approach.* Harrisburg, PA: VAWnet. Retrieved from: www.vawnet.org/summary.php?doc_id=1313&find_type=web_sum_AR.

Cohen, L., & Swift, S. (1999). The spectrum of prevention: Developing a comprehensive approach to injury prevention. *Injury Prevention, 5*(3), 203–207. doi: 10.1136/ip.5.3.203.

Cokkinides, V.E., Coker, A.L., Sanderson, M., Addy, C., & Bethea, L. (1999). Physical violence during pregnancy: Maternal complications and birth outcomes. *Obstetrics & Gynecology, 93*(5, Part 1), 661–666.

Connolly, A., Katz, V.L., Bash, K.L., Mcmahon, M.J., & Hansen, W.F. (1997). Trauma and pregnancy. *American Journal of Perinatology, 14*(6), 331–336.

Crooks, C.V., Goodall, G.., Hughes, R., Jaffe, P.G., & Baker, L.L. (2007). Engaging men and boys in preventing violence against women: Applying a cognitive-behavioral model. *Violence Against Women, 13*, 217–239.

de Moseson, B.A.G. (2004). *Intimate partner violence during pregnancy: Risk factors from the Oregon Pregnancy Risk Assessment Monitoring System.* MPH. Oregon Health & Science University.

Donovan, R., & Vlais, R. (2005). *VicHealth review of communication components of social marketing: Public education campaigns focusing on violence against women.* Melbourne: Victorian Health Promotion Foundation.

Douglas, U., Bathrick, D., & Perry, P.A. (2008). Deconstructing male violence against women: The Men Stopping Violence community accountability model. *Violence Against Women, 14*, 247–261.

Dubowitz, H. (2006). Where's Dad? A need to understand father's role in child maltreatment. *Child Abuse & Neglect, 30*(5), 461–465.

Dubowitz, H., Black, M.M., Kerr, M.A., Starr, R.H., & Harrington, D. (2000). Fathers and child neglect. *Archives of Pediatrics & Adolescent Medicine, 154*(2), 135–141.

Edleson, J.L., & Williams, O.J. (2007). Introduction: Involving men who batter in their children's lives. In J.L. Edleson & O.J. Williams (Eds.), *Parenting by men who batter* (pp. 3–18). New York: Oxford University Press.

Ehrensaft, M.K., Cohen, P., Brown, J., Smailes, E., Chen, H., & Johnson, J.G. (2003). Intergenerational transmission of partner violence: A 20-year prospective study. *Journal of Consulting and Clinical Psychology, 71*, 741–753.

El Kady, D., Gilbert, W.M., Xing, G., & Smith, L.H. (2005). Maternal and neonatal outcomes of assaults during pregnancy. *Obstetrics & Gynecology, 105*(2), 357–363.

Fellmeth, G.L., Heffernan, C., Nurse, J., Habibula, S., & Sethi, D. (2013). Educational and skills-based interventions for preventing relationship and dating violence in adolescents and young adults. *The Cochrane Library.* 6, Art. No.: CD004534, doi: 10.1002/14651858. CD004534.pub3.

Ferguson, H., & Gates, P. (2015). Early intervention and holistic, relationship-based practice with fathers: Evidence from the work of the Family Nurse Partnership. *Child & Family Social Work, 20*(1), 96–105.

Fernandez, F.M., & Krueger, P.M. (1999). Domestic violence: Effect on pregnancy outcome. *Journal of the American Osteopathic Association, 99*(5), 254–256.

Flood, M. (2007). Involving men in gender policy and practice. *Critical Half: Bi-Annual Journal of Women for Women International, 5*(1), 9–13.

Flood, M. (2011). Involving men in efforts to end violence against women. *Men and Masculinities, 14*(3), 358–377.

Florsheim, P., McArthur, L., Hudak, C., Heavin, S., & Burrow-Sanchez, J. (2011). The Young Parenthood Program: Preventing intimate partner violence between adolescent mothers and young fathers. *Journal of Couple & Relationship Therapy, 10*(2), 117–134.

Foshee, V.A., Bauman, K.E., Arriaga, X.B., Helms, R.W., Koch, G.G., & Linder, G.F. (1998). An evaluation of Safe Dates, an adolescent dating violence prevention program. *American Journal of Public Health, 88*(1), 45–50.

Foshee, V.A., Bauman, K.E., Ennett, S.T., Linder, G.F., Benefield, T., & Suchindran, C. (2004). Assessing the long-term effects of the Safe Dates program and a booster in preventing and reducing adolescent dating violence victimization and perpetration. *American Journal of Public Health, 94*(4), 619–624.

Foumbi, J., & Lovich, R. (1997). Role of men in the lives of children: A study of how improving knowledge about men in families helps strengthen programming for children and women. New York: UNICEF. Retrieved from: https://www.unicef.org/evaldatabase/files/Global_1997_Role_of_Men.pdf.

Fox, G.L., & Benson, M.L. (2004). Violent men, bad dads? Fathering profiles of men involved in intimate partner violence. In R. D. Day & M.E. Lamb (Eds.), *Conceptualizing and measuring father involvement* (pp. 359–384). Mahwah, NJ: Lawrence Erlbaum.

General Assembly resolution 48/104, Declaration on the elimination of violence against women, A/RES/48/104 (20 December 1993). Retrieved from: www.un.org/documents/ga/res/48/a48r104.htm.

Greene, A.D., & Moore, K.A. (2000). Nonresident father involvement and child well-being among young children in families on welfare. *Marriage & Family Review, 29*(2–3), 159–180.

Guterman, N.B., & Lee, Y. (2005). The role of fathers in risk for physical child abuse and neglect: Possible pathways and unanswered questions. *Child Maltreatment, 10*(136), 136–149. doi: 10.1177/1077559505274623.

Hart Research Associates, Inc. (2007). Father's Day poll. Retrieved from: www.caepv.org/membercenter/files/fathers_day_poll_07.pdf.

Haskett, M.E., Ahern, L.S., Ward, C.S., & Allaire, J.C. (2006). Factor structure and validity of the parenting stress index-short form. *Journal of Clinical Child and Adolescent Psychology, 35*(2), 302–312.

Heise, L.L. (1998). Violence against women: An integrated ecological framework. *Violence Against Women, 4*(3), 262-290.

Horn, W.F. (1999). Did you say "movement"? In W.F. Horn, D. Blankenhorn, & M.B. Pearlstein (Eds.), *The fatherhood movement: A call to action* (pp. 1–16). Lantham, MD: Lexington Books.

Horn, W.F., Blankenhorn, D., & Pearlstein, M.B. (1999). *The fatherhood movement: A call to action.* Lantham, MD: Lexington Books.

Instituto Promundo (2012). *Engaging men to prevent gender-based violence: A multi-country intervention and impact evaluation study.* Retrieved from: http://promundoglobal.org/resources/engaging-men-to-prevent-gender-based-violence-a-multi-country-intervention-and-impact-evaluation-study/.

Jaffe, P., Sudermann, M., Reitzel, D., & Killip, S.M. (1992). An evaluation of a secondary school primary prevention program on violence in relationships. *Violence and Victims, 7*, 129–146.

Jewkes, R., Flood, M., & Lang, J. (2015). From work with men and boys to changes of social norms and reduction of inequities in gender relations: A conceptual shift in prevention of violence against women and girls. *The Lancet, 385*(9977), 1580–1589. doi: 10.1016/S0140-6736(14)61683-4.

Jewkes, R., Gibbs, A., Jama-Shai, N., Willan, S., Misselhorn, A., Mushinga, M. et al. (2014). Stepping Stones and Creating Futures intervention: Shortened interrupted time series evaluation of a behavioural and structural health promotion and violence prevention intervention for young people in informal settlements in Durban, South Africa. *BMC Public Health, 14*(1), 1–10. doi: 10.1186/1471-2458-14-1325.

Kimball, E., Edleson, J. L., Tolman, R.M., Neugut, T.B., & Carlson, J. (2013). Global efforts to engage men in preventing violence against women: An international survey. *Violence Against Women, 19*(7), 924–939.

Labarre, M., Bourassa, C., Holden, G.W., Turcotte, P., & Letourneau, N. (2016). Intervening with fathers in the context of intimate partner violence: An analysis of ten programs and suggestions for a research agenda. *Journal of Child Custody, 13*(1), 1–29. doi: 10.1080/15379418.2016.1127793.

Lavoie, F., Hebert, M., Tremblay, R., Vitaro, F., Vezina, L., & McDuff, P. (2002). History of family dysfunction and perpetration of dating violence by adolescent boys: A longitudinal study. *Journal of Adolescent Health, 30*(5), 365–383.

Levtov, R., van der Gaag, N., Greene, M., Kaufman, M., & Barker, G. (2015). *State of the world's fathers: A MenCare advocacy publication.* Washington, DC: Promundo, Rutgers, Save the Children, Sonke Gender Justice, and the MenEngage Alliance.

Magdol, L., Moffitt, T.E., Caspi, A., & Silva, P.A. (1998). Developmental antecedents of partner abuse: A prospective-longitudinal study. *Journal of Abnormal Psychology, 107*, 375–389.

Marsiglio, W. (2008). Understanding men's prenatal experience and the father involvement connection: Assessing baby steps. *Journal of Marriage and Family, 70*(5), 1108–1113.

Marsiglio, W., Amato, P., Day, R.D., & Lamb, M.E. (2000). Scholarship on fatherhood in the 1990s and beyond. *Journal of Marriage and Family, 62*(4), 1173–1191.

MenEngage (2014). Declaration and call to action. Retrieved from: www.menengagedilli2014.net/delhi-declaration-and-call-to-action.html.

Miller, E., Tancredi, D.J., McCauley, H.L., Decker, M.R., Anderson, H.A., Stetkevich, N. et al. (2012). "Coaching Boys Into Men": A cluster-randomized controlled trial of a dating violence prevention program. *Journal of Adolescent Health, 1*(5), 431–438.

Minerson, T., Carolo, H., Dinner, T., & Jones, C. (2011). *Issue brief: Engaging men and boys to reduce and prevent gender-based violence.* Ottawa: Status of Women Canada. Retrieved from: www.deslibris.ca/ID/236976.

Morland, L.A., Leskin, G.A., Block, C.R., Campbell, J.C., & Friedman, M.J. (2008). Intimate partner violence and miscarriage: Examination of the role of physical and psychological abuse and posttraumatic stress disorder. *Journal of Interpersonal Violence, 23*(5), 652–669.

Olivier, D., Slaven, F., Pumla, S., and Vusizi, F. (2016). *MenCare+: Engaging men in a 4-country initiative: MenCare+ South Africa Outcome Measurement report.* Foundation for Professional Development Program Evaluation Unit. Retrieved from: http://men-care.org/resources/?type=publications.

Osofsky, J.D., Thompson, M.D., Shonkoff, J.P., & Meisels, S.J. (2000). Adaptive and maladaptive parenting: Perspectives on risk and protective factors. *Handbook of Early Childhood Intervention, 2*, 54–75.

PATH (2016). Evaluating the Male Norms Initiative in Ethiopia and Namibia. Retrieved from: http://sites.path.org/hivaidsandtb/closed-projects/male-norms-initiative/.

Pease, B. (2008). Engaging men in men's violence prevention: Exploring the tensions, dilemmas and possibilities. *Australian Domestic & Family Violence Clearinghouse, 17*, 1–20.

Perel, G., & Peled, E. (2008). The fathering of violent men: Constriction and yearning. *Violence Against Women, 14*(4), 457–482.

Pruett, K.D. (2000). *Fatherneed: Why father care is as essential as mother care for your child.* New York: Free Press.

Pulerwitz J., Martin S., Mehta M., Castillo, T., Kidanu, A., Verani, F. et al. (2010). Promoting gender equity for HIV and violence prevention: Results from the Male Norms Initiative evaluation in Ethiopia. Washington, DC: PATH. Retrieved from: www.path.org/publications/files/GVR_gen_eq_eth_rpt.pdf.

Rachana, C., Suraiya, K., Hisham, A.S., Abdulaziz, A.M., & Hai, A. (2002). Prevalence and complications of physical violence during pregnancy. *European Journal of Obstetrics & Gynecology and Reproductive Biology, 103*(1), 26–29.

Rosen, D., Seng, J.S. & Tolman, R.M. (2007). Intimate partner violence, depression, and posttraumatic stress disorder as additional predictors of low birth weight infants among low-income mothers. *Journal of Interpersonal Violence, 22*(10), 1305–1314.

Rothman, E., Mandel, D.G., & Silverman, J.G. (2007). Abusers' perceptions of the effect of their intimate partner violence on children. *Violence Against Women, 13*, 1179–1191.

Scott, K.L., & Lishak, V. (2012). Intervention for maltreating fathers: Statistically and clinically significant change. *Child Abuse & Neglect, 36*(9), 680–684. doi: 10.1016/j.chiabu.2012.06.003.

Self-Brown, S., Cowart-Osborne, M., Baker, E., Thomas, A., Boyd Jr, C., Chege, E. et al. (2015). Dad2K: An adaptation of SafeCare to Enhance positive parenting skills with at-risk fathers. *Child & Family Behavior Therapy, 37*(2), 138–155.

Shapiro, A.F., Krysik, J., & Pennar, A.L. (2011). Who are the fathers in healthy families Arizona? An examination of father data in at-risk families. *American Journal of Orthopsychiatry, 81*(3), 327.

Sharps, P.W., Laughon, K., & Giangrande, S.K. (2007). Intimate partner violence and the childbearing years: Maternal and infant health consequences. *Trauma, Violence, & Abuse, 8*(2), 105–116. doi: 10.1177/1524838007302594.

Smith, C.A., & Farrington, D.P. (2004). Continuities in antisocial behavior and parenting across three generations. *Journal of Child Psychology and Psychiatry, 45*(2), 230–247.

Stepping Stones (2015). Stepping Stones: Welcome. Retrieved from: www.steppingstonesfeedback.org.

Storer, H.L., Casey, E.A., Carlson, J., Edleson, J.L., & Tolman, R. (2016). Primary prevention is? A global perspective on how organizations engaging men in preventing gender-based violence conceptualize and operationalize their work. *Violence Against Women, 22*(2), 249–268. doi: 10.1177/1077801215601247.

Stover, C.S. (2015), Fathers for change for substance use and intimate partner violence: Initial community pilot. *Family Process, 54*(4), 600–609. doi: 10.1111/famp.12136.

Stover, C.S., & Morgos. D. (2013). Fatherhood and intimate partner violence: Bringing the parenting role into intervention strategies. *Professional Psychology: Research and Practice, 44*(4), 247–256.

UN Women (2014). HeForShe: UN Women solidarity movement for gender equality action kit. Retrieved from: www.heforshe.org/action-kit.

UNiTE to End Violence Against Women (2015). Orange Day 2015. The HeForShe Campaign. Retrieved from: www.un.org/en/women/endviolence/orangedayapril2015.shtml.

Walsh, T.B., Tolman, R.M., Davis, R.N., Palladino, C.L., Romero, V.C., Singh, V. (2014). Moving up the "magic moment": Fathers' experience of prenatal ultrasound. *Fathering: A Journal of Theory, Research, and Practice about Men as Fathers, 12*(1), 18–37.

Walsh, T.B., Tolman, R.M., Davis, R.N., & Singh, V. (in press). Fathers' presence at ultrasound: An opportunity for engagement. *Social Work Research.*

Weisz, A., & Black, B. (2001). Sexual assault and dating violence prevention with urban youth: Assessing effectiveness. *Social Work Research, 25*(2), 89–102.

Wells, L., Lorenzetti, L., Carolo, H., Dinner, T., Jones, C., Minerson, T., & Esina, E. (2013). *Engaging men and boys in domestic violence prevention: Opportunities and promising approaches.* Calgary, AB: University of Calgary. Retrieved from: http://blog.calgaryunitedway.org/socialvoice/wp-content/uploads/2013/03/Shift-Engaging-Men-and-Boys.pdf

Whitefield, C.L., Anda, R.F., Dube, S.R., & Felitti, V.J. (2003). Violent childhood experiences and the risk of intimate partner violence in adults: Assessment in a large health maintenance organization. *Journal of Interpersonal Violence, 18*(2), 166–185.

WHO (World Health Organization) (2002). *The world health report 2002: Reducing risks, promoting healthy life*. Geneva: WHO. Retrieved from: www.who.int/whr/2002/en/.

Wolfe, D. A., Crooks, C., Jaffe, P., Chiodo, D., Hughes, R., Ellis, W. et al. (2009). A school-based program to prevent adolescent dating violence: A cluster randomized trial. *Archives of Pediatrics & Adolescent Medicine, 163*(8), 692-699.

Wolfe, D.A., Wekerle, C., Scott, K., Straatman, A.-L., Grasley, C., & Reitzel-Jaffey, D. (2003). Dating violence prevention with at-risk youth: A controlled outcome evaluation. *Journal of Consulting and Clinical Psychology, 71*, 279–291.

FIVE

Gender-based Violence Assessment in the Health Sector and Beyond

Michele R. Decker, Elizabeth Miller, and Nancy Glass

Introduction

Over the past three decades, gender-based violence (GBV) has emerged as a primary threat to health and human rights globally. GBV is defined as types of violence that primarily women and girls experience, including physical violence (for example, being hit, punched, kicked, slapped, choked, hurt with a weapon, or otherwise physically hurt), sexual violence (for example, unprotected forced sex and coercive behaviors, which include sexual slavery and coerced abortion), and psychological harm (for example, controlling behaviors, stalking, threats of violence). Intimate partners, members of the woman or girl's family, acquaintances, and/or strangers perpetrate these acts of violence, in the home, community, and/or during armed conflict.

Globally, an estimated 35% of women experience physical and/ or sexual violence in their lifetime, including partner and non-partner violence (Bott et al., 2012; World Health Organization, 2013a). GBV confers profound health consequences, including physical, sexual, and mental health issues and homicide (Campbell, 2002; Decker et al., 2005; Ellsberg et al., 2008; Hathaway et al., 2000; Jewkes et al., 2010; Seth et al., 2010; Silverman et al., 2008; Stockl et al., 2013). Refugees fleeing conflicts and natural disasters are vulnerable to sexual violence; in humanitarian emergencies, refugee and displaced women and girls experience GBV within the context of war or conflict, during transit and displacement, and in the camp/settlement setting. Loss of secure housing, limited economic opportunities, lack of security, and family disruption among conflict-affected populations enable opportunistic violence as well as intimate partner violence (IPV) (Wirtz et al., 2016). A recent systematic review and meta-analysis of GBV among female refugees in complex humanitarian emergencies generated a pooled estimate of 21.4% (95%CI: 14.9–29.7%) sexual violence prevalence (Vu et al., 2013). There is substantial evidence indicating underreporting of GBV globally (Palermo et al., 2013) as well as in diverse humanitarian settings, where women and girls can be particularly vulnerable (Palermo & Peterman, 2011; Wirtz et al., 2013).

Global efforts often focus on a range of GBV perpetrators. Within the US, as elsewhere, intimate partners are the dominant perpetrators of GBV (Black et al., 2011), hence the domestic focus on IPV. In the US, an estimated one in three women experience IPV—that is, physical or sexual violence by a current or former spouse or boyfriend—with youth and young adult women at highest risk (Black et al., 2011). Gender differences persist in the nature and impact of IPV. Nationally, physical IPV prevalence is comparable for women (33%) and men (28%) (Black et al., 2011); however, women experience significantly more sexual IPV (9% vs. too small to report among men) (Black et al., 2011); more IPV with resulting fear, injury, or other health or social issues (29% vs. 10%) (Black et al., 2011); and more IPV homicide (Cooper and Smith, 2011; Stockl et al., 2013).

Women and girls in the sex industry; homeless and marginally housed youth; sexual minorities; and minority ethnic groups can face additional layers of vulnerability—often with impunity—that accumulate to produce risk for diverse forms of violence, including IPV, and undermine access to services and justice. To date, prevention and response efforts continue to be insufficient to make a significant difference in ending violence against women and girls globally.

Why screen for IPV and other forms of GBV?

"Screening" in public health refers to asymptomatic disease identification (generally prior to manifestation of symptoms) through the use of a rapid test, examination, or other procedure to enable early diagnosis and treatment. Routine screening in the health care sector has focused on IPV and has been one of the primary recommended means for advancing prevention and response strategies for survivors.

Specifically, early identification of survivors is supported for a variety of reasons, not least of which is the demonstrated negative impact of violence on women and girl's health and the responsibility of health providers to confidentially screen for IPV/GBV and provider referrals to local advocates and community-based programs. Moreover, GBV survivors are more likely than non-survivors to seek health services (Decker et al., 2005; Hathaway et al., 2000; Nasrullah et al., 2013), including those for sexual and reproductive health, making women's health centers an optimal setting for survivor identification and support. In more recent years, IPV screening efforts have begun in community settings beyond the formal health sector, such as through home visitation programs (Sharps et al., 2016).

Relying on survivor self-identification misses the vast majority of survivors. Globally and domestically, absent routine screening, the identification and care of survivors of IPV and other forms of GBV is generally reliant on women and girls self-reporting to health or service providers, or authorities such as police. However, survivors face complex, dangerous, and difficult safety decisions (Campbell et al., 2001; Campbell and Glass, 2009) when disclosing IPV. Moreover, significant barriers to disclosing IPV in health and justice systems exist, including fear; stigma; discrimination; lack of recognition of abuse; lack of knowledge of, or confidence in, existing health and social services; and lack of awareness of the negative health outcomes associated with IPV (Dienemann et al., 2003; Dutton, 2004; Garcia-Moreno et al., 2005; Hardesty and Campbell, 2004; Kalof, 2000; Koss et al., 1988). Low uptake of support services, coupled with limited prevention efforts and inadequate legal responses to survivors, likely maintain the status quo of impunity for perpetrators.

Limitations of the screening paradigm center on its relevance to IPV survivors, as many women are not truly "asymptomatic;" rather, the consequences of their violence exposure may be quite advanced, and for many women violence may be chronic. Yet the public health approach has served as a helpful model for advocating that health care providers routinely address IPV. In part, such a conversation can serve as primary prevention (for those never exposed to IPV), secondary prevention (for individuals with an IPV history), and tertiary prevention (intervention for those currently experiencing IPV) (Caralis and Musialowski, 1997; Gerbert et al., 1996; McCauley et al., 1998; Rodriguez et al., 1996).

IPV/GBV screening and response in health settings: The evidence base

The evidence base for IPV screening can be characterized as mixed and evolving. Several recent reviews have summarized the evidence to date on IPV screening and interventions based in health care. Thus, this section summarizes seminal developments in the field, and synthesizes the findings gleaned from these reviews.

One seminal trial, conducted with prenatal patients and published in 2000, compared brief provision of IPV-related information with a counseling intervention arm and an outreach arm. Abuse severity decreased in all three arms by 18-month follow-up, prompting the conclusion that abuse screening at a minimum may be the most effective way to prevent abuse against pregnant women (McFarlane et al., 2000). In 2004, a systematic review was undertaken to inform the US Preventive Services Task Force (USPSTF) recommendations; this review identified no trials of the effectiveness of health-based IPV screening on future harm, though screening instruments with reasonable consistency and validation parameters were identified (Nelson et al., 2004).

Several trials emerged in the years following the 2004 USPSTF review, including two screening trials with minimal intervention, which were found to be ineffective in reducing violence. One large randomized controlled trial, implemented with over 6,000 patients across 26 clinics, compared a self-administered IPV screening tool provided to the clinician before a health visit with standard of care, and found no impact of screening on IPV or quality of life at 18-month follow-up (MacMillan et al., 2009). In this study, IPV-related discussions and/or referrals were at the discretion of the treating clinician, without a systematic means to address any safety issues raised. One study implemented in emergency departments compared usual care with an intervention arm that received brief screening, risk assessment, and referral; at 3-month follow-up, recent violence exposure was comparable across treatment and control arms (Koziol-McLain et al., 2010).

Simultaneously, several trials provided brief clinic-based or home-based interventions in addition to assessment, generally with greater impact on health, safety, and social outcomes. In a 2010 trial, brief, individualized counseling with perinatal women yielded reductions in IPV victimization and improved birth outcomes—specifically, increased gestational age at delivery and reduced very preterm birth—relative to standard of care (Kiely et al., 2010). In Hawaii, a home visitation program that focused on supporting family functioning reduced physical IPV victimization compared with usual care, though intervention effects attenuated by long-term follow-up (Bair-Merritt et al., 2010). Where a wallet-sized IPV referral card was compared with a more extensive, 20-minute nurse case management protocol in primary care clinics, both approaches were equally effective in reducing threats of abuse and homicide risk factors, and in increasing safety behaviors (McFarlane et al., 2006). For perinatal women, home visiting and support provided by peer mother mentors generated significant reductions in abuse and trends favoring the intervention arm across domains of depression and physical and mental wellbeing (Taft et al., 2011). In family planning clinics, a brief intervention reduced pregnancy coercion among women experiencing IPV relative to standard care, and women in the intervention arm were more likely to terminate relationships due to safety concerns (Miller et al., 2011).

During this time, a related line of research addressed screening modality, including computer-based IPV screening. Results from several trials demonstrated increased detection with computerized screening compared with usual care (Ahmad et al., 2009; Rhodes et al., 2002; Trautman et al., 2007). Among those screened, referrals were also higher for those screened via computer (Trautman et al., 2007). The favorable detection rates identified via computer-based screening likely reflect, in part, significant differences in implementation—one study implemented in emergency departments revealed an implementation rate of 99.8% for computer-based screening, while in the usual care arm only 33% were screened for IPV (Trautman et al., 2007). A direct comparison of computerized vs. face-to-face IPV screening in Women, Infants, and Children (WIC) clinics yielded significantly higher disclosure rates of past-year verbal and sexual abuse, and any IPV, in face-to-face screening situations (Fincher et al., 2015). By contrast, in primary care settings, audio computer-assisted self-interviews yielded a higher disclosure rate than health care provider screening (Klevens et al., 2012).

These advances informed an updated USPSTF review in 2012, which concluded that IPV screening instruments can accurately identify patients experiencing IPV, and that screening can provide health and safety benefits with minimal adverse effects (Nelson et al., 2012). By contrast, in 2015, a Cochrane review on this topic found no evidence that screening decreased IPV (O'Doherty et al., 2015). The divergence in conclusions across these two reviews lies largely in their aims and inclusion criteria. The 2012 USPSTF sought to review evidence on health-based IPV screening and interventions (Nelson et al., 2012), while the Cochrane review sought to isolate the effect of screening and brief, feasible interventions, thus excluding interventions that went beyond an immediate response to disclosure—for example, clinical follow-up or further counseling (O'Doherty et al., 2015). Accordingly, the reviews differed in inclusion of several key trials. For example, the brief, clinic-based counseling in prenatal clinics that reduced violence and improved birth outcomes (Kiely et al., 2010) met inclusion criteria for the USPSTF 2012 review but was excluded from the Cochrane review, presumably because the intervention exceeded criteria for "brief."

Taken together, results indicate that IPV screening and intervention can identify survivors, and in some cases increase safety, reduce abuse, and improve clinical and social outcomes. However, the impact of screening without intervention appears to be quite limited. Concern regarding possible harms or unintended consequences of clinical assessment have been raised and considered in research trials, but thus far no evidence of such harm has emerged (Houry et al., 2008; MacMillan et al., 2006).

Other research illustrates the pathways through which discussing IPV with health providers can foster positive change and improved health outcomes. Research with female outpatients with a past-year history of IPV found that talking to health providers about the abuse increased likelihood of intervention use (for example, advocacy, shelter, restraining order); in turn, those who received an intervention were more likely to leave their abuser, which prompted better health outcomes (McCloskey et al., 2006). Qualitative research with IPV survivors has long emphasized providers taking initiative on IPV screening and make referrals available (Chang et al., 2003, 2005; Rodriguez et al., 1996).

Finally, screening is considered valuable even in the absence of disclosure for a host of reasons. Even when asked directly, women may not disclose current or past IPV/GBV for a multitude of reasons, including systems distrust, limited resources, and fear that reporting IPV could create a backlash (Caralis & Musialowski, 1997; Dienemann et al., 2003; Dutton, 2004; Gerbert et al., 1996; Hardesty & Campbell, 2004; McCauley et al., 1998; McNutt et al., 1999; Rodriguez et al., 1996). Thus, routine IPV screening in the health care context sends a valuable message that the clinic is open to discussing violence-related issues when the woman is interested or ready and feels that disclosure is safe. Given the documented barriers to disclosure, recommendations for health sector screening increasingly emphasize the use of screening as an opportunity to provide information and support to all female patients, rather than focusing on disclosure (American College of and Gynecologists, 2013). That is, screening is recognized as an awareness/educational opportunity that normalizes and contextualizes the health setting as a safe place to discuss IPV and other forms of GBV and its consequences, and to be connected to support services within the facility or larger community. Recognition of coercive behaviors is challenging for many survivors; for example, women may not define sexual assault experiences as meeting the definition of rape as rape (Kalof, 2000; Koss et al., 1988), especially in cases of a known perpetrator (Koss et al., 1988). In turn, screening efforts increasingly seek to define GBV through universal education—often focused in part on elements of coercion and control that survivors may not recognize as abusive—and behavioral strategies that can increase safety.

IPV/GBV screening: Policy context

The first wave of recommendations for IPV screening in the health care sector as routine practice emerged in the 1990s (American Congress of Obstetricians and Gynecologists, 2013; Council on Ethical and Judicial Affairs, American Medical Association, 1992; Lee et al., 1999;). In 2011, the Institute of Medicine recommended interpersonal and domestic violence screening and counseling for all women and adolescent girls, as part of women's clinical preventive services (Gee et al., 2011; Institute of Medicine, 2011). In turn, the US Department of Health and Human Services included violence-related screening and counseling in its *Women's preventive services guidelines*. In 2013, the USPSTF recommended IPV screening for all women of childbearing age, and provision of or referral to intervention services for those screening positive (Moyer, 2013). These recommendations resulted in inclusion of IPV screening and brief counseling for women as a component of required free preventive services endorsed and expected within the Affordable Care Act (ACA) (Anon, 2013a). This pivotal change in US health policy offers an opportunity to examine the current evidence on screening and counseling for IPV as "prevention," and to identify areas for research on the implementation of these screening and counseling recommendations. The US and international policy climates are largely aligned. In 2013, the World Health Organization (WHO) issued guidance on violence identification, assessment, and clinical care (WHO, 2013b). While stopping short of recommending universal screening, the WHO emphasized that providers assess for violence when health conditions could be caused or complicated by IPV or other forms of GBV.

In 2013, the US Department of Health and Human Services hosted a symposium on IPV screening and counseling research to guide effective practices based on the robust evidence available to date, with recommendations including: trauma-informed and women-centered care; integration of screening within clinical practice; harnessing electronic medical records to enable provider consistency; evaluation of screening; and brief counseling interventions.

Gaps in knowledge and recommendations

Advances over the past three decades have positioned the field for innovation and impact in reaching survivors and improving their health and wellbeing. However, multiple—and critical—barriers remain in terms of implementing evidence into practice gaps, at both individual and system levels. Identifying and supporting survivors remains difficult (Acierno et al., 1997; Cohen et al., 1997; Eisenstat & Bancroft, 1999; Erickson et al., 2001; Friedman et al., 1992; McCauley et al., 1998; McNutt et al., 1999; Rodriguez et al., 1999; Siegel et al., 1999; Sugg et al., 1999), in part due to provider discomfort (Elliott et al., 2002; Parsons et al., 1995; Sprague et al., 2012; Sugg et al., 1999) and lack of training (Deboer et al., 2013). Barriers for implementation of routine IPV/GPV screening and counseling in the health system are myriad, and include clinician concerns about time; limited incentives by facility and community program administration for screening (Colarossi et al., 2010); either nonexistent or poorly implemented policies to guide practitioners and clinical practices in conducting such screening; lack of knowledge and confidence about how to support a patient who discloses GBV (Cha & Masho, 2014; Jaffee et al., 2005; Tower et al., 2006; Weeks et al., 2008; Yonaka et al., 2007)—which may reflect a lack of reliable intervention services (Minsky-Kelly et al., 2005)—and inadequate cross-sector collaborations with victim service advocates (O'Campo et al., 2011; Rhodes et al., 2007).

Our recommendations therefore prioritize several critical gaps in knowledge to push the field forward, and allow us to realize the promise of harnessing health and other sectors to create safe environments to identify and support those in need. Given the evidence accumulated to date via randomized controlled trials, our recommendations emphasize translation of evidence to best practices, as well as a heavy focus on implementation science in order to determine the appropriate clinical and community settings, as well as the optimal methods for screening and intervention, and the health and social outcomes we can reasonably expect to see at a population level.

What do survivors do after they are screened?

While GBV interventions in the clinical setting have demonstrated success in improving health and mitigating abuse, the process by which these interventions create impact is less clear. Implementation science—which evaluates and monitors the translation of policy and evidence-based interventions into routine practice, and identifies facilitators and barriers in the process (Glasgow et al., 2012) —can help us understand how the health and violence support sectors operate in systems, and where they can be strengthened (Decker et al., 2012). Priority areas include understanding if and where women go for services (formal and informal) after they are screened and receive brief counseling in the health setting, and whether the support and resources provided in a screening encounter with a skilled provider are sufficient to meet their needs for safety. Further, implementation research can inform providers in challenging settings where advocacy and community-based supports are limited regarding the minimum package of GBV services required—from the perspective of the survivors, providers, and community leaders—to safely integrate GBV screening and brief counseling in health programs. Additionally, the use of mixed methods research (triangulation of qualitative and quantitative techniques) from multiple key stakeholders on harm reduction strategies and safety trajectories after GBV screening and brief counseling can help researchers, advocates, and policy makers to better understand *how* screening and brief interventions improve health and social outcomes—and for whom.

What are the most meaningful and feasible outcomes that can result from screening/brief intervention?

To date, the research base on GBV screening has focused heavily on health improvements and reductions in violence, but demonstrating impact on these endpoints is challenging within the constraints of most study designs (for example, short follow-up periods). Further, these endpoints are not always aligned with the multiple complex influences and priorities of survivors themselves (for example, economic and resource needs, feelings for the abusive partner, privacy, safety and wellbeing of children). Clarity and consensus on outcomes that are both feasible and meaningful—for example, clarity of decisions related to safety; awareness of options for safety within formal (hotlines, shelters, supervised visitation for children) and informal (trusted friends or family members) networks; reducing economic and emotional dependence on the abusive partner—are needed to ensure we are truly meeting the primary safety needs of survivors and are positioning our interventions and evaluation designs for impact on health (such as to reduce depression/anxiety and chronic pain, which is often a more distal outcome). Researchers and funders meaningfully engaging with survivors and advocates through a consensus meeting—one that includes survivors' voices—is recommended to fill this gap in the evidence for appropriate and meaningful outcomes when implementing interventions in the formal health system and in informal settings.

What is the minimum package needed to implement screening/brief intervention?

Recommendations that GBV screening and brief intervention only be implemented in health settings in which sufficient training and support services exist are well intended, but can prompt communities to continue to accept the consequences of inaction. This is especially the case in resource-limited settings. With the availability of eHealth interventions and resources globally—which provide evidence-based screening tools with guidance on confidentiality and implementation, as well as support diverse facility- and community-based health providers in collaborating with women and girls on safety planning in the absence of formal services—the frequent excuse of the lack of formal services in the community is somewhat less relevant. Yet to date, few standards and little empirical evidence have emerged on the minimum standards necessary for initiating GBV screening and brief safety interventions in health and informal sectors. Again, implementation science with input from survivors and key stakeholders is essential here.

Combination prevention/intervention

Structural interventions—that is, those that change the broader social–structural climate that gives rise to perpetration of GBV—are increasingly recommended for primary and secondary prevention.

Given these needs, coupled with evidence of efficacy of GBV screening and intervention, there exists a need to understand optimal packages of interventions—that is, combination prevention/intervention, including that which pairs GBV screening with larger-scale structural interventions such as safe and affordable housing, employment with a living wage, and trauma-informed and survivor-centered services. This type of research typically requires collaborations among multiple partners from diverse disciplines, governmental and nongovernmental organizations, and survivor groups, in distinct geographic communities, to avoid issues of contamination; as such, it is more resource-intensive.

Recent innovation

We close with a review of specific key knowledge gaps and recent innovations that address them through three case studies, spanning eHealth, screening paired with brief intervention, and a cross-sector systems-strengthening effort.

Harm reduction and safety strategies

The emphasis on screening implementation and health outcomes in GBV screening research to date, coupled with connecting women to formal support services, has created critical gaps in our knowledge of women's own harm reduction and safety strategies. Qualitatively and quantitatively understanding patterns of safety behavior and harm reduction from women themselves—particularly those who have not sought formal services—will help interventionists to craft harm reduction and safety messages that can be meaningfully integrated into clinic-based screening, as well as within other sectors such as legal and social services.

A key innovation over the past decade is the development of information and communication technology (ICT) applications aimed at improving health and wellbeing. The World Health Assembly's eHealth resolution of 2005 called on countries to use eHealth solutions to address their health needs, and defined eHealth as the "cost-effective and secure use of information and communications technologies in support of health and health-related fields, including healthcare services, health surveillance, health literature, and health education, knowledge and research" (558th World Health Assembly, 2005, p. 121). Opportunities exist within resource-rich and limited settings to integrate eHealth initiatives for improved identification, assessment, and safety planning with survivors. For example, given the new guidance in the ACA that IPV/GBV screening and brief counseling is a component of preventive care, clinicians need efficient tools for implementation. Validated screening questions can be integrated into electronic medical records (EMR) to remind providers to ask the questions to all patients as the protocol directs for the setting. Further, clinical decision aids can support informed safety-related patient decision-making for those identified as IPV survivors (Stacey et al., 2014). Decision aids provide information and help patients clarify personal values—and, critically, are intended to complement (not replace) professional services (Ottawa Hospital Research Institute, 2013).

Case study 1

One innovative approach to meeting the needs of survivors who lack access to formal services is the creation of a safety decision aid (SDA). The SDA was originally developed prior to smartphone technology and applications ("apps"), and thus has been updated to the myPlan app for female IPV survivors, which can be adapted for survivors of other forms of GBV—including with survivors in low-resource settings— based on existing evidence in violence prevention and decisional conflict research. The SDA is individualized and helps abused women understand their risk of repeat and near-lethal violence, set safety priorities, and plan for safety (Glass et al., 2010).

Among IPV survivors in shelters (n=90) who tested the original SDA via a laptop, decisional conflict was significantly reduced after just one use (Glass et al., 2010). eHealth interventions hold unique promise in meeting survivor needs—in part because, while abused women often experience isolation, many have safe internet access through computers, tablets, and/or smartphones, and actively search for IPV help and information online (Westbrook, 2008). The SDA was found to significantly lower total decisional conflict relative to women in the usual safety planning control group, controlling for baseline value of decisional conflict ($p=0.002$, effect size$=.12$), immediately following women's first use of the SDA. Controlling for baseline values, the SDA group also had significantly greater reduction in uncertainty ($p=0.006$, effect size$=.07$) and lack of support ($p=0.008$, effect size$=.07$) for safety relative to the usual safety planning group (Eden et al., 2015).

These findings support the underlying premise that a personalized and interactive SDA based on a woman's own assessment of safety priorities and level of danger in the relationship, as well as relationship characteristics and previous protective actions, is more effective in reducing decisional conflict over safety than providing usual safety planning information (emergency safety plans, phone numbers, and websites). Just one session (typically 45 minutes) using an internet-based SDA was effective at reducing decision conflict and thereby supporting the decision-making process of IPV survivors, with no adverse events (Eden et al., 2015). This work represents an important and promising innovation to connect abused women—who most often do not access safety planning through formal services—with the information and resources they need on their own terms. While facility-based IPV/GBV screening is best done in an environment that enables immediate access to established support services, tremendous support needs exist in resource-poor settings where health and social program infrastructure is frequently absent; thus, innovation is needed in safety planning post-screening for survivors. Implementing eHealth technology through an SDA application (app) can increase survivors' access to survivor-centered health and safety messages, with an individualized safety plan for self and family in an abusive relationship, and, for example, when seeking protection in conflict and post-conflict settings, refugee camps, and settlements.

Evidence-based best practices on screening implementation

Providers have long requested specific direction on how to respond briefly and effectively in cases of violence. A clear, efficient, and limited clinician role is key for sustained implementation: provide information about the relationship of GBV to health to all patients; conduct a validated GBV assessment in private; refer and facilitate connections with an advocate, a community agency, or other safety planning; and validate survivors' experiences with messages such as "you are not alone" and "you deserve to live free of violence" (Decker et al., 2012; McCaw et al., 2001). These steps are aligned with the trauma-informed approach recommended for responding to violence. Trauma-informed care is grounded in recognizing and responding to trauma, emphasizes safety and healing, and provides opportunities to regain a sense of control and empowerment (Hopper et al., 2010). In practice, trauma-informed care anticipates the prevalence and impact of accumulated trauma, and responds appropriately by providing sustained support and linkage to care—within an environment that is calm, safe, and empowering, and within a system that supports providers and collaborates with related services (Machtinger et al., 2015).

This guidance is ever more important in light of the shift to EMR, and the resulting opportunity for seamless integration of GBV assessment within the standard patient history. GBV screening questions embedded in the EMR do not supplant the need for a trauma-informed approach and trained clinicians; rather, they make clinician training and processes even more critical. For success in meeting the health and support needs of GBV survivors and those at risk, any screening questions must be accompanied by a brief scripted intervention that includes validation of experiences and provision of support resources, even for individuals who do not disclose abuse.

Addressing barriers, developing protocols, and improving screening practices requires attention to multiple levels within the health care delivery system to create a safe, trusting environment for clients/patients (McCaw et al., 2001). Strategies include provider education (Hamberger et al., 2004; Hamberger & Phelan, 2006; McNulty et al., 2005; O'Campo et al., 2011); client support and engagement; policies and protocols with tools for clinical settings (Coker et al., 2007; Hamberger & Phelan, 2006; Scholle et al., 2003; Thurston et al., 2007); collaboration with GBV advocates; environmental cues; reminders within the electronic health record; and quality incentives integrated into clinic flow (Hamberger & Phelan, 2006; Sprague et al., 2013). Studies are needed on how to implement clinical guidelines for GBV screening and assessment with attention to barriers and testing strategies to increase screening and counseling efficiency, effectiveness, and sustainability.

Case study 2

GBV screening paired with brief intervention demonstrates success in improving health and reducing reproductive coercion (RC). For example, a universal education and brief counseling intervention for female clients seeking care in family planning (FP) clinics incorporates an introduction to local advocates as part of the clinician and staff training at each clinical site. The intervention provides universal assessment for all female FP clients about IPV and RC—which includes screening, education, and discussion of harm reduction strategies to reduce risk for unintended pregnancy and IPV, and lets women know the clinic can help make referrals to IPV support services ("warm referrals," meaning facilitating women calling or connecting with an advocate). All women are offered a palm-size information card (or several to share with their friends) containing harm reduction strategies and national hotline numbers. During intervention training, providers meet with designated advocates from local support services to enhance the referral system.

The emphasis on harm reduction and connection of FP clinics with IPV services underscores that the FP clinic is a safe place for all women to seek care for unhealthy relationships. Patients who disclose abuse can receive immediate support. The intervention evaluation followed women over 4 months, and documented a 71% reduction in pregnancy pressure (an element of RC) among women experiencing recent IPV. Women receiving the intervention were also 60% more likely to terminate a relationship due to safety concerns (Miller et al., 2011). As each site is introduced to their local domestic and sexual violence advocates through formal and informal staff meetings, clinician comfort related to implementing this IPV assessment appears to increase. In formal interviews with providers, they shared the ease of intervention implementation:

> [The safety card] made me feel empowered because . . . you can really help somebody . . . somebody that might have been afraid to say anything or didn't know how to approach the topic, this is a door for them to open so they can feel . . . more relaxed about talking about it.

> [The safety card] is a tool that (the clinic staff) could use and hand to the patient so it . . . broke that barrier. I think it was a comfort thing for the staff to be able to hand something like that to them.

> [Giving the safety card to a patient] made me feel like I wasn't just helping this patient but empowering her to discuss it with someone. Once she read it, maybe it was her sister, her mom, cousin, friend . . . that might be dealing with issues [of IPV/RC]. (Miller, McCauley, Decker, Levenson, Zelazny, Jones et al., 2017)

A larger cluster randomized controlled trial in 24 FP clinics in Pennsylvania found that women receiving this intervention had significant increases in knowledge of IPV-related resources, as well as increased self-efficacy to enact harm reduction behaviors. Additionally, women who were experiencing higher levels of RC at baseline also reported significant reductions in RC one year later (Miller et al., 2016).

Evidence-based best practices on systems strengthening

GBV screening and brief safety interventions shift the goal from an emphasis on patient disclosure to making safer spaces for survivors with connections to supports, services, and protection. Evidence suggests that, when health care providers facilitate patients' connection to an advocate through the aforementioned "warm referral," patients are more likely to use an intervention (Hathaway et al., 2002; McCloskey et al., 2006). Health providers report, however, that they often are unfamiliar with local resources and do not know what to do if a patient discloses IPV to them (Erickson et al., 2001; Friedman et al., 1992; McCauley et al., 1998; Minsky-Kelly et al., 2005; Rodriguez et al., 1999; Siegel et al., 1999; Sugg & Inui, 1992). To date, little guidance exists on how to build connections with advocacy services, strengthen local connections, nurture a collaborative relationship, and evaluate systems as they strengthen and evolve to meet the needs of survivors.

Case study 3

In 2009, Project Connect: A Coordinated Public Health Initiative to Prevent Violence Against Women was launched by Futures Without Violence (a national nonprofit organization dedicated to ending violence against women and children), with support from the federal Office on Women's Health (OWH), as part of the Violence Against Women Act's health title funds. Project Connect's coordinated public health response to GBV entailed developing, implementing, and evaluating new ways to identify, respond to, and prevent domestic and sexual violence. Diverse sites received funding to create comprehensive GBV prevention and intervention models, with the aim of improving health and safety for women and children. Each Project Connect site developed policy and public health responses to domestic and sexual violence within FP, adolescent health, home visitation, or other maternal child health or perinatal programs. The project emphasized training health care providers in these settings to implement the aforementioned screening and brief counseling interventions.

Following two cycles of funding (grantees are 14 states and five Native communities), a major emphasis of Project Connect was the development of coordinated state-level Leadership Teams (LTs), which included representation from public health programs and domestic violence and sexual assault coalitions for each of the sites involved. The goal of the LTs was creating sustained policy change, implementation of best practices, and systems-level coordination of response for victims. These teams guided project development, planning, and implementation, and created practice and policy changes, with the goal of sustained collaborations beyond the project period. Policy changes achieved through this effort included adding domestic and sexual violence assessment into statewide nursing guidelines and clinical assessment forms, requiring RC training in state-funded teen pregnancy prevention programs, and improving data collection by adding domestic and sexual violence questions to statewide surveillance systems. Project Connect is a promising strategy for creating coordinated systems within public health to implement best practices and evidence-informed clinical screening and counseling interventions to prevent domestic and sexual violence.

Conclusion

The prevalence and health impact of GBV are well-established and demand an evidence-based response. The formal health sector and informal community sectors have much to offer in identifying survivors and providing the validating, empathetic response that GBV survivors request. The next decade of research and clinical and community practice must focus on advancing interventions to promote the health and safety of women globally, including integrating promising screening and brief counseling practices in low-resource settings and ensuring connection to services based on women's and girls' needs.

References

558th World Health Assembly (2005). *eHealth resolution WHA58.28*. Geneva: WHO. Retrieved at http://www.who.int/healthacademy/media/WHA58-28-en.pdf?ua=1.

American Congress of Obstetricians and Gynecologists (ACOG) (2012). ACOG Committee Opinion No. 518: Intimate partner violence. *Obstetrics & Gynecology*, *119*, 412–417.

Acierno, R., Resnick, H.S., & Kilpatrick, D.G. (1997). Health impact of interpersonal violence, 1: Prevalence rates, case identification, and risk factors for sexual assault, physical assault, and domestic violence in men and women. *Journal of Behavioral Medicine*, *23*, 53–64.

Ahmad, F., Hogg-Johnson, S., Stewart, D.E., Skinner, H.A., Glazier, R.H., & Levinson, W. (2009). Computer-assisted screening for intimate partner violence and control: A randomized trial. *Annals of Internal Medicine, 151*, 93–102.

American College of Obstetrics & Gynecologists (ACOG) (2013). ACOG Committee opinion no. 554: Reproductive and sexual coercion. *Obstetrics & Gynecology, 121*, 411–415.

Anon (2013a). Coverage of certain preventive services under the Affordable Care Act: Final rules. *Federal Register, 78*, 39869–39899.

Bair-Merritt, M.H., Jennings, J.M., Chen, R., Burrell, L., Mcfarlane, E., Fuddy, L., & Duggan, A.K. (2010). Reducing maternal intimate partner violence after the birth of a child: A randomized controlled trial of the Hawaii Healthy Start Home Visitation Program. *Archives of Pediatrics & Adolescent Medicine, 164*, 16–23.

Black, M.C., Basile, K.C., Breiding, M.J., Smith, S.G., Walters, M.L., Merrick, M.T. et al. (2011). *The National Intimate Partner and Sexual Violence Survey (NISVS): 2010 summary report*. Atlanta, GA: National Center for Injury Prevention and Control, Centers for Disease Control and Prevention.

Bott, S., Guedes, A., Goodwin, M., & Mendoza, J. (2012). *Violence against women in Latin America and the Carribean: A comparative analysis of population-based data from 12 countries*. Washington, DC: Pan American Health Organization.

Campbell, J.C. (2002). Health consequences of intimate partner violence. *Lancet, 359*, 1331–1336.

Campbell, J.C., & Glass, N. (2009). Safety planning, danger, and lethality assessment. In C.E. Mitchell (Ed.), *Intimate partner violence: A health-based perspective* (pp. 319–334). Oxford: Oxford University Press.

Campbell, J.C., Sharps, P., & Glass, N.E. (2001). Risk assessment for intimate partner homicide. In G.F. Pinard & L. Pagani (Eds.), *Clinical assessment of dangerousness: Empirical contributions* (pp. 136-157). London: Cambridge University Press.

Caralis, P., & Musialowski, R. (1997). Women's experiences with domestic violence and their attitudes and expectations regarding medical care of abuse victims. *Southern Medical Journal, 90*, 1075–1080.

Cha, S., & Masho, S.W. (2014). Intimate partner violence and utilization of prenatal care in the United States. *Journal of Interpersonal Violence, 29*, 911–927.

Chang, J.C., Decker, M., Moracco, K.E., Martin, S.L., Petersen, R., & Frasier, P.Y. (2003). What happens when health care providers ask about intimate partner violence? A description of consequences from the perspectives of female survivors. *Journal of the American Medical Women's Association, 58,* 76–81.

Chang, J.C., Decker, M.R., Moracco, K.E., Martin, S.L., Petersen, R., & Frasier, P.Y. (2005). Asking about intimate partner violence: Advice from female survivors to health care providers. *Patient Education and Counseling, 59,* 141–147.

Cohen, S., De Vos, E., & Newberger, E. (1997). Barriers to physician identification and treatment of family violence: Lessons from five communities. *Academic Medicine, 72,* S19–S25.

Coker, A.L., Flerx, V.C., Smith, P.H., Whitaker, D.J., Fadden, M.K., & Williams, M. (2007). Intimate partner violence incidence and continuation in a primary care screening program. *American Journal of Epidemiology, 165,* 821–827.

Colarossi, L.G., Breitbart, V., & Betancourt, G.S. (2010). Screening for intimate partner violence in reproductive health centers: An evaluation study. *Women & Health, 50,* 313–326.

Cooper, A., & Smith, E. (2011). *Homicide trends in the United States, 1980–2008.* Washington, DC: Bureau of Justice Statistics.

Council on Ethical and Judicial Affairs, American Medical Association (1992). Physicians and domestic violence: Ethical considerations. *Journal of the American Medical Association, 267,* 3190–3193.

Deboer, M.I., Kothari, R., Kothari, C., Koestner, A.L., & Rohs, T., Jr. (2013). What are barriers to nurses screening for intimate partner violence? *Journal of Trauma Nursing, 20,* 155–160.

Decker, M.R., Frattaroli, S., Mccaw, B., Coker, A.L., Miller, E., Sharps, P. et al. (2012). Transforming the healthcare response to intimate partner violence and taking best practices to scale. *Journal of Women's Health (Larchmont), 21,* 1222–1229.

Decker, M.R., Silverman, J.G., & Raj, A. (2005). Dating violence and sexually transmitted disease/HIV testing and diagnosis among adolescent females. *Pediatrics, 116,* e272–e276.

Dienemann, J., Campbell, J., Wiederhorn, N., Laughon, K., & Jordan, E. (2003). A critical pathway for intimate partner violence across the continuum of care. *Journal of Obstetrics & Gynecology Neonatal Nursing, 32,* 594–603.

Dutton, M.A. (2004). Complexity of women's response to violence: Response to Briere and Jordan. *Journal of Interpersonal Violence, 19,* 1277–1282.

Eden, K.B., Perrin, N.A., Hanson, G.C., Messing, J.T., Bloom, T.L., Campbell, J.C. et al. (2015). Use of online safety decision aid by abused women: Effect on decisional conflict in a randomized controlled trial. *American Journal of Preventive Medicine*, *48*, 372–83.

Eisenstat, S.A., & Bancroft, L. (1999). Domestic violence. *New England Journal of Medicine*, *341*, 886–892.

Elliott, L., Nerney, M., Jones, T., & Friedmann, P.D. (2002). Barriers to screening for domestic violence. *Journal of General Internal Medicine*, *17*, 112–116.

Ellsberg, M., Jansen, H.A., Heise, L., Watts, C.H., Garcia-Moreno, C., Health, WHO Multi-country Study on Women's Health, & Domestic Violence against Women Study Team (2008). Intimate partner violence and women's physical and mental health in the WHO multi-country study on women's health and domestic violence: An observational study. *Lancet*, *371*, 1165–1172.

Erickson, M.J., Hill, T.D., & Siegel, R.M. (2001). Barriers to domestic violence screening in the pediatric setting. *Pediatrics*, *108*, 98–102.

Fincher, D., Vanderende, K., Colbert, K., Houry, D., Smith, L.S., & Yount, K.M. (2015). Effect of face-to-face interview versus computer-assisted self-interview on disclosure of intimate partner violence among African American women in WIC clinics. *Journal of Interpersonal Violence*, *30*, 818–838.

Friedman, L.S., Samet, J.H., Roberts, M.S., Hudlin, M., & Hans, P. (1992). Inquiry about victimization experiences. A survey of patient preferences and physician practices. *Archives of Internal Medicine*, *152*, 1186–1190.

Garcia-Moreno, C., Jansen, H.A., Ellsberg, M., Heise, L., & Watts, C. (2005). *WHO multi-country study on women's health and domestic violence against women*. Geneva: WHO.

Gee, R.E., Brindis, C.D., Diaz, A., Garcia, F., Gregory, K., Peck, M.G., & Reece, E.A. (2011). Recommendations of the IOM clinical preventive services for women committee: Implications for obstetricians and gynecologists. *Current Opinion in Obstetrics & Gynecology*, *23*, 471–480.

Gerbert, B., Johnston, K., Caspers, N., Bleecker, T., Woods, A., & Rosenbaum, A. (1996). Experiences of battered women in health care settings: A qualitative study. *Women & Health*, *24*, 1–17.

Glasgow, R.E., Vinson, C., Chambers, D., Khoury, M.J., Kaplan, R.M., & Hunter, C. (2012). National Institutes of Health approaches to dissemination and implementation science: Current and future directions. *American Journal of Public Health*, *102*, 1274–1281.

Glass, N., Eden, K.B., Bloom, T., & Perrin, N. (2010). Computerized aid improves safety decision process for survivors of intimate partner violence. *Journal of Interpersonal Violence*, *25*, 1947–1964.

Hamberger, K.L., Guse, C., Boerger, J., Minsky, D., Pape, D., & Folsom, C. (2004). Evaluation of a health care provider training program to identify and help partner violence victims. *Journal of Family Violence*, *19*, 1–11.

Hamberger, K.L., & Phelan, M.B. (2006). Domestic violence screening in medical and mental health care settings: Overcoming barriers to screening, identifying and helping partner violence victims. *Journal of Aggression, Maltreatment and Trauma*, *13*, 61–99.

Hardesty, J., & Campbell, J.C. (2004). Safety planning for abused women and their children. In P.G. Jaffe, LLB., & A.J. Cunningham (Eds.), *Protecting children from domestic violence: Strategies for community intervention* (pp. 89–100). New York: Guilford Press.

Hathaway, J.E., Mucci, L.A., Silverman, J.G., Brooks, D.R., Mathews, R., & Pavlos, C.A. (2000). Health status and health care use of Massachusetts women reporting partner abuse. *American Journal of Preventive Medicine*, 19, 302–307.

Hathaway, J.E., Willis, G., & Zimmer, B. (2002). Listening to survivors' voices: Addressing partner abuse in the health care setting. *Violence Against Women*, *8*, 687–719.

Hopper, E.K., Bassuk, E.L., & Olivet, J. (2010). Shelter from the storm: Trauma-informed care in homelessness services settings. *Open Health Services and Policy Journal*, *3*, 80–100.

Houry, D., Kaslow, N.J., Kemball, R.S., Mcnutt, L.A., Cerulli, C., Straus, H. et al. (2008). Does screening in the emergency department hurt or help victims of intimate partner violence? *Annals of Emergency Medicine*, *51*, 433–442, 442 e1–e7.

Institute of Medicine. (2011). *Clinical preventive services for women: Closing the gaps*. Washington, DC: Institute of Medicine.

Jaffee, K.D., Epling, J.W., Grant, W., Ghandour, R.M., & Callendar, E. (2005). Physician-identified barriers to intimate partner violence screening. *Journal of Women's Health (Larchmont)*, *14*, 713–720.

Jewkes, R.K., Dunkle, K., Nduna, M., & Shai, N. (2010). Intimate partner violence, relationship power inequity, and incidence of HIV infection in young women in South Africa: A cohort study. *Lancet*, *376*, 41–48.

Kalof, L. (2000). Ethnic differences in female sexual victimization. *Sexuality & Culture*, *4*, 75–97.

Kiely, M., El-Mohandes, A.A., El-Khorazaty, M.N., Blake, S.M., & Gantz, M.G. (2010). An integrated intervention to reduce intimate partner violence in pregnancy: A randomized controlled trial. *Obstetrics & Gynecology*, *115*, 273–283.

Klevens, J., Sadowski, L., Kee, R., Trick, W., & Garcia, D. (2012). Comparison of screening and referral strategies for exposure to partner violence. *Women's Health Issues*, *22*, e45–e52.

Koss, M., Dinero, T.E., Seibel, C.A., & Cox, S. L. (1988). Stranger and acquaintance rape: Are there differences in women's experiences? *Psychology of Women Quarterly*, *12*, 1–24.

Koziol-Mclain, J., Garrett, N., Fanslow, J., Hassall, I., Dobbs, T., Henare-Toka, T.A., & Lovell, V. (2010). A randomized controlled trial of a brief emergency department intimate partner violence screening intervention. *Annals of Emergency Medicine*, *56*, 413–423, e1.

Lee, D., James, L., & Sawires, P. (1999). *Preventing domestic violence: Clinical guidelines on routine screening*. San Francisco, CA: Family Violence Prevention Fund.

Machtinger, E.L., Cuca, Y.P., Khanna, N., Rose, C.D., & Kimberg, L.S. (2015). From treatment to healing: The promise of trauma-informed primary care. *Women's Health Issues*, *25*, 193–197.

Macmillan, H.L., Wathen, C.N., Jamieson, E., Boyle, M., Mcnutt, L.A., Worster, A. et al. (2006). Approaches to screening for intimate partner violence in health care settings: A randomized trial. *Journal of the American Medical Association*, *296*, 530–536.

Macmillan, H.L., Wathen, C.N., Jamieson, E., Boyle, M.H., Shannon, H.S., Ford-Gilboe, M. et al. (2009). Screening for intimate partner violence in health care settings: A randomized trial. *Journal of the American Medical Association*, *302*, 493–501.

McCauley, J., Yurk, R.A., Jenckes, M.W., & Ford, D.E. (1998). Inside "Pandora's box": Abused women's experiences with clinicians and health services. *Journal of General Internal Medicine*, 13, 549–555.

McCaw, B., Berman, W.H., Syme, S.L., & Hunkeler, E.F. (2001). Beyond screening for domestic violence: A systems model approach in a managed care setting. *American Journal of Preventive Medicine*, 21, 170–176.

McCloskey, L.A., Lichter, E., Williams, C., Gerber, M., Wittenberg, E., & Ganz, M. (2006). Assessing intimate partner violence in health care settings leads to women's receipt of interventions and improved health. *Public Health Reports*, *121*, 435–444.

McFarlane, J.M., Groff, J.Y., O'brien, J.A., & Watson, K. (2006). Secondary prevention of intimate partner violence: A randomized controlled trial. *Nursing Research*, *55*, 52–61.

McFarlane, J., Soeken, K., & Wiist, W. (2000). An evaluation of interventions to decrease intimate partner violence to pregnant women. *Public Health Nursing*, *17*, 443–451.

McNulty, A., Andrews, P., & Bonner, M. (2005). Can screening for domestic violence be introduced successfully in a sexual health clinic? *Sexual Health*, *3*, 179–182.

Mcnutt, L.A., Carlson, B.E., Gagen, D., & Winterbauer, N. (1999). Reproductive violence screening in primary care: Perspectives and experiences of patients and battered women. *Journal of the American Medical Women's Association*, *54*, 85–90.

Miller, E., Decker, M.R., Mccauley, H.L., Tancredi, D.J., Levenson, R.R., Waldman, J. et al. (2011). A FP clinic partner violence intervention to reduce risk associated with reproductive coercion. *Contraception*, *83*, 274–280.

Miller, E., McCauley, H.L., Decker, M.R., Levenson, R., Zelazny, S., Jones, K.A., et al. (2017). Implementation of a family planning clinic-based partner violence and reproductive coercion intervention: Provider and patient perspectives. *Perspectives on sexual and reproductive health*. doi: 10.1363/psrh.12021.

Miller, E., Tancredi, D.J., Decker, M.R., Mccauley, H.L., Jones, K.A., Anderson, H. et al. (2016). A FP clinic-based intervention to address reproductive coercion: A cluster randomized controlled trial. *Contraception*, *94*, 58–67.

Minsky-Kelly, D., Hamberger, L.K., Pape, D.A., & Wolff, M. (2005). We've had training, now what? Qualitative analysis of barriers to domestic violence screening and referral in a health care setting. *Journal of Interpersonal Violence*, *20*, 1288–1309.

Moyer, V.A. (2013). Screening for intimate partner violence and abuse of elderly and vulnerable adults: US Preventive Services Task Force recommendation statement. *Annals of Internal Medicine*, *158*, 478–486.

Nasrullah, M., Oraka, E., Breiding, M.J., & Chavez, P.R. (2013). HIV testing and intimate partner violence among non-pregnant women in 15 US states/territories: Findings from behavioral risk factor surveillance system survey data. *AIDS and Behavior*, *17*, 2521–2527.

Nelson, H.D., Bougatsos, C., & Blazina, I. (2012). Screening women for intimate partner violence: A systematic review to update the US Preventive Services Task Force recommendation. *Annals of Internal Medicine*, *156*, 796–808, W-279–W-282.

Nelson, H.D., Nygren, P., Mcinerney, Y., Klein, J., & US Preventive Services Task Force. (2004). Screening women and elderly adults for family and intimate partner violence: A review of the evidence for the US Preventive Services Task Force. *Annals of Internal Medicine, 140*, 387–396.

O'Campo, P., Kirst, M., Tsamis, C., Chambers, C., & Ahmad, F. (2011). Implementing successful intimate partner violence screening programs in health care settings: Evidence generated from a realist-informed systematic review. *Social Science & Medicine, 72*, 855–866.

O'Doherty, L., Hegarty, K., Ramsay, J., Davidson, L.L., Feder, G., & Taft, A. (2015). Screening women for intimate partner violence in healthcare settings. *Cochrane Database of Systematic Reviews*, CD007007.

Ottawa Hospital Research Institute (2013). *Patient decision aids.* Retrieved from: http://decisionaid.ohri.ca/.

Palermo, T., Bleck, J., & Peterman, A. (2013). Tip of the iceberg: Reporting and gender-based violence in developing countries. *American Journal of Epidemiology, 179*(5), 602–612.

Palermo, T., & Peterman, A. (2011). Undercounting, overcounting and the longevity of flawed estimates: Statistics on sexual violence in conflict. *Bulletin of the World Health Organization, 89*, 924–925.

Parsons, L.H., Zaccaro, D., Wells, B., & Stovall, T.G. (1995). Methods of and attitudes toward screening obstetrics and gynecology patients for domestic violence. *American Journal of Obstetrics & Gynecology, 173*, 381–387.

Rhodes, K.V., Frankel, R.M., Levinthal, N., Prenoveau, E., Bailey, J., & Levinson, W. (2007). "You're not a victim of domestic violence, are you?" Provider patient communication about domestic violence. *Annals of Internal Medicine, 147*, 620–627.

Rhodes, K.V., Lauderdale, D.S., He, T., Howes, D.S., & Levinson, W. (2002). "Between me and the computer": Increased detection of intimate partner violence using a computer questionnaire. *Annals of Emergency Medicine, 40*, 476–484.

Rodriguez, M.A., Bauer, H.M., Mcloughlin, E., & Grumbach, K. (1999). Screening and intervention for intimate partner abuse: Practices and attitudes of primary care physicians. *Journal of the American Medical Association, 282*, 468–474.

Rodriguez, M., Quiroga, S., & Bauer, H. (1996). Breaking the silence: Battered women's perspectives on medical care. *Archives of Family Medicine, 5*, 153–158.

Scholle, S.H., Buranosky, R., Hanusa, B.H., Ranieri, L., Dowd, K., & Valappil, B. (2003). Routine screening for intimate partner violence in an obstetrics and gynecology clinic. *American Journal of Public Health*, *93*, 1070–1072.

Seth, P., Raiford, J.L., Robinson, L.S., Wingood, G.M., & Diclemente, R.J. (2010). Intimate partner violence and other partner-related factors: Correlates of sexually transmissible infections and risky sexual behaviours among young adult African American women. *Sexual Health*, 7, 25–30.

Sharps, P.W., Bullock, L.F., Campbell, J.C., Alhusen, J.L., Ghazarian, S.R., Bhandari, S.S., & Schminkey, D.L. (2016). Domestic violence enhanced perinatal home visits: The DOVE randomized clinical trial. *Journal of Women's Health (Larchmont)*, *25*(11), 1129-1138.

Siegel, R.M., Hill, T.D., Henderson, V.A., Ernst, H.M., & Boat, B.W. (1999). Screening for domestic violence in the community pediatric setting. *Pediatrics*, *104*, 874–877.

Silverman, J.G., Decker, M.R., Saggurti, N., Balaiah, D., & Raj, A. (2008). Intimate partner violence and HIV infection among married Indian women. *Journal of the American Medical Association*, *300*, 703–710.

Sprague, S., Madden, K., Simunovic, N., Godin, K., Pham, N.K., Bhandari, M., & Goslings, J.C. (2012). Barriers to screening for intimate partner violence. *Women & Health*, *52*, 587–605.

Sprague, S., Swinton, M., Madden, K., Swaleh, R., Goslings, J.C., Petrisor, B., & Bhandari, M. (2013). Barriers to and facilitators for screening women for intimate partner violence in surgical fracture clinics: A qualitative descriptive approach. *BMC Musculoskeletal Disorders*, *14*, 122.

Stacey, D., Legare, F., Col, N.F., Bennett, C.L., Barry, M.J., Eden, K.B. et al. (2014). Decision aids for people facing health treatment or screening decisions. *Cochrane Database of Systematic Reviews*, CD001431.

Stockl, H., Devries, K., Rotstein, A., Abrahams, N., Campbell, J., Watts, C., & Moreno, C.G. (2013). The global prevalence of intimate partner homicide: A systematic review. *Lancet*, *382*, 859–865.

Sugg, N.K., & Inui, T. (1992). Primary care physicians' response to domestic violence: Opening Pandora's box. *Journal of the American Medical Association*, *267*, 3157–3160.

Sugg, N.K., Thompson, R.S., Thompson, D.C., Maiuro, R., & Rivara, F.P. (1999). Domestic violence and primary care: Attitudes, practices, and beliefs. *Archives of Family Medicine*, *8*, 301–306.

Taft, A.J., Small, R., Hegarty, K.L., Watson, L.F., Gold, L., & Lumley, J.A. (2011). Mothers' AdvocateS In the Community (MOSAIC): Non-professional mentor support to reduce intimate partner violence and depression in mothers: a cluster randomised trial in primary care. *BMC Public Health*, *11*, 178.

Thurston, W.E., Tutty, L.M., Eisener, A.E., Lalonde, L., Belenky, C., & Osborne, B. (2007). Domestic violence screening rates in a community health center urgent care clinic. *Reseach in Nursing and Health*, *30*, 611–961.

Tower, M., McMurray, A., Rowe, J., & Wallis, M. (2006). Domestic violence, health & health care: Women's accounts of their experiences. *Contemporary Nurse*, *21*, 186–198.

Trautman, D.E., Mccarthy, M.L., Miller, N., Campbell, J.C., & Kelen, G.D. (2007). Intimate partner violence and emergency department screening: Computerized screening versus usual care. *Annals of Emergency Medicine*, *49*, 526–534.

Vu, A., Adam, A., Wirtz, A., Pham, K., Rubenstein, L., Glass, N., & Singh, S. (2014). The prevalence of sexual violence among female refugees in complex humanitarian emergencies: A systematic review and meta-analysis. *PLOS Currents Disasters*, *18*, 6.

Weeks, E.K., Ellis, S.D., Lichstein, P.R., & Bonds, D.E. (2008). Does health care provider screening for domestic violence vary by race and income? *Violence Against Women*, *14*, 844–855.

Westbrook, L. (2008). Understanding crisis information needs in context: The case of intimate partner violence survivors. *Library Quarterly: Information, Community, Policy*, *78*, 237–261.

WHO (World Health Organization) (2013a). *Global and regional estimates of violence against women: Prevalence and health effects of intimate partner violence and nonpartner sexual violence.* Geneva: WHO, London School of Hygiene and Tropical Medicine, & South African Medical Research Council.

WHO (2013b). *Responding to intimate partner violence and sexual violence against women: WHO clinical and policy guidelines.* Geneva: WHO.

Wirtz, A.L., Glass, N., Pham, K., Aberra, A., Rubenstein, L.S., Singh, S., & Vu, A. (2013). Development of a screening tool to identify female survivors of gender-based violence in a humanitarian setting: Qualitative evidence from research among refugees in Ethiopia. *Conflict and Health*, *7*, 13.

Wirtz, A. L., Glass, N., Pham, K., Perrin, N., Rubenstein, L.S., Singh, S., & Vu, A. (2016). Comprehensive development and testing of the ASIST-GBV, a screening tool for responding to gender-based violence among women in humanitarian settings. *Conflict and Health*, *10*, 7.

Yonaka, L., Yoder, M.K., Darrow, J.B., & Sherck, J.P. (2007). Barriers to screening for domestic violence in the emergency department. *Journal of Continuing Education in Nursing, 38,* 37–45.

SIX

Emergent Research and Practice Trends in Contextually Addressing the Complexity of Women's Use of Force

Lisa Y. Larance and Susan L. Miller[1]

Introduction

This chapter provides an overview of the research about, and community-based programmatic responses to, battered[2] women's use of force in their intimate heterosexual relationships[3]. By highlighting emerging issues, we hope to stimulate discussion and a more fully informed response to the complexity introduced by criminalizing women's responses to violence and abuse in their intimate relationships. Three decades ago, efforts to efficaciously and compassionately address the needs of battered women were in their infancy. A grassroots coalition comprised of survivors, advocates, attorneys, and practitioners elevated the personal experiences of battered women to an issue of social prominence, and challenged the system's trivialization and tolerance of violence and abuse occurring between intimate partners and former partners. Changes in the ways that the criminal legal system[4] (CLS) responded to intimate violence are directly attributed to these early efforts of battered women's advocates and members of the feminist movement; perhaps the most significant change is the manner in which police handle intimate partner violence (IPV) calls, by implementing mandatory (or presumptive) arrest policies requiring arrest if probable cause exists that demonstrates that an act of violence occurred. This *Gemeinschaft*—advocating arrest for "non-stranger" crime—facilitated research promoting the deterrence aspects of pro- or mandatory arrest policies (Sherman, 1992; Sherman & Berk, 1984). Following the widely publicized findings that arrest deters future IPV, many jurisdictions quickly enacted mandatory, preferred, or pro-arrest statutes.

IPV arrest policies are lauded for increasing abused women's protection and encouraging offender accountability. They do so by removing police discretion at the time of arrest. When enforced properly, the changes ensure an appropriate arrest is made, hopefully serve as a deterrent to future violence, and show the state is no longer tolerant of IPV. At the same time, however, mandatory arrest policies may in some instances do more harm than good. Adverse consequences result because the CLS rests on an incident-driven model, void of context, which removes women's decision-making power. Furthermore, police officers typically do not consider the full context of the incident, even if they are legally required to do so (Finn & Bettis, 2006). As a result, police officers continue to make inappropriate arrests of victims, despite extensive training. This has been attributed to patriarchal police force culture, organized along paramilitary contours, in addition to a misinformed reliance on the myth of mutual combat (O'Dell, 2007).

When police fail to consider the full context of the presenting abusive situation, victim arrests naturally occur, given the disproportionate representation of female victims and male offenders (Black et al., 2011). Of particular concern is the growing evidence of women's increased arrests for IPV when they are either the sole offender or arrested as part of a dual arrest (Miller, 2005; Osthoff, 2002; Rajan & McCloskey, 2007). Furthermore, women are often wrongly arrested for defending themselves. Additionally, when police arrive at the scene of the incident, abusive male partners often manipulate the situation to their own advantage (Larance & Rousson, 2016; Miller, 2005; Muftic et al., 2007; Osthoff, 2002; Roy, 2012). For example, in Pollack et al.'s (2005) research, 10 of the 19 women arrested for using force against a partner "reported that their male partner used his knowledge of the criminal justice system (including how mandatory charge policies work) to portray her as the primary aggressor and have her arrested and charged" (p. 11). Pollack et al.'s (2005) findings are similar to those of Dichter (2013, 2015), Larance and Rousson (2016), Miller (2005), and Roy (2012). Similarly, women's use of force is increasingly used against them in custody and/or visitation disputes, a phenomenon often exacerbated by men's rights groups (see Dragiewicz, 2011).

"Paper abuse" is an additional consideration regarding abusive men manipulating the system against women (Dragiewicz, 2011; Miller & Smolter, 2011). Paper abuse incorporates routine acts used by batterers against their former partners to continue victimization and includes a range of behaviors such as filing frivolous lawsuits, making false reports of child abuse, and taking other legal actions as a means of exerting power, forcing contact, and financially burdening their ex-partners. In addition, some jurisdictions charge mothers of minor children with "failure to protect" if the children are exposed to IPV (Kantor & Little, 2003).

A thorough understanding of why women use force is a critical aspect of placing the violence in context, undertaking informed research, and implementing effective programming. Swan et al.'s (2012) work addresses the need for more thorough investigation into women's aggression. They argue that a gendered analysis accurately portrays women's experiences of IPV, pointing out that women's aggression is distinctly different from women's victimization. The work of Swan et al. (2012) and Swan and Snow (2002) concluded that, in comparison with men who perpetrate IPV, women are more likely to be motivated by self-defense and fear. Hamberger and Guse (2002) found that women's motivation for using violence against an intimate partner is dramatically different from men's; men use IPV as a means of control whereas women do so in self-defense (Hamberger & Guse, 2002; Saunders, 2002).

Women have stated a range of motives for using force (Caldwell et al., 2009; Dasgupta, 1999, 2002, 2007; Hamberger & Potente, 1994; Hamberger et al., 1997; Larance, 2006, 2007, 2012; Larance & Miller, forthcoming; Miller & Meloy, 2006; Swan et al., 2008; Weston et al., 2007). Their reasons include, but are not limited to, physically defending themselves; defending who they are as individuals; "turning the tables" of power and control; protecting their children; retaliating for past relationship wrongs; demanding attention; feeling jealous; expressing anger; regaining lost respect; using his abusive actions against him; and attempting to escape abuse while asserting their dignity. This understanding explains the complex power and control dynamics that contribute to the difficulty of accurately assessing the situation. Such an explanation is necessary for more thorough research and effective intervention.

It is clear that police often circumvent arrest policies. Some police officers refuse to make arrests even when mandatory arrest policies exist (Frye et al., 2007), while others rely upon their own beliefs about what behavior is "normative" for offenders and victims and make arrests guided by their own positions (Miller, 2005; O'Dell, 2007; Stalans & Finn, 1995). Overall, studies reveal that police officers do not always find abused women credible, and may still blame them for the violence (DeJong et al., 2008; Ferraro & Pope, 1993; Goodmark, 2008; Stalans & Finn, 2006). Thus, as Ritmeester and Pence (1992) suggest, CLS agents contribute to women's criminalization through the way in which they process and categorize women's experiences.

The CLS's response blurs the boundaries between victims and offenders. It also highlights the CLS's lack of capacity for taking multiple factors into account. There is hope, however, given examples from a coordinated community response in Washtenaw County, MI (Gondolf, 2015; Larance & Rousson, 2016), and a growing informed awareness of the problem among advocates, CLS staff, and academics, who actively challenge misleading arrest statistics, the lack of appropriate programming, and entrenched structural and gender inequalities, which all contribute to the complexity of this issue (Larance & Miller, 2015).

Perspectives of criminal justice professionals

Although police officers act as the gatekeepers to the CLS, other criminal legal and social service professionals struggle with how best to respond to women's use of force in intimate relationships. Research reflecting this ambiguity reveals a different accounting, such as those described in Miller's (2005) analysis of police, prosecutors, defense attorneys, and other CLS and social service professionals who dismiss the idea of mutual combatants; reveal an understanding of power and control dynamics and men's primary power; attribute women's increased IPV arrests to changes in policy; believe male offenders manipulate women and the CLS; and find that misguided police motivation exacerbates the problem. The court process in general is often mysterious for women, because they are baffled by how their efforts to protect themselves and their children could possibly result in arrest or any punitive measures from a system founded upon the philosophy of seeking justice. Current strategies are underway to address how alienating the legal/court process can be for women survivors of domestic violence who have used force, such as instituting primary aggressor guidelines so police and prosecutors can more effectively distinguish between victims and offenders. It is still the case that, when police cannot determine the primary aggressor, they arrest one or both parties and let the courts figure out the end result (Bohmer et al., 2002; Miller 2005). The Center for Court Innovation (CCI), which seeks to aid victims by improving public trust in justice, is on the cutting edge of ameliorating this situation through support of domestic violence specialty courts in the US. By facilitating open houses around the nation—as well as providing other resources, including webinars (CCI, 2013) —the CCI promotes best practices geared toward more equitable courtroom treatment.

The focus on early and more enhanced police training stems from the research of O'Dell (2007) and Finn and Bettis (2006), which found that police officers are neither trained nor prepared to identify primary aggressors. In a review of 128 domestic violence cases over 6 years, Hester (2012) found that women identified by police as "perpetrators" rarely exerted the power and control inherent in battering tactics. With the decontextualized approach, women in Hester's sample were three times as likely as their male partners to be arrested. Hester (2012) also emphasized that women who were heavy drinkers or much younger than their male partners were more likely to be arrested. She notes that police understanding of gendered dynamics is central to their ability to accurately identify the primary aggressor. This does not abnegate women's responsibility for retaliatory violence, but by contextualizing such behavior, it can be effectively dealt with while increasing women's safety.

How police evaluate, blame, and interpret behavior affects arrest patterns as well. For instance, Leisenring (2011) looked at women's understanding of their interactions with police, and suggested that women's self-presentation fails to convince officers that they are victims; consequently, they are arrested. Similarly, some women are unable to convince officers that they were *not* victims—but the officers still arrested their partners (Leisenring, 2011, p. 358). This perpetuates the practice of implicit bias—using images or assumptions of what a "good" victim looks and acts like to understand behavior or assess presentation. It is common for a woman to hear from police officers that she did not fit the profile of a "good" victim because she called first for police help but then failed to leave the man. From the officer's point of view, a "good" victim would have left. Therefore, she was arrested.

Other women who were arrested openly admitted their violent acts to police for self-defense or frustration reasons. Police then arrested them for "damaging property." Still other women believed their emotional state—for example, crying and visibly upset—harmed their credibility, causing police to take their claims less seriously. Leisenring's findings confirm Miller's (2001, 2005) earlier research, which revealed women's partners/ex-partners used the women's emotions as evidence that they were crazy, thereby diminishing the women's credibility. Who was able to proactively define the situation—such as who called 911 first—also influenced who the police believed. Again, this supports Miller's (2001, p. 1354) research that abusers have learned how to manipulate the system. It also exemplifies how cases are often assessed differently by police officers, could explain why stereotypes of "normative" characterizations of victims still influence arrest decisions (DeJong et al., 2008; Dichter, 2013), and shows that officers interpret mandatory arrest policies differently (Crager et al. 2003; O'Dell, 2007).

Perceptions of women who have used force

The lay public and the CLS continue to rely on visual cues that highlight the physicality of IPV, such as visible bruises or broken bones. Many researchers, however, maintain that coercive control is more likely part and parcel of abuse, and this tactic is often gendered, as well as invisible to those outside the relationship (Anderson, 2009; Brush, 2009; Pence & Dasgupta, 2006; Stark, 2007). Dichter (2013) mentions how coercive control fits into victims' use of force in response to forms of IPV "that are not as clearly identifiable to outsiders but may be as damaging as, or more damaging than, physical attacks; examples include isolating the victim from social supports, controlling the victim's activities and access to resources, and using verbal threats and nonphysical forms of intimidation" (p. 83; see also Smith et al., 1999). The collateral damage of arresting women who use force includes implications for how a criminal record affects employment; housing; financial aid; voting rights; immigration status; the right to bear arms; child custody; and accrued costs for court-ordered intervention/ treatment, legal counsel, and childcare—not to mention an often greater use of violent retaliation from the true abuser. Dichter's (2013) study provides examples of monetary expenses incurred by women as a result of arrest, in addition to other costs, such as trouble finding employment and/or losing a job. Women also described how arrests led to clinical depression, suicide attempts, substance abuse, financial problems, loss of employment, and parenting challenges.

Emerging trends in research

This section presents an overview of emerging trends identified by advocates and researchers.

The symmetry question

Despite the abundant research resoundingly demonstrating that women's use of force is typically not equivalent to men's battering, critics of contextually based research and scholars who conduct quantitative surveys or use large samples that measure IPV using acontextual checklists (that is, "If you ever do X, check yes or no") continue to assert that violence is symmetrical and that there are scant gender-based differences in its use (Straus, 1995, 2009). Context is crucial in unpacking motivations and mechanisms of abuse; failure to consider the panoply of research that reveals the nuanced and complicated nature of women's use of force means the presentation of summed up checklists is inaccurate and misleading. While we believe that gaining insight through research is an important enterprise in knowledge building, if the tenets it rests on are unsteady or collapsing, the message is both disingenuous and dangerous.

We echo the admonishment in Johnson et al.'s (2014) recent article: quantitative researchers must think about problems inherent in using large general survey data to analyze IPV perpetration, and endeavor to uncover gender differences in the use of force. Johnson et al. (2014) detail a new operationalization of intimate terrorism and situational couple violence using ex-spouse data from the National Violence Against Women Survey, demonstrating that it is possible to use quantitative survey data to expose gender asymmetry. Their work not only confirms differences between intimate terrorism and situational couple violence, but also establishes that "intimate terrorism is much more likely to be perpetrated by men, it involves more frequent and more injurious violence, and it has debilitating psychological consequences for victims" (Johnson et al., 2014, pp. 202–203).

Similarly, Gondolf's (2012) investigation into the differences between the violence of men enrolled in batterer intervention programs (BIPs) and the violence of their female partners refutes claims that BIP participants and their partners are primarily engaged in "mutual violence." Gondolf's work illustrates that women's reports of using force against their partners largely stop when their male partners reduce their abuse and violence, and in relationships with continuing severe violence, the women's behavior is best characterized as "violent resistance" rather than a "both victim" dyad (Gondolf, 2014). Straus (2014), however, dismisses these findings by reinterpreting Gondolf's (2014) data and calling for an emphasis on programming for female partners, asserting that only then will violence by women be reduced.

Culture and diversity

Although broad observations are made about women's use of force, recent work acknowledges the differential impact and response of women hailing from varied backgrounds and circumstances. This acknowledgment is especially important given the CLS's tendency to overcriminalize poor women of color (Potter, 2008; Richie, 1995, 2012; Sokoloff, 2005; West, 2002, 2012). Other women are also disenfranchised based on their multiple identities: "race"/ethnicity, immigration status (Dasgupta, 2002; Roy, 2012), poverty, sexuality, gender identity, disability (Ballan & Freyer, 2012), and/or age (Collins, 2015).

There is a related concern that some women from these groups would avoid approaching the police as a resource for help, which could increase the likelihood that an individual will use violence as a means of self-protection (Miller, 2005). For instance, West (2007) looks at Black women—whom she calls "victim–defendants"—and develops the concept of bidirectional asymmetric violence. She argues that Black women use aggression to protect themselves and/or their children or in retaliation against their abusers. Black women are therefore disproportionately labeled as mutual combatants and/or arrested, but the possibility of arrest for Black women increases in jurisdictions with mandatory arrest policies (see also Melton & Belknap, 2003; Simpson et al., 2006). Swan and Snow's (2002) work with a sample of predominately Black low-income women (108) found that, although women and men committed equivalent levels of verbal abuse and women more moderate physical violence (throwing objects, pushing, and shoving), men committed significantly more severe physical violence (choking, sexual aggression, and coercive control) and were better able to control the women's behavior. The findings of West (2007), and other scholars, suggest that Black women are overrepresented in arrests due to:

> the association among poverty, residence in economically
> disadvantaged neighborhoods, and Black female-perpetrated

IPV. Low-income urban areas are often characterized by racial segregation, social isolation, rampant unemployment, and community violence, including high rates of non-IPV homicide. In these communities, the appearance of physical or emotional weakness can be dangerous, making at least the show of violence essential for survival. When violence is routinely modeled for Black women (and men) as a way of achieving one's goals, as a means of self-protection, or as a conflict resolution strategy, this aggressive behavior can easily spill over into intimate relationships. (West, 2007, p. 100; see also Benson & Fox, 2004; Websdale, 2001)

Coinciding with these findings, after pro-arrest legislation was expanded in Maryland, arrests of women increased for all groups but more drastically for Black women (25.3% and 38% respectively, before and after the policy) (Simpson et al., 2006).

Focusing on the intersectional nature of women's experiences is critical: "Strategies based on the experiences of women who do not share the same class and race backgrounds will be of limited utility for those whose lives are shaped by a different set of obstacles" (Crenshaw, 1991, p. 86). It is necessary to move beyond regarding "race," class, and gender as individual identity characteristics; instead, by including the standpoints of diverse women, these issues should be seen as interlocking structures that interact with other forms of inequality and oppression—such as racism, ethnocentrism, class privilege, and heterosexism—to constrain and/or shape women's lives and choices (Collins, 2015; Crenshaw, 1991; Larance, 2012; Smith, 1987). Diversity raises issues of "culture"—how to account for different cultures defining IPV differently—without allocating blame to an immigrant's culture, for example, or excusing/tolerating cultural practices in ways that justify batterers who use cultural defenses. We need a sociocultural context, but cannot elevate cultural difference so that structural power is erased (Sokoloff & Dupont, 2005). Swan and Snow (2006) use an intersectional approach—with particular emphasis placed on social, historical, and cultural contexts—to understand the complex nature of women's use of force. Their:

> model proposes a number of risk and protective factors that appear to be related to women's use of violence with male partners, including the male partners' violence against women, experiences of childhood trauma, women's strategies for coping with problems in their relationships,

> women's motivations for using violence, and the outcomes
> of depression, anxiety, substance abuse, and PTSD. (p. 1039)

Cultural issues often overlap with the methodological issues noted earlier in this section. Mainstream IPV research, however, lacks necessary sociocultural contexts. Greater attention to cultural context requires multi-methods approaches to investigate the nuances and complexities of women's circumstances. As Yoshihama (1999) points out, turning over a dining table is a culturally specific form of abuse in Japan because it questions women's legitimate role in the family, while dousing a woman with liquid in Japan conveys she is impure or contaminated. Garfield's (1991) life history interviews with African American women reveal that the women "did not always regard physical aggression as violence, whereas acts of racism were uniformly experienced as such" (p. 42), and so could raise concerns that calling the police would subject Black men to racist treatment by the CLS and confirm racist stereotypes. Similarly, Bui and Morash (1999) report that Vietnamese women—who have been taught that saving face and family unity are more important than individual safety—may be at a disadvantage in a system that believes otherwise. Women's responses to these actions reflect a distinct cultural milieu that may be misunderstood by outsiders.

Sexuality complicates the gendered use of force. Being cognizant of the similarities and differences introduced by LGBTQ relationships and IPV is as vital to include in research and practice as is highlighting cultural issues. Early research conducted by Renzetti (1998) asserted that, although power and control over one's partner is inherent in both heterosexual and lesbian IPV, we cannot lose sight of the homophobic social context in which abuse occurs. For instance, Ristock (2002) reminds us that lesbians who are not "out" to their friends, family, landlord, or employer are at risk from an abusive partner, who may disclose their sexual identity. Fear of a homophobic response from the CLS or social services could also prevent an abused lesbian from seeking help or thorough assessment of which partner is using force. Furthermore, the legal system has been hard pressed to appropriately address the needs of transgender women caught in violent relationships (Goodmark, 2013). Thus, intersectional approaches to examining women's use of force need to take sexuality and gender identity into account, in addition to culture, "race"/ethnicity, immigration status, disability, social class, and age (Collins, 2015).

Faulty assumptions of "real" victims

Assumptions about what a "real" victim looks like perpetuates the problem in research, CLS response, and programming. This is a complicated issue; it was important in the early days of the battered women's movement to construct an image of a "blameless" battered woman in order to garner public sympathy, understanding, and resource support, and to underscore the message that "battering affects every woman" and "it could be anyone." However, this "trivializes both the dimensions that underlie the experiences of these particular abuse victims" (Kanuha, 1996, p. 41) and suggests that there is universal risk. When battered women are portrayed as blameless "good women," they are touted as passive, nonviolent, and visibly afraid of the abuser (Berns, 2004; Lamb, 1999; Loseke, 1992). This image is harmful when it prevents service providers or CLS personnel from further assessing situations that are far more nuanced than initial presentation may suggest (Creek & Dunn, 2011; Dunn, 2008; Larance & Miller, forthcoming; Larance & Rousson, 2016). It also ignores the structural issues that complicate women's daily lives, such as when poor women of color are "most likely to be in both dangerous intimate relationships and dangerous social positions" (Richie, 2000, p. 1136).

Trauma-informed approach

The emerging focus on trauma-informed, gender-responsive practice (Bloom et al., 2004) acknowledges survivorship histories in ways useful for practitioners and researchers. It is very appealing because it validates how early trauma could have a long-lasting impact, and can help to understand why adults traumatized by violence may have frightening flashbacks and fears. For survivors who blame themselves for their victimization, understanding research that finds this connection could absolve them of their internalized shame or guilt. Finally, trauma research has facilitated treatment interventions that have been very helpful for victims.

However, there are limitations. If trauma is understood as an individual psychological response, it could be seen as a "psychological condition caused by exposure to violence/extreme stress, leading to the assumption that all types of traumatic events are precursors of psychological symptomatology, unless the victim is exceptionally resilient" (Gilfus, 1999, p. 1241). Additionally, an individual pathology-oriented explanation could ignore victims' agency, and may be used to excuse men's violence if they too experienced trauma (Gilfus, 1999). If we focus too much on childhood traumatic experiences, we risk losing structural factors—including racism, poverty, and other forms of oppression—that could also be just as traumatic. By focusing on the trauma victim, we also ignore the person who has hurt them. We must not lose sight of the social and political context and the gendered nature of the inequalities of power within which IPV occurs.

Service utilization issues

Research and practice (Dichter, 2013; Miller, 2005; Osthoff, 2002) reveal that, for many women, it often takes being arrested to receive the services they need. One woman in Dichter's (2013) study said: "[Arrest] saved my life – but it shouldn't work like that." When a woman receives help only after she is arrested, it is a wakeup call for the spectrum of violence prevention programs. In some jurisdictions, advocacy organizations believe they cannot help victims who are arrested because of the organization's rules or funding restrictions. This means many women do not receive emotional support, tangible assistance, shelter opportunities, and other resources they desperately need from their local advocacy organizations. In addition, many women are court-ordered by judges to "anger management" groups; this demonstrates a fundamental misunderstanding of the women's circumstances, and wastes the women's time and limited resources on services that do not address their needs. Those needs include opportunities to address the gendered power and control dynamics of IPV, heal from possible survivorship issues, and explore viable alternatives to using force in a safe, nonjudgmental space.

Women who have used force: Emerging issues from arrest to intervention

Connie's[5] story illustrates the complexity of understanding and addressing one woman's situation. Of course Connie's story is unique, as is each woman's story, but understanding common themes will facilitate tailored intervention innovations that lead to violence reduction.

Case study

When Connie and Steve first met, it was "like a romance novel," according to Connie. But all of that quickly changed after Steve convinced Connie to quit her job, leave her children, move to the US, and marry him. As soon as she married him the physical and emotional abuse began. He controlled everything. She relied on him for transportation, her right to remain in the US, and her daily needs. Late one evening, after she had prepared to go to bed, Connie heard Steve talking on the phone to a member of his extended family. After the call, she begged him to finally introduce her to his extended family members. During the argument, he put his clenched fists up to her face to threaten her. She grabbed his fists to protect herself, and when he jerked his hands away, one of her fingernails inadvertently caught the skin on his cheek. Connie panicked, thinking Steve would hit her. Instead, he calmly encouraged her to go to the garden, not to worry, and have a cigarette. While in the garden Connie heard the doorbell ring. When it continued to ring, Connie went to see who it could be. She was shocked to find two police officers at her front door. The officers were responding to Steve's call, made while Connie was in the garden. He alleged that Connie had attacked him and showed the police the scratch to prove it. During questioning, Connie took responsibility for scratching Steve. She did not detail the abuse she had suffered and how she feared his clenched fists. Connie went to jail and was threatened with being deported.

Arrest

Connie's situation provides a framework for understanding the gendered differences in behavior at the time of police intervention. In contrast to men who batter, women who have used force in their intimate heterosexual relationships typically take complete responsibility for their use of force—from the time of police response, through court proceedings, and during group intervention sessions. Like Steve, men who batter women often minimize, deny, and/or blame women for the violence. In many situations, the only difference between a woman who is referred to a battered women's/domestic violence shelter and a woman who is sent to jail and/or an intervention program for her use of force is whether or not she is arrested.

Connie's situation can be generalized to many women's situations. When the police arrive at the scene, a woman is often crying, detailing her abusive actions, and asking how she can help him. In contrast, he often remains calm, quiet, and apologetic for wasting the police officers' time. His manipulative presentation to the (often male) police officers typically escalates her frustration and impassioned "truth telling." As first responders, the police then see a calm man who may be bleeding and what many have described as a "hysterical" woman. Her perceived hysteria contributes to the perception that she is unbalanced and "obviously" guilty. Similar to Connie, she is reluctant to disclose her survivorship story to the responding officers, because she sees her partner as having power well beyond the presenting incident. She may be asking herself: Will I need to go back to him? What will happen to my children? Where will I live if he kicks me out? Answers to these questions may discourage her from telling the officers about her survivorship history. From her perspective, she is initially relieved that the police are there because she believes they will serve as the neutral presence needed to calm him down; she is not aware that most officers believe they must leave having made an arrest. Unfortunately, she often finds that police intervention results in her being labeled the "perpetrator" and his being identified as the "victim" (Frye et al., 2007; Larance, 2006, 2007).

In many states, women who are charged with domestic violence lose jobs that are contingent upon state licensure (such as child care providers, cosmetologists, doctors, lawyers, social workers, and nurses), as well as their public housing and financial aid (Bible & Osthoff, 1998; Worcester, 2002). Native women may be prevented from returning to the reservation, while immigrant woman can be and often are deported. Renzetti (1999) notes that these collateral consequences are examples of widespread gendered injustice, and Pence (2012) frames this as a human rights issue.

Courtroom

The gendered distinctions in behavior at the time of women's arrest are present in the courtroom as well. There women are much more likely than men to detail their actions, with the belief that telling "the whole truth" to the judge will result in justice being served. Men, however, often obfuscate their role in the altercation. Attorneys often complicate women's cases because they typically do not understand the complex dynamics of IPV. In addition, many women have explained that their attorneys have discouraged them from taking the case to trial for a range of reasons—including the expense and the need for them to get back to the children, who are typically being cared for by a family member—and attorneys may remind the woman that he has more money and will drag the case out as long as possible in order to bankrupt her. Women are urged to plead "no contest," which will result in a domestic violence charge but will "get [her] out of court faster." Many women take their attorney's advice, not realizing the long-term implications of a guilty plea (Miller, 2005; Larance & Rousson, 2016).

Community supervision

Once on probation or parole, women in the community are often much more vulnerable to the men who are abusing them. Ann, a member of a group created for women who have used force (Gondolf, 2015; RENEW, www.csswashtenaw.org/renew), explained: "Because he was the 'victim' he knew more about my probation than I did . . . the prosecuting attorney explained everything in detail to him . . . and now he knows where I live!" Due to the vulnerability Ann describes, a gender-responsive (Bloom et al., 2004), contextual approach to probation and parole is critically important to positive outcomes for women (Cross, 2013; Morash, 2010; Neal, 2007).

To meet this need, probation and parole agents must be aware of gender-specific challenges to women's compliance (Cross, 2013), particularly intentional manipulation of women's probation/parole status by their abusers. Abusers' tactics include, but are not limited to, making false allegations to probation/parole agents if women do not have sex the way they demand, do not buy drugs for them, and/or refuse to sign over child custody. This attempted, and often successful, manipulation of probation/parole agents also includes abusers self-inflicting wounds and using these as "proof" that the women are abusing them (Larance & Miller, forthcoming; Larance & Rousson, 2016). Probation/parole agents must also be aware that blanket conditions for the women's compliance often set the women up for failure. Such conditions may include, for example, requiring low-income women who have never used drugs to complete weekly drug tests at their own expense and/or enroll in excessive programming (in areas such as parenting and budgeting)—also at their own expense—within an unreasonable period of time. This constellation of events sets women up for failure, when it is the system that has failed them.

Toward tailored intervention

Community supervisors' challenges are, in many ways, shared by those providing community-based intervention. For example, many intervention providers across the nation place women in groups designed for men who batter, and/or with men in the same intervention group. This is revictimizing and ineffective. By using a "one size fits all" (Gardner, 2007; Miller et al., 2005) approach to intervention, practitioners may be unintentionally escalating the violence in the women's lives rather than providing necessary support and opportunities for change. Indeed, domestic violence service providers struggle with how to philosophically and practically assist battered women caught in the legal system for using force. Those in a movement focused on providing safety to battered women are justifiably concerned that shifting attention away from men's violence against women will be detrimental to the movement and the women they hope to serve.

As Gardner (2007) points out, intervention for battered women who have used force presents practitioners with the ethical quandary of how to effectively serve these women in a manner that addresses the violence but is not punitive and shaming. According to Dasgupta (2002), identifying the women as batterers and "resocializing them to be nonviolent through education classes that are similar to men's programs seems illogical and inappropriate" (p. 1368). However, referring women to voluntarily seek survivor services and discuss their use of violence within that setting does not seem promising either (Larance & Rousson, 2016). When female survivors of domestic violence begin to use violence as a strategy to navigate their relationships, it increases their male partner's violence against them (Dieten et al., 2014; Larance, 2006; Swan & Snow, 2002). It also increases the likelihood that the women will be severely injured by their male partners, as well as the probability that the women will use force again.

Given the risks to women and their families, there is a need for contextual intervention tailored to their circumstances. Such intervention, Larance (2006) suggests, is possible from a "healing place" approach that builds upon traditional survivor support group strengths, yet is distinctly different from batterers intervention programs. This approach, grounded in Bronfenbrenner's (1977) ecological nested model, holds promise for reducing violence and rebuilding lives.

Curricula

An early "guide book" meeting this need was written by Erin House (n.d.) of the Domestic Violence Project/SAFE House in Ann Arbor, MI. This guidebook provides an essential grassroots resource for antiviolence practitioners, and a framework for community-based[6] violence intervention with women. Since the guidebook's creation, three main curricula were developed to meet the evolving needs of programs serving women in the community who were court-ordered to intervention for their use of force: Vista: A Program for Women Who Use Force (Dieten et al., 2014; Larance, 2006; Larance et al., 2009); Turning Points: A Nonviolence Curriculum for Women (Pence, Connelly, & Scaia, 2011); and Beyond Anger and Violence: A Program for Women (Covington, 2014).

The Vista Program curriculum outlines 20 sessions focused on providing women the opportunity to heal from the past while exploring viable future options. During group participation, the women plan for their safety; address feelings of shame and/or guilt related to their use of force, and strategies for moving beyond that shame and/or guilt; are encouraged to identify appropriate levels of responsibility, rather than responsibility for everything that "went wrong" in the relationship; explore personal skills and resources in light of cultural messages they have received about "appropriate female behavior"; and increase their awareness of alternatives to using force.

The goal of the Turning Points curriculum is to help women understand connections between the violence they experience and the violence they use—and to end both. The three-part curriculum focuses on domestic violence and its impact on relationships and family; different aspects of violence, such as feelings of guilt, feeling justified, and feeling trapped; living with anger; talking to children about the violence; and understanding the impact the use of force has had on their partners.

Beyond Anger and Violence is a manualized intervention for women that focuses on anger and use of force. It utilizes a multimodal approach and a variety of evidence-based therapeutic strategies: psycho-education, role playing, mindfulness activities, cognitive behavioral restructuring, and grounding skills for trauma triggers. The companion DVD, *What I want my words to do to you* (by Eve Ensler), is incorporated throughout the 21 program sessions. Beyond Anger and Violence offers a comprehensive framework for addressing the role past trauma plays in the lives of women who struggle with anger. It includes detailed empowerment tools, exercises, and activities focused on self-examination, self-soothing, and managing anger.

As curricula have gradually developed to meet programming needs, professionals' resource-sharing opportunities have evolved. In 2007, the W-Catch22 Listserv (2007) was established to provide such opportunities to activists, advocates, law enforcement, the judiciary, and service providers, while also streamlining gender-responsive, context-focused responses to women's use of force. In 2014 and 2016, the W-Catch22 Listserv international membership of 321 agency representatives was informally surveyed regarding whether or not they had community-based programming for women who use force; if so, which curriculum they used in their work; and what, if any, evaluation tools were in place to assess outcomes. Forty-one service providers from six countries—Australia, Canada, China (Hong Kong), Malta, the UK, and the US—and 21 different US states responded to the survey. While two respondents (in Australia and Malta) said they were in the process of implementing programs (Australia would be implementing Turning Points; Malta planned to implement Vista), the other 38 respondents indicated that they either used Vista, Turning Points, or Beyond Violence exclusively; integrated Vista, Turning Points, and Beyond Violence curricula content; modified existing curricula from the program for men who batter; or created a separate in-house curriculum that met program and agency needs. Two programs (in Michigan and Wisconsin) assessed for recidivism and utilized pre- and post-tests to measure program effectiveness. The RENEW Program in Michigan also utilized quarterly evaluations to gage program impact. Five programs (from Alabama, Delaware, Indiana, Ohio, and Wisconsin) distributed satisfaction surveys at program completion.

Hong Kong's Nurturing Heart Program, based at Harmony House, provided an example of how Hong Kong's first shelter program innovatively addressed a complex issue according to cultural needs. The Nurturing Heart program was initially part of a 3-year pilot project to address women's use of force (Queenie Tao, Executive Director, Harmony House, personal communication). The pilot project began in July 2011 and was completed in November 2014. One result of the pilot project was a Chinese-language training manual on working with women using force. The program, which secured renewed funding in 2016, involves 10 psycho-educational group sessions and a curriculum culturally adapted from the Vista model. Additional wraparound services include individual counseling, family relationship enhancement support programs, and workshops and sharing sessions for multidisciplinary professionals. To date, the agency has worked with 99 women who identify as having used force against their family members.

Recommendations for work with women who have used force

As programs identify curricula that meet the needs of the women they serve, there are essential programmatic components necessary for effectively serving this population.

First and foremost, ongoing assessment is crucial to women's healing and sustainable intervention. Not only are women's situations constantly changing, but also women who have used force are not a homogenous group. Women court-ordered to programming for their use of force may need a range of concurrent services, such as counseling for sexual assault, substance abuse, mental health, and/or domestic violence survivorship. Note that when assessing for domestic violence survivorship, women who have used force will typically not initially self-identify as "victims" or "survivors." Therefore, assessment questions must focus on specific situations women may have experienced, such as: "Has your partner ever kicked/punched/slapped you?" The questions must also assess for coercive control, which women may have experienced or may be currently experiencing, such as: "Are there ways that your partner can hurt you that may seem crazy or misunderstood by other people?" Likewise, gaining a deeper understanding of whether or not women dread a partner's presence or involvement in a particular situation are critical (Larance, 2017). Questions about the extent of an abuser's micro-management or surveillance of daily life may be more informative for assessment purposes than those that focus primarily on whether or not someone self-reports fearing their partner.

In addition to ongoing assessment, the group session structure and process are critical. Although many women may state that they prefer individual sessions to group intervention, group sessions are generally more beneficial, as they have the capacity to promote social networks and long-term supportive relationships among women who are often isolated due to the abuse they have suffered. However, group intervention sessions for women who have used force must be comprised only of women. In the event that there are not enough women for a group, individual sessions may then be a short-term alternative. During each contact with the women, practitioners must reinforce that behavior change within an abusive relationship can potentially place women at increased risk of harm. Thus, using new behaviors encouraged in group are at her discretion. Each woman knows her situation and knows when (or if) it is safe to integrate new behaviors. Safety and support planning must be a priority, particularly in the forms of promoting healthy relationships and raising awareness of available community resources. Sessions must also raise awareness of power and control dynamics of abuse and the impact of the abuse on extended relationships with children, family, and friends. Space must also be provided for women to explore any shame and/or guilt they may feel for their situations, while encouraging healing and promoting awareness of viable alternatives to using force. In order to encourage successful participation and completion, onsite childcare and sliding-fee scales and/or scholarships are a necessity; these enable women to attend group sessions at little or no personal cost.

Policies and procedures must be in place to ensure that women are not penalized for missing group sessions due to extenuating circumstances, particularly abusers manipulating the women's attendance with the goal of having women violate the terms of their probation/parole. During each woman's program participation, there must be communication with and education for the CLS personnel (probation/parole agents) involved in the women's lives. Such communication and education must focus on the intervention program's role as a support, intervention, and advocacy opportunity for the women—a role that is separate from the monitoring function of probation/parole. For additional recommendations, see Cross (2013), Dieten et al. (2014), House (n.d.), Larance (2006), Neal (2007), and Guidelines for Programs Working with Women Who Use Force (2011).

Upcoming challenges

In an effort to more closely standardize and supervise BIPs that serve men who abuse their partners, most states have implemented standards for programs providing intervention to service participants (Ferency, 2016; Kernsmith & Kernsmith, 2009). A looming issue for many states is how to—and even whether or not to—implement standards for programs serving women who have used force. This is particularly challenging—and potentially problematic—due to a lack of understanding among CLS, police, advocates and practitioners of the dynamics of women's use of force and effective intervention.

States struggle with the issue, utilizing a variety of approaches. For example, Section 4.2 of Michigan's intervention standards states

> This document refers to batterers who are male, reflecting the predominant pattern of domestic violence. Most men are not batterers, but most batterers are men. Female battering towards males occurs, as does battering in lesbian and gay relationships, but until more is known about appropriate intervention in such relationships, these standards will apply to a [Batterer Intervention Program] for men who batter. (Batterer Intervention Standards for the State of Michigan, 1998)

It is clear that further collaborative investigation, by researchers and practitioners, is critical to informing these conversations so that state standards ultimately reflect the nuances of programmatic needs.

Conclusion

Ellen Pence (2012) reminds us that achieving justice involves the actions of exposing the truth, repairing the harm that the injustice caused, and changing the social conditions that brought about the injustice. In the case of addressing the complexity of women's use of force, context-based research exposes this truth, while innovative, gender-responsive programming may provide promising avenues toward forging a form of justice for these women. The larger task will be creating social conditions that recognize the ripple effects of men's violence against women, as well as the continued fortitude needed to work toward prevention. In a culturally competent manner, we must continue to think beyond the established paradigm of relying so heavily upon a CLS response to IPV. While such a response has saved many lives, it has also led to dire consequences for many women, who continue to be at risk.

Notes

1. The authors' equal contributions pertain to their respective research and practice expertise.
2. We recognize that not all women who use force are survivors of IPV. However, in our research of 208 women court-ordered to programming for using force, only one of the women who had used aggressive violence did not indicate a history of domestic violence.
3. Although we recognize that women use force in same-sex relationships, our focus in this chapter is on heterosexual IPV. More details will be provided in a subsequent section.

4. Women often do not experience it as a "justice" system; therefore, we use the term criminal legal system (CLS).
5. Women's names and certain identifying details have been changed and/or omitted to protect their privacy.
6. For programming for incarcerated women, refer to Larance et al.'s (2012) *Meridians for incarcerated women: Facilitator manual* and *Meridians for incarcerated women: Participant workbook*, and Covington's (2013) *Beyond violence: A prevention program for criminal justice-involved women.*

References

Anderson, K.L. (2009). Gendering coercive control. *Violence Against Women, 14*(12), 1444–1457.

Ballan, M.S., & Freyer, M.B. (2012). Self-defense among women with disabilities: An unexplored domain in domestic violence cases. *Violence Against Women, 18*(9), 1083–1107.

Batterer Intervention Standards for the State of Michigan (1998). *Governor's taskforce on batterer intervention standards: Domestic Violence Prevention and Treatment Board.* Lansing, MI: Domestic Violence Prevention and Treatment Board. Retrieved from: www.biscmi.org/aboutus/docs/michigan_standards_final.html.

Benson, M.L., & Fox, G.L. (2004). *When violence hits home: How economics and neighborhood play a role.* Washington, DC: US Department of Justice, National Institute of Justice.

Berns, N. (2004). *Framing the victim: Domestic violence, media, and social problems.* New York: Aldine de Gruyter.

Bible, A., & Osthoff, S. (1998). When battered women are charged with assault. *Double-Time: Newsletter of the National Clearinghouse for the Defense of Battered Women, 6*(1/2), 8–10.

Black, M.C., Basile, K.C., Brieding, M.J., Smith, S.G., Walters, M.L., Merrick, M. T., Chen, J., & Stevens, M.R. (2011). *National Intimate Partner and Sexual Violence Survey (NISVS): 2010 summary report.* Atlanta, GA: National Center for Injury Prevention and Control, Center for Disease Control and Prevention.

Bloom, B., Owen, B., & Covington, S. (2004). Women offenders and the gendered effects of public policy. *Review of Policy Research, 21*(1): 31–48.

Bohmer, C., Brandt, D., & Hartnett, H. (2002). Domestic violence law reforms: Reactions from the tranches. *Journal of Sociology and Social Welfare, 29*, 71–87.

Bronfenbrenner, U. (1977). Toward an experimental ecology of human development. *American Psychologist, 32*(7), 513–531.

Brush, L.D. (2009). Editor's introduction: Special issue focusing on Evan Stark's *Coercive Control. Violence Against Women, 15*(12), 1423–1431.

Bui, H.N., & Morash, M. (1999). Domestic violence in the Vietnamese immigrant community: An exploratory study. *Violence Against Women, 5*, 769–795.

Caldwell, J.E., Swan, S.C., Allen, C.T., Sullivan, T.P., & Snow, D.L. (2009). Why I hit him: Women's reasons for intimate partner violence. *Journal of Aggression, Maltreatment, & Trauma, 18*, 672–697.

CCI (Center for Court Innovation) (2013). *A community's experience addressing the complexity of women's use of force in their intimate heterosexual relationships.* Presenters: Lisa Y. Larance (Domestic Violence Intervention Services Coordinator), The Honorable Elizabeth Pollard Hines (Chief Judge, 15th District Court), & Brant Funkhouser (Former Director of Model Cities Legal Services). Webinar series (September 18). Retrieved from: https://courtinnovation.ilinc.com/.

Collins, P.H. (2015). Intersectionality's definitional dilemma. *Annual Review of Sociology, 41*, 1-20.

Covington, S. (2013). *Beyond violence: A prevention program for criminal justice-involved women.* Hoboken, NJ: John Wiley & Sons.

Covington, S. (2014). *Beyond anger and violence: A program for women.* Hoboken, NJ: John Wiley & Sons.

Crager, M., Cousin, M., & Hardy, T. (2003). *Victim-defendants: An emerging challenge in responding to domestic violence in Seattle and the King County region.* St Paul, MN: Minnesota Center Against Violence and Abuse.

Creek, S.J., & Dunn, J.L. (2011). Rethinking gender and violence: Agency, heterogeneity, and intersectionality. *Sociology Compass, 5*(5), 311–322.

Crenshaw, K. (1991). Mapping the margins: Intersectionality, identity politics, and violence against women of color. *Stanford Law Review, 43*(6): 1251–1299.

Cross, C. (2013). *Victimized again: How the reentry process perpetuates violence against survivors of domestic violence.* Philadelphia, PA: National Clearinghouse for the Defense of Battered Women. Retrieved from: www.ncdbw.org/CC%20NCDBW%20paper--%207-31-14%20 clean.pdf.

Dasgupta, S.D. (1999). Just like men? A critical view of violence by women. In M.F. Shepard & E.L. Pence (Eds.), *Coordinating community response to domestic violence: Lessons from Duluth and beyond* (pp. 195–222). Thousand Oaks, CA: Sage.

Dasgupta, S.D. (2002). A framework for understanding women's use of nonlethal violence in intimate heterosexual relationships. *Violence Against Women, 8*(11), 1364–1389.

Dasgupta, S.D. (2007). Exploring South Asian battered women's use of force in intimate relationships. *Manavi Occasional Paper, 1,* 1–24. Retrieved from: www.manavi.org/documents/OccasionalPaper1.pdf.

DeJong, C., Burgess-Proctor, A., & Elis, L. (2008). Police officer perceptions of partner violence: An analysis of observational data. *Violence and Victims, 23,* 683–696.

Dichter, M.E. (2013). "They arrested me – and I was the victim": Women's experiences with getting arrested in the context of domestic violence. *Women and Criminal Justice, 23,* 81–98.

Dichter, M.E. (2015). Women's experiences of abuse as a risk factor for incarceration: A research update. *VAWnet.* Retrieved from: http://vawnet.org/material/womens-experiences-abuse-risk-factor-incarceration-research-update.

Dieten, M.V., Jones, N.J., & Rondon, M. (2014). *Working with women who perpetrate violence: A practice guide.* Silver Spring: National Resource Center on Justice-Involved Women. Retrieved from: https://cjinvolvedwomen.org/wp-content/uploads/2015/09/Working-With-Women-Who-Perpetrate-Violence-A-Practice-Guide6-23.pdf.

Dragiewicz, M. (2011). *Equality with a vengeance: Men's rights groups, battered women and antifeminist backlash.* Boston, MA: Northeastern University Press.

Dunn, J. (2008). Accounting for victimization: Social constructionist perspectives. *Sociological Compass, 2,* 1601–1620.

Ferency, D.J. (2016). Solutions for domestic violence: The state of batterer intervention programs in Michigan. *Michigan Family Law Journal, 46*(1), 6–10.

Ferraro, K.J., & Pope, L. (1993). Irreconcilable differences: Police, battered women, and the law. In N.Z. Hilton (Ed.), *The legal response to battering* (pp. 36–61). Newbury Park, CA: Sage.

Finn, M.A., & Bettis, P. (2006). Punitive action or gentle persuasion: Exploring police officers' justifications for using dual arrest in domestic violence cases. *Violence Against Women, 12,* 268–287.

Frye, B., Haviland, M., & Rajah, V. (2007). Dual arrest and other unintended consequences of mandatory arrest in New York City: A brief. *Journal of Family Violence, 22,* 397–405.

Gardner, D. (2007). Victim-defendants in mandated treatment: An ethical quandary. *Journal of Aggression, Maltreatment and Trauma, 15*(3–4), 75–93.

Garfield, G. (1991). *Constructing boundaries: Defining violence against women.* Unpublished manuscript.

Gilfus, M. (1999). The price of the ticket: A survivor-centered appraisal of trauma theory. *Violence Against Women, 5*(11), 1238–1257.

Gondolf, E. (2012). Physical threats of female partners against male batterer program participants, *Violence Against Women: Special Issue, 18*(9), 1027–1044.

Gondolf, E. (2014). Why Straus' "reanalysis" of physical tactics used by female partners is wrong. *Violence Against Women, 20*(12), 1539–1546.

Gondolf, E. (2015). *Gender based perspectives on batterer programs: Program leaders on history, approach, research and development.* Lanham, MD: Lexington Books.

Goodmark, L. (2008). When is a battered woman not a battered woman? When she fights back. *Yale Journal of Law and Feminism, 20*(75), 75–129.

Goodmark, L. (2013). Transgender people, intimate partner abuse, and the legal system. *Harvard Civil Rights–Civil Liberties Law Review, 48,* 51–104.

Hamberger, L.K., & Guse, C.E. (2002). Men's and women's use of intimate partner violence in clinical samples. *Violence Against Women, 8,* 1303–1331.

Hamberger, L.K., Lohr, J.M., Bonge, D., & Tolin, D.E. (1997). An empirical classification of motivations for domestic violence. *Violence Against Women, 3,* 401–423.

Hamberger, L.K., & Potente, T. (1994). Counseling heterosexual women arrested for domestic violence: Who presents the greater threat? *Journal of Family Violence, 19*(2), 69–80.

Hester, M. (2012). Portrayal of women as intimate partner domestic violence perpetrators. *Violence Against Women, 18*(9): 1067–1082.

House, E. (n.d.). *When women use force: An advocacy guide to understanding this issue and conducting an assessment with individuals who have used force to determine their eligibility for services form a domestic violence agency.* Ann Arbor, MI: Domestic Violence Project/SAFE House. Retrieved from: http://csswashtenaw.org/wp-content/uploads/2014/01/wwuferinhouse.pdf.

Johnson, M.P., Leone, J.M., & Xu, Y. (2014). Intimate terrorism and situational couple violence in general surveys: Ex-spouses required. *Violence Against Women, 20*(2), 186–207.

Kantor, G.K., & Little, L. (2003). Defining the boundaries of child neglect: When does domestic violence equate with parental failure to protect? *Journal of Interpersonal Violence, 18,* 338–355.

Kanuha, V. (1996). Domestic violence, racism and the battered women's movement in the United States. In J.L. Edelson and Z.C. Eiskovits (Eds.), *Future interventions with battered women and their families* (pp. 34–50). Thousand Oaks, CA: Sage.

Kernsmith, P., & Kernsmith, R. (2009). Treating female perpetrators: State standards for batterer intervention services. *Social Work, 54*(4), 341–350.

Lamb, S. (1999). Constructing the victim: Popular images and lasting labels. In S. Lamb (Ed.), *New versions of victims: Feminists struggle with the concept* (pp. 108–138). New York: New York University Press.

Larance, L.Y. (2006). Serving women who use force in their intimate heterosexual relationships: An extended view. *Violence Against Women, 12*(7), 622–640.

Larance, L.Y. (2007). When she hits him: Why the institutional response deserves reconsideration. *Violence Against Women Newsletter: Prosecuting Attorney's Association of Michigan, 5*(4), 11–19.

Larance, L.Y. (2012). Commentary on Wilson, Woods, Emerson and Donenberg: The necessity for practitioner vigilance in assessing the full context of an individual's life experiences. *Psychology of Violence: Special Issue on Interconnections Among Different Types of Violence, 2*(2), 208–210.

Larance, L.Y. (2017). A practitioner's response to "Addressing violence by female partners is vital to prevent or stop violence against women: Evidence from the Multisite Batterer Intervention Evaluation," by Murray Straus'. *Violence Against Women, 1–2*, online only. Retrieved from: http://www.vaw.sagepub.com. doi: 10.1177/1077801216662340.

Larance, L.Y., Cape, J.K., & Garvin, D.J.H. (2012). *Meridians for incarcerated women: Facilitator manual*. Ann Arbor, MI: Catholic Social Services of Washtenaw County. Retrieved from: http://csswashtenaw.org/wp-content/uploads/2013/07/MeridiansIWFacilitatorManual09152012.pdf.

Larance, L.Y., Cape, J.K., & Garvin, D.J.H. (2012). *Meridians for incarcerated women: Participant workbook*. Ann Arbor, MI: Catholic Social Services of Washtenaw County. Retrieved from: http://csswashtenaw.org/wp-content/uploads/2013/07/MeridiansIWParticipantWorkbook09152012.pdf.

Larance, L.Y., Hoffman, A., & Shivas, J.B. (2009). *VISTA program curriculum: An extended view of serving women who use force*. Morristown, NJ: Jersey Center for Nonviolence. Retrieved from: www.jbws.org/publications.html.

Larance, L.Y., & Miller, S.L. (2015). Finding the middle ground: Re-imagining responses to women's use of force. *University of Miami Law Review Special Issue: CONVERGE! Conference Contributions, 5,* 437–443.

Larance, L.Y., & Miller, S.L. (Forthcoming). In her own words: Women describe their use of force resulting in court-ordered intervention. *Violence Against Women.* doi: 10.1177/1077801216662340.

Larance, L.Y., & Rousson, A. (2016). Facilitating change: A process of renewal for women who have used force in their intimate heterosexual relationships. *Violence Against Women, 22*(7), 876–891.

Leisenring, A. (2011). "Whoa! They could've arrested *me!*": Unsuccessful identity claims of women during police response to intimate partner violence. *Qualitative Sociology, 34,* 353–370.

Loseke, D.R. (1992). *The battered woman and shelters: The social construction of wife abuse.* Albany, NY: State University of New York Press.

Melton, H.C., & Belknap, J. (2003). He hits, she hits: Assessing gender differences and similarities in officially reported intimate partner violence. *Criminal Justice and Behavior, 30*(3), 328–348.

Miller, S.L. (2001). The paradox of women arrested for domestic violence: Criminal justice professionals and service providers respond. *Violence Against Women, 7*(12), 1339–1376.

Miller, S.L. (2005). *Victims as offenders: The paradox of women's use of violence in relationships.* New Brunswick, NJ: Rutgers University Press.

Miller, S.L., Gregory, C., & Iovanni, L. (2005). One size fits all? A gender-neutral approach to a gender-specific problem: Contrasting batterer treatment programs for male and female offenders. *Criminal Justice Review, 16*(3), 336–359.

Miller, S.L., & Meloy, M.L. (2006). Women's use of force: Voices of women arrested for domestic violence. *Violence Against Women, 12*(1), 89–115.

Miller, S.L., & Smolter, . (2011). "Abuse by paper": When all else fails, there's procedural stalking. *Violence Against Women, 17*(5), 637–650.

Morash, M. (2010). *Women on probation and parole: A feminist critique of community programs and services.* Boston, MA: Northeastern University Press.

Muftic, L.R., Bouffard, J.A., & Bouffard, L.A. (2007). An exploratory study of women arrested for intimate partner violence: Violent women or violent resistance? *Journal of Interpersonal Violence, 22,* 753–774.

Neal, C. (2007). Women who are victims of domestic violence: Supervision strategies for community corrections professionals. *Corrections Today, 69*(4), 34–43.

O'Dell, A. (2007). Why do police arrest victims of domestic violence: The need for comprehensive training and investigative protocols. *Journal of Aggression, Maltreatment and Trauma, 15*, 53–73.

Osthoff, S. (2002). But Gertrude, I beg to differ, a hit is not a hit is not a hit. *Violence Against Women, 8*, 1521–1544.

Pence, E. (2012). Foreword. *Violence Against Women, 18*(9), 1000–1003.

Pence, E., Connelly, L., & Scaia, M. (2011). *Turning points: A nonviolence curriculum for women.* Grand Rapids: Turning Points, LLC.

Pence, E., & Dasgupta, S.D. (2006). *Re-examining "battering": Are all acts of violence against intimate partners the same?* Duluth: Praxis International. Retrieved from: http://dvturningpoints.com/wp-content/uploads/downloads/2011/01/ReexaminingBattering1.pdf.

Pollack, S., Battaglia, M., & Allspasch, A. (2005). *Women charged with domestic violence in Toronto: The unintended consequences of mandatory charge policies.* Toronto: Woman Abuse Council of Toronto.

Potter, H. (2008). *Battle cries: Black women and intimate partner violence.* New York: New York University Press.

Rajan, M., & McCloskey, K.A. (2007). Victims of intimate partner violence: Arrest rates across recent studies. *Journal of Aggression, Maltreatment and Trauma, 15*(3/4), 27–52.

Renzetti, C.M. (1998). Violence and abuse in lesbian relationships: Theoretical and empirical issues. In R.K. Bergen (Ed.), *Issues in intimate violence* (pp. 117–127). Thousand Oaks, CA: Sage.

Renzetti, C. (1999). The challenge to feminism posed by women's use of violence in intimate relationships. In S. Lamb (Ed.), *New visions of victims: Feminists struggle with the concept* (pp. 42–56). New York: New York University Press.

Richie, B.E. (1995). *Compelled to crime: The gender entrapment of battered black* women. New York: Routledge.

Richie, B.E. (2000). A Black feminist reflection on the antiviolence movement. *Signs: Journal of Women in Culture and Society, 25*(4), 1133–1137.

Richie, B.E. (2012). *Arrested justice: Black women, violence, and America's prison nation.* New York: University Press.

Ristock, J. (2002). *No more secrets: Violence in lesbian relationships,* New York: Routledge.

Ritmeester, T., & Pence, E. (1992). A cynical twist of fate: How processes of ruling in the criminal justice system and the social science impede justice for battered women. *Southern California Review of Law and Women's Studies, 2*(1), 255–292.

EMERGENT RESEARCH AND PRACTICE TRENDS...

Roy, D. (2012). South Asian battered women's use of force against intimate male partners: A practice note. *Violence Against Women, 18*(9), 1108–1118.

Saunders, D.S. (2002). Developing guidelines for domestic violence offender programs: What can we learn from related fields and current research? *Journal of Aggression, Maltreatment, & Trauma, 5*, 235–248.

Sherman, L.W. (1992). *Policing domestic violence: Experiments and Dilemmas.* New York: Free Press.

Sherman, L.W., & Berk, R.A. (1984). The specific deterrent effects of arrest for domestic assault. *American Sociological Review, 49*(2), 261–272.

Simpson, S.S., Bouffard, L.A., Garner, J., & Hickman, L. (2006). The influence of legal reform on the probability of arrest in domestic violence cases. *Justice Quarterly, 23*(3), 297–316.

Smith, D. (1987). *The everyday world as problematic: A feminist sociology.* Evanston, IL: Northwestern University Press.

Smith, P.H., Smith, J.B., & Earp, J.L. (1999). Beyond the measurement trap: A reconstructed conceptualization of woman battering. *Psychology of Women Quarterly, 23*, 177–193.

Sokoloff, N.J. (Ed.) (2005). *Domestic violence at the margins: Readings on race, class, gender, and culture.* New Brunswick, NJ: Rutgers University Press.

Sokoloff, N.J., & DuPont, I. (2005). Domestic violence at the intersections of race, class, and gender: Challenges and contributions to understanding violence against marginalized women in diverse communities. *Violence Against Women, 11*(1), 38–64.

Stalans, L.J., & Finn, M.A. (1995). How novice and experienced officers interpret wife assaults: Normative and efficiency frames. *Law and Society Review, 29*, 287–321.

Stalans, L. J., & Finn, M. A. (2006). Public's and police officers' interpretation and handling of domestic violence cases: Divergent realities. *Journal of Interpersonal Violence, 21*, 1129–1155.

Stark, E. (2007). *Coercive control: The entrapment of women in personal life.* New York: Oxford University Press.

Straus, M.L. (1995). Trends in cultural norms and rates of partner violence: An update to 1992. In National Council on Family Relations (Series Ed.) and S. Stith & M.A. Straus (Vol Eds.), *Families in focus: Understanding partner violence: Prevalence, causes, consequences, and solutions* (Vol.2) (pp. 30–33). Minneapolis, MN: National Council on Family Relations.

Straus, M.L. (2009). Why the overwhelming evidence on partner physical violence by women has not been perceived and is often denied. *Journal of Aggression, Maltreatment and Trauma, 18*(6), 552–571.

Straus, M.L. (2014). Addressing violence by female partners is vital to prevent or stop violence against women: Evidence from the multisite batterer intervention evaluation. *Violence Against Women, 20,* 889–899.

Swan, S.C., Gambone, L.J., Caldwell, J.E., Sullivan, T.P., & Snow, D.L. (2008). A review of research on women's use of violence with male intimate partners. *Violence and Victims, 23*(3), 301–314.

Swan, S.C., Gambone, L.J., Van Horn, M.L., Snow, D.L., & Sullivan, T.P. (2012). Factor structures for aggression and victimization among women who used aggression against male partners. *Violence Against Women, 18*(9), 1045–1066.

Swan, S.C., & Snow, D.L. (2002). A typology of women's use of violence in intimate relationships. *Violence Against Women, 8*(3), 286–319.

Swan, S.C., & Snow, D.L. (2006). The development of a theory of women's use of violence in intimate relationships. *Violence Against Women, 12*(11), 1026–1045.

Websdale, N. (2001). *Policing the poor: From slave plantation to public housing.* Boston, MA: Northeastern University Press.

West, C.M. (2002). Lesbian intimate partner violence: Prevalence and dynamics. *Journal of Lesbian Studies, 6*(1), 121–127.

West, C.M. (2007). "Sorry, we have to take you in": Black battered women arrested for intimate partner violence. *Journal of Aggression, Maltreatment and Trauma, 15*(3/4), 95–121.

West, C.M. (2012). Partner abuse in ethnic minority and gay, lesbian, bisexual, and transgender populations. *Partner Abuse, 3*(3), 336–357.

Weston, R., Marshall, L.L., & Coker, A.L. (2007). Women's motives for violent and nonviolent behaviors in conflicts. *Journal of Interpersonal Violence, 22*(8), 1043–1065.

Women Who Use Force Ad Hoc Committee of Ohio Domestic Violence Network (2011). *Guidelines for programs working with women who use force.* Retrieved from: www.ncdsv.org/images/odvn_guidelinesforprgrmswkgwomenwhouseforce_7-2011.pdf.

Worcester, N. (2002). Women's use of force: Complexities and challenges of taking the issue seriously. *Violence Against Women, 8*(11), 1390–1415.

Yoshihama, M. (1999). Domestic violence against women of Japanese descent in Los Angeles: Two methods of estimating prevalence. *Violence Against Women, 5*(8), 869–897.

SEVEN

Research on Restorative Justice in Cases of Intimate Partner Violence

James Ptacek

Introduction

This chapter will review the evaluation research on restorative justice (RJ) in cases of intimate partner violence (IPV). What do we know about how well RJ ensures the safety and immediate needs of survivors? What do we know about whether survivors feel a sense of justice as a result of these practices? What do we know about the ability of these practices to hold offenders accountable, and to prevent further offending?

The discussion begins with a brief description of the three most common forms of RJ, and a brief look at some of the evaluation research conducted on these practices. Next, the research literature on RJ and IPV will be reviewed. Following this review, attention will be paid to some recent developments in RJ and other alternative approaches to crimes of sexual assault and severe violence. The research literature on RJ and IPV is remarkably small, and as a result the potential of RJ might best be seen by also considering its application to other serious forms of victimization.

Common forms of RJ

There are three forms of RJ that are commonly used in cases of IPV—namely, victim–offender mediation (VOM), family group conferencing, and peacemaking and sentencing circles—all of which share a set of goals. They seek to hold offenders accountable; empower those who are victimized; allow for the expression of feelings; clarify facts about the crime; provide an opportunity to address the impact of the crime on the survivors and those around them; and come to an agreement about how the offender can make amends.

Victim–offender mediation (VOM)

VOM involves a direct, mediated interaction between victims and offenders. This is sometimes called victim–offender dialog (VOD), or (as will be discussed later) victim–offender conferencing (VOC). The power of this process lies in the emotional exchange between the parties. Extensive preparation of both victims and offenders is essential to effective practice. The mediator must explain the process and the potential outcomes to both parties. Mediators also need to assess whether the victims and offenders are ready for such an encounter. Arising in Canada and the US in the early 1970s, VOM is now a global phenomenon; there are now over 1,200 programs worldwide (Victim Offender Mediation Association, 2014).

Family group conferencing

Family group conferencing (often called community conferencing, or sometimes just conferencing) brings many more people into a facilitated dialog about crime. Family members, friends, justice officials, school officials, and service providers can be involved in the process. Support people are included both for those who are victimized and those who offend. The power of this practice lies in the moral authority of supporters, relatives, and community members therein; since this includes supporters for both parties, the offenders should have a stake in the process, and thus should be affected by the dialog with the survivor. This practice originated in New Zealand, with the indigenous Maori community. What is now called family group conferencing is a modified version of a traditional Maori way of handling conflict and crime. In the 1980s, Maori communities were critical of the treatment of their youth in the New Zealand legal system. In 1989, a law was passed that made family group conferencing the official way in which all but the most serious youth offenses are handled (McCold, 2006).

Peacemaking and sentencing circles

Peacemaking and sentencing circles are adaptations of traditional justice practices in First Nations communities in Canada and Native American communities in the US. A "circle" is a community meeting, arranged in a circle, that is organized and led by a "keeper," or facilitator. The goal of the circle is to address conflict through a consensual process that restores family and community responsibilities. A "talking piece" is often passed around the circle, and individuals can only talk when they are holding this piece. One of the practices discussed in this chapter, Navajo Peacemaking, is an authentic indigenous tradition. In Canada, Judge Barry Stuart recognized circles as a legitimate form of sentencing in a 1992 legal decision (Stuart, 1992). But many circle processes are adaptations of such traditions by white people. Stuart, who has been influential in popularizing this practice in Canada and the US, has detailed how different kinds of circles can be used for sentencing, healing, and the wider community (Stuart, 1997).

Evaluation of RJ programs

There is much evaluation research on RJ, although this largely focuses on youth crime (Bonta et al., 2006; Gilligan & Lee, 2005; Hayes, 2007; Shapland et al., 2011; Strang, 2002; Strang et al., 2013; Umbreit et al., 2006a). The findings are generally positive, both for the effects of the practices on victim satisfaction and for the reduction of offender recidivism. For instance, in a review of a number of studies, Umbreit et al. (2006a, p. 2) found that 80–90% of victims and offenders reported satisfaction with both the process and the outcomes of VOM, and that 90% of the participants would recommend the practice to others.

Among the better-designed evaluations are the Reintegrative Shaming Experiments in Canberra, Australia. These compared the experiences of victims who participated in family group conferencing with victims whose cases were processed by the courts. Following an experimental design, cases of property and violent crime were randomly assigned to either conferencing or the court process. Domestic and sexual violence were not eligible crimes for this study;

because of the seriousness of these offenses, the police and prosecutors wanted to keep them within the court system.

The results were supportive of RJ as an effective means of meeting the needs of victims. Those whose cases went to conferencing reported more satisfaction with the process (60% versus 46%), lower levels of fear and anxiety, and increased feelings of dignity, self-respect, and self-confidence. Offenders also reported greater satisfaction when their cases went to conferences rather than the courts (Strang, 2002).

A study of recidivism rates in the Reintegrative Shaming Experiments is quite promising. Sherman et al. (2000, p. 3) found that family group conferencing cases involving violent crime had a 38% lower recidivism rate than the court cases at the 1-year mark.

A more recent review of RJ evaluations using an experimental design was published by Strang et al. (2013). They identified 10 evaluations using randomized control trials, drawn from the UK, Australia, and the US. The types of crimes that were addressed by these programs were adult and youth crimes—specifically, assaults, property crime, street crime, and burglary. They found that conferencing programs reduced offender recidivism in 9 out of 10 of these studies, which they saw as "clear and compelling" evidence (Strang et al., 2013, p. 4). Further, they stated that: "The effect of conferencing on victims' satisfaction with the handling of their cases is uniformly positive" (Strang et al., 2013, pp. 4–5).

Some programs that draw upon RJ values and practices depart from the three most popular aforementioned practices. The Resolve to Stop the Violence Project (RSVP), located in the San Francisco, CA's Sheriff's Office, has existed since 1997 (Gilligan & Lee, 2005). RSVP works with adult offenders who commit a broad range of violent crimes, and mostly operates within the jail itself.

RSVP says it is influenced by restorative justice models; it emphasizes "victim restoration, offender accountability, and community involvement." This is an intensive treatment regimen for offenders, featuring a "12-hours-a-day, 6-days-a-week program consisting of workshops, academic classes, theatrical enactments, counseling sessions and communications with victims of violence" (Gilligan & Lee, 2005, p. 144).

A group of 101 inmates who participated in RSVP for at least 8 weeks was followed up at the 1-year point for evidence of recidivism. Since there is a long waiting list to enroll in the program, a control group was randomly selected from the waiting list. Compared to the control group, inmates who took part in RSVP had a 46% lower arrest rate for violent crime (Gilligan & Lee, 2005, p. 143). RSVP also seeks to alter the violence-supporting inmate culture of jails. In the year before this program was implemented in one area of the jail, 24 incidents of violence had occurred; in the 12 months following implementation, there was only one incident (Lee & Gilligan, 2005, p. 149).

Even the most severe cases of violence, including homicide, are addressed by restorative programs, and some of these have been evaluated (Gustafson, 2005; Roberts, 1995). Umbreit et al. (2006b) studied the outcomes of VOD in Texas and Ohio. VOD programs are survivor-driven, post-conviction practices, and they are designed to have no role in reducing the offenders' sentences. Umbreit and his colleagues interviewed 40 victims (including victims' family members) and 39 offenders in this multistate study. While there was no control group, this sample included all of the victims who participated in the Ohio program since its inception, and all but five of those who were involved in VOD in Texas. Half of the crimes involved murder or manslaughter; the length of time between the crime and the dialog session ranged from 2 to 27 years (Umbreit et al., 2006b, pp. 34, 40). Asked about their satisfaction with their participation in the dialog, all but one of the victims and offenders reported satisfaction; 91% (71 of 78) selected the highest rating, "very satisfied." Some 85% of victims and 97% of offenders said they would recommend the process to others (Umbreit et al., 2006, p. 41). The departments of corrections in 25 states now support VOD programs for crimes of severe violence (Umbreit & Armour, 2010, p. 235). A model program in Delaware and its evaluation are discussed at the end of the chapter.

This brief review of RJ evaluations indicates why many are seeking to use these practices in cases of IPV. The evidence of an impact on offender recidivism is strong; there is much evidence of victims being satisfied with the practice and its outcomes; and restorative practices involving a variety of crimes have been found to be beneficial. Still, Stubbs (2004) points out that many of the studies of victim satisfaction have been simplistic, and that knowledge about the long-term consequences of RJ practices on victims is limited.

Feminist perspectives on RJ in cases of IPV

It is worth noting that the three main forms of RJ all arose to address the needs of offenders (Ptacek & Frederick, 2008). What is now known as VOM began as an alternative sentence for two youth who had vandalized a number of homes and businesses in Kitchner, ON in 1974 (Peachey, 2003). Family group conferencing became the official way to address youth crime in New Zealand because of charges from Maori leaders that the legal system was racist, locked up too many of their youth, and had a negative impact on their communities (Love, 2000; Sharpe, 1998). The aforementioned establishment of circles as a sentencing practice in Canada by Judge Barry Stuart was an effort to better meet the needs of offenders and address recidivism (Stuart, 1992).

It is therefore not surprising that many feminist activists and scholars have been critical of using RJ in cases of IPV and sexual assault (Coker 1999, 2002; Daly & Stubbs, 2006, 2007; Stubbs, 2002, 2004). Three themes are consistent in these critiques. First, there is a concern that the needs of survivors, especially for safety, are not central. RJ. Smith (2010, p. 259) observed that "in many Native American communities, these models are often pushed on domestic violence survivors in order to pressure them to 'reconcile' with their families and 'restore' the community without sufficient concern for their personal safety." Second, there is a concern that offenders will not be held accountable in these informal practices. There is an emphasis on offender apologies in RJ that can create particular problems for addressing IPV, in which false and manipulative apologies are commonplace. Such processes can thus be too easy on offenders, and as a result may deliver little justice for survivors. And third, there is a concern about the politics of gender and "race." Many feminists have stated that RJ lacks an awareness of the gender inequality that forms the background of violence against women. Some have also argued that there has been a lack of awareness of colonialism and racial inequality in governmental talks with First Nations communities in Canada about RJ in cases of violence against women (Stubbs, 2010).

At the same time, some feminists have made the opposite arguments. Joan Pennell and Gale Burford, whose work will be discussed later, see RJ as a way to "widen the circle" of community involvement in families in which IPV and child abuse occur. They claim this helps to protect survivors and stop the violence better than existing legal interventions (Pennell & Burford, 1994). Mary Koss (whose feminist/ restorative approach to sexual assault is reviewed shortly) believes that, since restorative practices are not focused on imprisonment, there is an opportunity to invite communities into these informal processes that view the criminal legal system (CLS) as racist and oppressive (Koss & Achilles, 2008).

Evaluations of RJ in cases of IPV

While the application of RJ to IPV is prohibited in many jurisdictions (Daly & Stubbs, 2007), there are nonetheless many programs that take such cases. One 2010 report identified RJ or mediation programs accepting domestic violence cases in the US, UK, Austria, Belgium, Finland, Germany, Romania, Jamaica, Columbia, Australia, New Zealand, the Gambia, South Africa, and Thailand (Liebmann & Wootton, 2010). A 2005 survey identified 72 respondents in 17 countries who said their family group conferencing programs accepted cases of domestic or family violence (Nixon et al., 2005). With the evidence of such widespread practice, it is therefore astonishing that so little evaluation research has been conducted on these programs. A small number of RJ projects addressing IPV have been evaluated. In most cases, the evaluation methods employed are problematic. A close review of seven of these studies may be useful to assess just how these projects treat crimes of IPV, and what we know about their impact on survivors (a more appropriate term than victims for cases of IPV) and offenders.

Family group decision making in Canada

To date, the most comprehensive evaluation of a restorative approach to IPV is that conducted by Joan Pennell and Gale Burford. This was one of the earliest uses of family group conferencing in North America (Pennell & Burford, 1994, 2000). The goal of the project was "to eliminate or reduce violence against child and adult family members and to promote their well-being" (Pennell & Burford, 2000, p. 137). They called their version of conferencing *family group decision making* "to emphasize that the family group, made up of the immediate family and its relatives, friends, and other close supports, would decide what steps needed to be taken to stop the maltreatment" (Pennell & Burford, 2000, p. 137).

The project aimed to mobilize community networks to address domestic violence and child abuse. This approach was influenced by the feminist, Aboriginal, and RJ movements. The researchers consulted women's advocates, child and youth advocates, offender programs, and academic researchers—as well as the police, and government officials from social services; corrections; victim services; and prosecution—regarding the design and implementation of the project (Pennell & Burford, 2002). Joan Pennell was one of the founders of the first shelter in Newfoundland and Labrador for abused women and their children. Pennell and Burford see this project as extending aspects of the coordinated community response model of the well-known Duluth Domestic Abuse Intervention Project (Pennell, 2006). For these reasons, this approach may be best understood as a feminist/ restorative hybrid model.

Family group decision-making conferences seek to bring together both formal and informal resources to assist families. Such resources include programs for abused children, advocacy for abused women, counseling for abusers, and drug and alcohol treatment. The conference itself is seen as a planning forum—not as therapy or mediation. The facilitator of the conference prepares extensively with survivors and offenders before the conference. During the conference, a plan to stop the abuse is created by the families, after receiving input from community agencies. This plan must be approved by the facilitator of the conference, with consultation from legal officials. In Pennell's view, the family group decision-making conference widens the circle of people who can keep survivors safe and hold offenders accountable.

Evaluation research was built into this project. Pennell and Burford conducted follow-up interviews with the 32 families who participated in conferences. There were no reports of violence during the conferences, and no reports of violence that occurred because of the conferences (Pennell, 2005). Two thirds of those interviewed said the family was "better off" following the conference; one fifth said the family was "the same," and 7% said it was "worse." A comparison group of 31 families was drawn from families who had come to the attention of child protection authorities. Pennell and Burford reported that, for families that went through the conferencing process, measures of maltreatment declined by half (using a scale of 31 indicators). This was true for abuse of both mothers and their children. For families in the comparison group, measures of maltreatment rose over the test period (Pennell & Burford, 2000, pp. 145–147).

Despite the success of this project in achieving its stated goals, Pennell and Burford remain cautious about the use of this practice, saying they:

> were (and continue to be) wary of applying restorative processes to abuse of women in cases where children are not involved . . . children maintain ties between partners, whether or not they stay together; the presence of children is particularly effective at galvanizing extended family involvement to stop the abuse; and the involvement of child

protection, along with law enforcement, exerts controls over the proceedings to safeguard participants. (Pennell & Koss, 2011, pp. 203–204)

After relocating to North Carolina, Pennell began work on a new project to address IPV and child abuse. Instead of simply implementing the family group decision-making model, she drew together everyone working on these issues to create a new approach. This new feminist/restorative hybrid involved input from domestic violence shelters, batterers' counseling programs, services for children, child protection workers, the domestic violence court, the police, and the North Carolina Coalition Against Domestic Violence. In designing this project, Pennell conducted focus groups with a multiracial group of shelter residents and shelter staff. She named this approach "safety conferencing," to indicate that the safety of survivors and their children was prioritized in this design. Based on input about this approach, it was not even clear that abusers would be included in the conferences (Pennell & Francis, 2005). Unfortunately, the inability to obtain funding brought this project to an end before the design was completed (Pennell, personal communication, April 7, 2014).

Navajo Peacemaking in the Navajo Nation, AZ

In 1999, Donna Coker published an important study of Navajo Peacemaking—an indigenous circle process—as it is applied to cases of IPV. Along with reviewing Peacemaking files in two Navajo communities and observing a Peacemaking session, she conducted interviews with Peacemakers, judges, prosecutors, advocates for abused women, shelter staff, attorneys working with abused women, and batterers' counselors. She focused on 20 cases of IPV brought to the peacemaking divisions in these communities (Coker, 2006). In this practice, the parties in the case meet with a Peacemaker—someone chosen by the local leaders, who has knowledge of Navajo traditions. After an opening prayer, there is an explanation of the rules, followed by the presentation of the complaint by the petitioner. The respondent to the complaint then speaks, and then the Peacemaker gives a description of the problem. Other members of the circle, which may include family members, then participate, offering their explanation of the matter. The Peacemaker guides the group in creating recommendations and an agreement to address the problem. Agreements may include alcohol treatment plans, healing ceremonies, victim compensation, and "stay away" elements (Coker, 2006).

Coker found four benefits for abused women who use this practice. First, this is an alternative to standard legal interventions, which may see separation as the only remedy—something many abused women do not want. Second, because Peacemaking involves a survivor's family, this practice helps to mobilize financial and social resources for survivors and overcome the separation that often occurs between survivors and their families in the wake of abuse. Third, this practice creates a space in which Peacemakers, families, and other community members can challenge abusers and their denials. Lastly, through the agreements created by the group, this process assists in the rehabilitation of abusive partners (Coker, 2006).

Coker reports that none of the Navajo advocates would support the use of Peacemaking in cases of domestic violence. Some felt the process could be adapted to better serve abused women; others said the power imbalance between abusers and the people they victimized could not be remedied, even if the practice was reformed (Coker, 2006). Two limitations that Coker raises are important, because they are concerns commonly raised by feminists about restorative and alternative justice approaches to violence against women. First, there is the "coercion problem." Coercion can undermine the benefits of Peacemaking. The intimidation that abusive partners use to dominate a relationship can appear in the circle process and can undermine both safety and the fairness of the agreement. Coker reports that some women have been assaulted just after participating in a Peacemaking session (Coker, 1999).

Second, there is what Coker calls the "cheap justice problem." Noting that many restorative practices prioritize the importance of offender apologies, she is concerned that this focus on rehabilitation may serve to coerce forgiveness from survivors, and thus present a false and unjust resolution (Coker, 1999). Further, emphasizing apologies over actual behavioral changes cheapens the value of the process.

VOM in Austria

Crista Pelikan has published two studies of VOM in cases of IPV in Austria. In her 2000 study, she observed 30 VOM sessions, interviews with both parties following the sessions, and another set of interviews with the parties 3 to 4 months later. These are diversionary mediation processes, meant to keep these cases from going to a criminal trial. She further observed an equal number of court cases of IPV that did not use VOM, and again, interviews and follow-up interviews with both parties in these cases. Oddly, in neither of the two articles on this study (2000, 2002) does the author offer a clear comparison of the outcomes of the VOM and non-VOM court cases.Mediation in these cases is described as a "mixed doubles" process, drawing on a metaphor from mixed double tennis (2002). Each of the parties is assigned a same-gender mediator who meets with them individually. The mediator asks about the state of the relationship, the violence, the future of the relationship, and the expectations concerning an agreement. Both material and non-material compensation are included in the agreements. Following these individual sessions, both parties and their mediators meet together. The mediators report what they have learned, after which the parties join in the conversation. The goal is recognition, understanding, and empowerment of the survivor.

Pelikan concludes that some cases of IPV are inappropriate for VOM. These are cases "where the domination of the male partner is demonstrated, ascertained and defended by the use of physical violence; the concrete incidence constituting just one of many acts of that kind" (Pelikan, 2000, p. 10). Abusive men in these cases "cannot be reached by an intervention, aiming at insight and cooperation" (Pelikan, 2000, p. 10). Cases that are more suitable involve either what she sees as "mutual" violence, or cases in which the violence is unusual and is seen even by the perpetrator as "disturbing and distressing" (Pelikan, 2000, p. 10).

For the latter two kinds of cases, Pelikan claims that VOM is "highly satisfactory" for abused women; it was empowering and contributed to change for women, although she does not indicate what percentage of the women fall into this category. At the same time, however, she states that VOM appeared to have little effect on men. "Only very rarely does a conversion, or a reformation of the alleged perpetrator take place" (Pelikan, 2000, p. 17).

It is unclear exactly how this squares with the previous claim of satisfaction for survivors. Pelikan does say that in a number of cases—again, it is not stated how many—the mediation did not stop the violence. "For VOM, promoting and enhancing a process of empowerment, the existence of resources—of both victim and offender—is a prerequisite. Otherwise the intervention remains futile," she concludes (Pelikan, 2000, p. 18). In particular, Pelikan's view is that if the women involved are economically dependent on their abusers and lack job skills, the intervention may be useless.

Pelikan's 2010 study again draws from cases of IPV in Austria. She contacted roughly 900 abused women who went through

VOM in 2006. Since only 20% responded, her quantitative findings clearly cannot represent women's experiences of this process. She further observed 33 VOM cases, and interviewed 21 women. These interviews took place from 1.5 to 2 years after the mediation sessions. The mediations followed the same "mixed double" process previously discussed.

The findings on the quality of the process from women's perspectives were mixed. Based on her quantitative data on 162 questionnaires (out of some 900 that were sent out), over 75% of the women said they were listened to, and felt understood and supported in the process. Over 80% reported that the abusive behavior was taken seriously by the mediators. Yet, in only 57% of the cases did women find that their partners understood "in which way and to what extent he had harmed you" (Pelikan, 2010, pp. 54–55), and only 40% said their abusive partners felt sincere remorse.

The VOM seemed to have spurred many women to separate from their partners. Of those who continued living with or remained in contact with their abusive partners, one third experienced further violence (Pelikan, 2010, p. 55). Pelikan admits that, since she cannot compare them to a court sample that did not use VOM, these figures are difficult to interpret. She nonetheless calls these figures "impressive." But an even greater problem is the self-selection bias noted earlier: If only 20% of women who went through VOM responded, we simply do not know what happened in most of the cases.

Victim–offender conferencing in South Africa

In 2003, Amanda Dissel and Kindiza Ngubeni presented a research paper on a version of VOM used in South Africa known as victim–offender conferencing (VOC). While VOC is commonly applied to cases of IPV, it was not designed for such cases; the initial assumption was that it would be used for crimes between strangers. This is a diversionary process; a trial will be postponed if the conference takes place. A magistrate must approve the agreement created in the conference. If the agreement is adequately completed, the criminal case is withdrawn (Dissel & Ngubeni, 2003).

Conferencing will only proceed if the abused party requests it. Mediators meet with survivors and offenders separately. In the meetings with individuals who have been abused, the mediator addresses safety concerns and advises them of their rights to report abuse to the police, seek orders of protection, and refer the case to trial. The mediators also meet with support people, that is family or friends, who are named by the parties. In this version of VOM, support people are allowed to participate in the conference; however, in general this does not occur. Dissel and Ngubeni interviewed a total of 21 abused women whose cases went through a VOC. All but one of the offenders were men; one case of same-sex IPV was included. The interviews took place 6 to 18 months after the VOC. The researchers admit this was not a representative sample, and it is not clear how the cases were selected.

Most of the women felt safe during the mediation session, although one was threatened during the VOC and the offender had to be warned by the mediator. Most women reported they were not allowed to speak freely at home, and so they appreciated the safe space to speak in the conference. All of the women reported positive changes in the abuser's behavior, and all stated there was no physical abuse since the mediation. The VOC facilitated separation for some of the women. For those who remained with their partners, all said the relationship had improved since the conference. While these are intriguing findings, as in the 2010 Pelikan study the small and unrepresentative sample cannot reveal the experience of most women who went through the process.

VOM and community panels in New Zealand

Venezia Kingi, Judy Paulin, and Laurie Porima (2008) authored a study of five sites in New Zealand using restorative practices in cases of family violence. The five sites used somewhat different restorative practices; two used VOM, while three used "community panels." The community panels included community members—and, at one site, a police coordinator—along with family or friends chosen by the survivors and offenders. There is similarity here with VOM, since these support people may also attend VOM sessions. At four sites, these mediations were mostly held at the pre-sentence point; at one site, they were pre-trial community diversion practices. The study also involved observing the practices and interviewing mediators, victim "advisers," police, judges, and attorneys about the programs.

Interviews were conducted with 20 survivors and 19 offenders, drawn from the five sites. The cases of "family violence" included a range of relationships. Fifteen of the 20 cases involved abuse between intimate partners; the remainder were cases of child abuse, sibling abuse, abuse of a parent, or abuse of an in-law. Most of the survivors were female, and most of the offenders were male. There were similar numbers of interviewees with Maori and European ancestry. The interviews were conducted from several months to more than a year after the mediations.

Kingi and her colleagues reported that most survivors and offenders saw the meetings as positive experiences. They felt they were treated with respect and were able to express their views. In their comments, survivors highlighted the open dialog, the healing process, and the ability to talk with their offenders in a safe place. Offenders highlighted "being able to put things right," being supported, and being treated respectfully (Kingi et al., 2008, n.p.). The agreements created in these meetings generally included some kind of counseling program, and sometimes community work. Some 79% of survivors and 93% of offenders were satisfied with the agreement.

Most of the survivors (63%) said the offender had been held accountable for their behavior, and yet half said the offender had not fully made up for their actions. A number of survivors felt the offenders needed more help to stop their abusive behavior. One third of the survivors said the abuse had stopped; one third said the abuse had changed form—from physical violence to psychological abuse. All of the offenders and most of the survivors (84%) reported they would recommend the practice to others for cases of family violence.

In the interviews with program providers, judges, police, and attorneys, there were mixed views about the appropriateness of RJ in family violence cases. One third supported the practice unconditionally; 29% opposed it in these cases; and 38% offered conditional support. In their survey of 24 RJ programs in New Zealand, they reported that 21 (88%) accepted cases of family violence.

It is not possible to draw clear conclusions from this evaluation because the research was conducted in different sites, somewhat different practices were used at each site, different kinds of abuse were included in the study, and only a small number of interviews with survivors and offenders were conducted.

Circles of Peace in Nogales, AZ

Circles of Peace is a Nogales, AZ domestic violence treatment program. It is a court-referred program that uses the circle process to work with domestic violence offenders. The program was created by Mary Helen Maley (AZ judge) and Linda Mills (Director of the New York University (NYU) Center on Violence and Recovery).

Mills et al. (2013) compared Circles of Peace to a local treatment program for batterers by using a randomized experimental design.

The study randomly assigned 152 domestic violence cases to either Circles of Peace or the program for batterers. All of the individuals had been charged with a domestic violence crime and pleaded guilty. The majority of offenders were men (81%). Both programs lasted for 26 weeks. The effect of the treatment for these two groups of offenders was measured in terms of a single factor—recidivism, both in terms of subsequent domestic violence and non-domestic violence arrests. This was measured at 6-, 12-, 18-, and 24-month periods from the beginning of treatment. The circle model involves a number of participants in the 26-week practice. There is a circle keeper, who facilitates the process; the offender; the offender's support person; a trained volunteer community member; and members of the offender's family. Survivors may attend for a few sessions, or not at all; their participation is strictly voluntary. In this study, most circles contained survivors at some point, and no harm occurred as a result of having survivors and offenders in the same circle. The participants sit in a circle and use a "talking piece" to symbolize that only the person holding this object has a right to speak. The goal of the circle is to "focus on the impact of the crime committed and the desire, potential, and capacity for changing behavior to prevent such an event in the future" (Mills et al., 2013, p. 71).

The study experienced a high attrition rate. Of the 152 cases assigned to the two treatment programs, only 70 individuals (46% of the sample) completed the treatment process. Attrition was higher for the counseling program for batterers. When recidivism was measured at the 6-, 12-, 18-, and 24-month periods, recidivism was higher at all points for the standard program for batterers. But there was only one period during which the difference was statistically significant (at the $p<.05$ level); at the 12-month point, Circles of Peace had a statistically lower recidivism rate for the *non*-domestic violence arrests. In a finding that must have disappointed the study authors, there were no significant differences for domestic violence arrests at any point. In an article that is sharply critical of batterer intervention programs (BIPs), Mills et al. (2013) are also critical of Circles of Peace: "It is important to note that the CP [Circles of Peace] treatment, at least under the present conditions, may not be effective for domestic violence batterers" (p. 84). The study sought to demonstrate the superiority of Circles of Peace to the local BIP, but instead found that Circles of Peace was merely "no worse" (Mills et al., 2013, p. 65).

Promising recent developments

Victims' Voices Heard in Delaware

In 2002, Kim Book created an innovative restorative program for crimes of severe violence. The program was developed in the aftermath of a horrible crime; in 1995, Book's 17-year-old daughter was murdered by a 16-year-old male acquaintance (Miller, 2011, p. 24). Book's frustrating experience with the CLS led her to explore new ways of meeting the needs of survivors. Victims' Voices Heard (VVH) offers face-to-face mediation between survivors and offenders in a victim-centered way. In her book-length evaluation of this program, Susan Miller (2011) delineates between "diversionary" and "therapeutic" RJ programs. Most of the restorative practices discussed earlier are diversionary; they are alternatives to the CLS process, and they are centered more on the needs of offenders than those of survivors. In contrast, VVH is a therapeutic model, like the other VODs for severe violence discussed earlier. It is a post-conviction program that focuses on the healing process for survivors of crime and their families.

VVH is not designed to offer offenders an alternative to the CLS, and the mediation process cannot be used to reduce the offender's sentence. The structure of this program therefore avoids many of the criticisms raised by feminists about RJ concerning safety, coercion, and the "cheap justice" problem raised by Donna Coker. The cases VVH has dealt with include IPV, child sexual abuse, rape, murder, and vehicular homicide. While these are obviously very different kinds of violence, many states have programs that take on crimes of this severity, including the Texas and Ohio programs discussed earlier. Like the VOD programs in Texas and Ohio, VVH facilitates dialog between survivors and offenders long after the crime occurred. Book believes that this may be better for both survivors and offenders. Survivors might have a clearer sense of the information they need from the offenders, and the offenders may have the chance to develop empathy for their survivors. In order to be eligible for the dialog, offenders must accept responsibility for their crimes.

Only survivors can initiate the process. A request does not guarantee that a dialog will take place; many requests do not go forward, often because the offender does not accept responsibility or is not sufficiently remorseful. Sometimes survivors are seen as too angry to become involved in a dialog. If a survivor makes a request, and the offender is judged to be eligible, a period of extensive preparation begins, where Book meets separately with the survivor and the offender. She reviews the mediation process and helps both parties anticipate what may take place. Book may decide that, based on these meetings, a mediation session should not take place. This preparation process takes from 6 months to a year. The dialog is a one-time-only event. It takes place in the correctional facility in which the offender is incarcerated. There is a facilitator present, and at times also support people for the survivor and the offender. After the dialog, there are debriefings with the survivor and offender immediately after the meeting, 3 days later, and finally 2 months after the dialog. VVH offers a range of other services to the survivor: a tour of the prison, information about the offenders and the crime, opportunities to participate in victim impact panels, meetings with family members of the offender, and assistance concerning contact with state agencies (Miller, 2011, pp. 14–21).

Susan Miller conducted a qualitative evaluation of VVH, studying 9 of the 10 cases that went through the program between 2002 and 2007 (Miller, 2011, p. 214). There was no control group in this study. Miller conducted open-ended interviews with Kim Book, the survivors, the offenders, and some of the key people associated with the cases, such as victim advocates. She viewed videotapes of the dialogs. After drafting chapters for a book based on this investigation, she shared the drafts with the survivors and asked for their input on how well she represented their stories (Miller, 2011, pp. 214–218). Miller judges the program to be a "crystal clear" success for both survivors and offenders (Miller, 2011, p. 187). Drawing from follow-up interviews with both parties, conducted several years after her first set of interviews, Miller concludes:

> The victims/survivors' comments clearly displayed how buoyant they still felt; the victims continued to define their participation as a watershed moment, seeing VVH as essential in breaking the silence and mystery surrounding their victimization and providing a mechanism to combat feelings of being trivialized, condescended to, and disempowered by the criminal justice process. The offenders, too, believed that the program helped them to better understand the consequences of their choices and actions. (Miller, 2011, p. 187)

RESTORE in Arizona

One of the most imaginative approaches to sexual assault in recent years combines feminist principles with restorative practices. This is the RESTORE Program in Arizona, a pilot study created by the psychologist Mary Koss. RESTORE stands for Responsibility and Equity for Sexual Transgressions Offering a Restorative Experience. Like the project created by Joan Pennell and Gale Burford, Koss developed this approach with extensive community collaboration. She consulted with sexual assault providers in its development and implementation, making this another feminist/restorative hybrid model. She also reviewed her project with public health and CLS officials (Koss et al., 2004). The RESTORE process begins with a criminal investigation of sexual assault. Cases are referred to RESTORE by prosecutors if they feel the offenders stand a chance of being convicted. RESTORE is survivor-driven, and this process is only offered to offenders if survivors agree to participate. Psychosexual evaluations of offenders are required to assess their suitability for RESTORE. If survivors agree to the process and offenders are also willing to participate, extensive preparation is made for a conference, which can include family members and friends of the survivor and offender. The survivor's support group may also include pro-survivor community members.

Two coordinators are present at the conference. The offender, now referred to as the "responsible person," describes the offending behavior, and then the "survivor victim" describes the impact of this crime. Following this, the friends and family members of both parties share their experiences. The responsible person listens and responds to what has been said. Next, a redress plan is created to identify what the responsible person will do to repair the harm done. Elements of the plan may include restitution, offender treatment, community service, payment of the survivor's medical or counseling costs, restraining orders, and apologies. The final stage of the process concerns accountability and reintegration. The responsible person is supervised for a 12-month period, during which regular contact is made with a case manager to assess progress with the redress plan. If the individual fails to comply with the plan, the case can be returned to the prosecutor. A "community accountability and reintegration board" reviews compliance with the redress plan; if the plan is completed, the board formally closes the case (Koss, 2010). An evaluation of 22 cases that went through RESTORE has now been published (Koss, 2014). This addressed many elements of the process, including the reasons for participating; the fidelity of the actual process to the intended design; the psychological and physical health of survivor victims, both at intake and following the conferences; the safety of survivor victims during the conferences; satisfaction with preparation for the conferences; satisfaction with the conferences and the redress agreements; the completion of the redress plans; and re-offenses during the 12-month supervision period. The views of the supporters of both survivor victims and responsible persons who attended conferences were also evaluated.

This evaluation of RESTORE must be viewed as encouraging. No physical safety issues were reported during the preparation period, at the conferences, or following the conferences. Satisfaction with the conferences was high (over 90%) among all parties; the highest satisfaction was reported by survivor victims and their supporters. Koss reports that over 90% of all participants would recommend the RESTORE process to others.

Community-based responses to IPV

Lastly, it is important to note that there are alternative approaches to IPV that lie beyond the orbit of RJ. Most of the programs discussed so far have a formal relationship with the CLS, often operating as pre-trial diversion for offenders, or otherwise involving supervision by legal officials over the process or the agreements reached in the practices. But in this age of mass incarceration—in which there is compelling evidence of racism at multiple levels of the CLS (Alexander, 2010; Tonry, 2011) —antiviolence activists from many racialized and marginalized communities want nothing to do with the law, seeing the system as a perpetrator of violence against them (Dabby & Autry, 2003; Durazo et al., 2011–2012; Incite, 2006; Kim, 2010; Mogul et al., 2011; Richie, 2012; Smith, 2010). The national activist organization Incite! Women, Gender Non-Conforming, and Trans People of Color Against Violence seeks to disseminate solutions to IPV that avoid any reliance upon the police, courts, and prisons (Incite, 2006). The alternative programs that these activists promote are being called "community-based approaches" or "community accountability approaches" (Durazo et al., 2011–2012; Kim, 2010). While some activists are interested in restorative practices—because they are not based on punishment and imprisonment (Kim, 2011–2012)—some are critical of the close relationship between most RJ programs and the state (Smith, 2010).

Conclusion

This review of the evaluation research on RJ in cases of IPV reveals many methodological shortcomings. There are problems with small samples; poorly drawn samples that combine different practices, different locations, and different kinds of crimes; and confusing findings. Of the studies using quantitative methods, only Pennell and Burford (2000) and Mills et al. (2013) employ control groups in a rigorous fashion.

What do we know from this literature about the outcomes of these practices for survivors and offenders? While there are suggestions of effectiveness in most of these studies, we actually know very little. The family decision-making project in Canada is an early benchmark for building evaluation research into the program, as well as for its complex assessment of subsequent abuse, its creation of a comparison group, and its positive findings regarding recidivism. The groundwork done by Pennell and Burford to develop this approach is further noteworthy for its consultation with advocates for abused women and a range of community agencies in its design and implementation. Despite the fact that the first publication by Pennell and Burford on this project is now 20 years old, only the RESTORE program shows a similar collaborative involvement in the creation of these practices. In a more recent publication, Pennell and her colleagues have further outlined how to practice family group conferencing in ways that prioritize the safety of women and children (Pennell & Anderson, 2005). Donna Coker's qualitative research is also important. She examined and critically questioned the use of Navajo Peacemaking in cases of IPV, discovering both benefits and shortcomings for abused women. The cautions she raises offer guidelines for all restorative practices addressing these crimes.

The various practices in this review illustrate that RJ can be used in ways that involve both survivors and offenders; survivors, offenders, and community members; only offenders; and only survivors. But clearly, more research conducted with the sophistication demonstrated by Joan Pennell, Donna Coker, Susan Miller, and Mary Koss is long overdue. Given the thinness of the evaluation research on RJ and IPV, there is much to be done. Clearly, there are many existing practices that need rigorous follow-up research. This research should go beyond simple measures of recidivism and victim satisfaction to explore—using both qualitative and quantitative methods—the experience of the practices upon survivors, offenders, and their families, both in the short and the long term. Since there is a long history of practice that has not been evaluated, it would be worthwhile to explore the experience of practitioners as part of such research.

Currently, there are a number of feminist antiviolence projects that are using or investigating restorative practices. There is an RJ pilot program in Duluth, MN, which is coordinated with the well-known Duluth Domestic Violence Intervention Programs (Gaarder, 2014). The Domestic Violence Safe Dialogue (DVSD) program in Portland, OR, offers mediated dialog between survivors and surrogate offenders, and offenders and surrogate survivors (DVSD, 2014). No evaluation research has yet been conducted on this program. In the author's own community in Boston, MA, one domestic abuse shelter uses restorative practices in its work with survivors, and two other shelters recently sponsored a training session on circles and domestic violence work led by Kay Pranis, a nationally known restorative practitioner. We need to carefully examine the different ways in which restorative practices are being used in cases of intimate partner abuse. We also need to create new programs that are worth evaluating.

References

Alexander, M. (2010). *The new Jim Crow*. New York: The New Press.

Bonta, J., Rugge, T.A., Cormier, R.B., & Jesseman, R. (2006). Restorative justice and recidivism: Promises made, promises kept? In D. Sullivan & L. Tifft (Eds.), *Handbook of restorative justice: A global perspective* (pp. 108–118). London: Routledge.

Communities Against Rape and Abuse (CARA) (2006). Taking risks: Implementing grassroots community accountability strategies. In Incite! Women of Color Against Violence (Ed.), *Color of violence: The Incite! anthology* (pp. 250–256). Cambridge, MA: South End Press.

Coker, D. (1999). Enhancing autonomy for battered women: Lessons from Navajo Peacemaking. *UCLA Law Review, 47*(1), 1–111.

Coker, D. (2002). Transformative justice: Anti-subordination processes in cases of domestic violence. In H. Strang & J. Braithwaite (Eds.), *Restorative justice and family violence* (pp. 128–152). Cambridge: Cambridge University Press.

Coker, D. (2006). Restorative justice, Navajo Peacemaking and domestic violence. *Theoretical Criminology, 10*(1), 67–85.

Dabby, C., & Autry, A. (2003). *Activist dialogues: How domestic violence and child welfare systems impact women of color and their communities*. San Francisco, CA: Futures Without Violence. Retrieved from: www.futureswithoutviolence.org/userfiles/file/Children_and_Families/Activist.pdf.

Daly, K., & Stubbs, J. (2006). Feminist engagement with restorative justice. *Theoretical Criminology, 10*(1), 9–28.

Daly, K., & Stubbs, J. (2007). Feminist theory, feminist and anti-racist politics, and restorative justice. In G. Johnstone & D.W. Van Ness (Eds.), *Handbook of restorative justice* (pp. 149–170). Cullompton, Devon: Willan Publishing.

Dissel, A., & Ngubeni, K. (2003). *Giving women their voice: Domestic violence and restorative justice in South Africa.* Paper presented at the XIth International Symposium on Victimology, Stellenbosch, South Africa. Retrieved from: www.csvr.org.za/docs/crime/givingwomenvoice. pdf.

Domestic Violence Safe Dialogue (DVSD) (2014). *Dialogue program.* Portland, OR: DVSD. Retrieved from: http://www.dvsdprogram. com/dialogue-program.html.

Durazo, A., Rojas, C., Bierria, A, & Kim, M. (2011–2012). Community accountability: Emerging movements to transform violence. *Social Justice, 37*(4), 1–12.

Gaarder, E. (2014, November). *Restorative justice meets the Duluth Model: Integrating restorative justice with a community coordinated response to partner abuse.* Presentation at the American Society of Criminology annual meeting, San Francisco, CA.

Gilligan, J., & Lee, B. (2005). The Resolve to Stop the Violence Project: Reducing violence in the community through a jail-based initiative. *Journal of Public Health, 27*(2), 143–148.

Gustafson, D. (2005). Exploring treatment and trauma recovery implications of facilitating victim offender encounters in crimes of severe violence: Lessons from the Canadian experience. In E. Elliott & R.M. Gordon (Eds.), *New directions in restorative justice: Issues, practice, evaluation* (pp. 193–227). Cullompton, Devon: Willan Publishing.

Hayes, H. (2007). Reoffending and restorative justice. In G. Johnstone & D. Van Ness (Eds.), *Handbook of restorative justice* (pp. 426–444) Cullompton, Devon: Willan Publishing.

Incite! Women of Color Against Violence (Eds.) (2006). *Color of violence: The Incite! anthology.* Cambridge, MA: South End Press.

Kim, M. (2010). Alternative interventions to intimate violence: Defining political and pragmatic strategies. In J. Ptacek (Ed.), *Restorative justice and violence against women* (pp. 193–217). New York: Oxford University Press.

Kim, M. (2011–2012). Moving beyond critique: Creative interventions and reconstructions of community accountability. *Social Justice, 37*(4), 14–35.

Kingi, V., Paulin, J., & Porima, L. (2008). *Delivery of restorative justice in family violence cases by providers funded by the Ministry of Justice.* Wellington, New Zealand: Ministry of Justice. Retrieved from: www.justice.govt.nz/publications/global-publications/r/review-of-the-delivery-of-restorative-justice-in-family-violence-cases-by-providers-funded-by-the-ministry-of-justice-may-2008.

Koss, M.P. (2010). Restorative justice for acquaintance rape and misdemeanor sex crimes. In J. Ptacek (Ed.), *Restorative justice and violence against women* (pp. 218–238). New York: Oxford University Press.

Koss, M.P. (2014). The RESTORE program of restorative justice for sex crimes: Vision, process, and outcomes. *Journal of Interpersonal Violence, 29*(9), 1629–1660.

Koss, M. P., & Achilles, M. (2008). Restorative justice approaches to sexual assault. *VAWnet.* Retrieved from: http://new.vawnet.org/Assoc_Files_VAWnet/AR_RestorativeJustice.pdf.

Koss, M.P., Bachar, K., Hopkins, C.Q., & Carlson, C. (2004). Expanding a community's justice response to sex crimes through advocacy, prosecutorial, and public health collaboration: Introducing the RESTORE program. *Journal of Interpersonal Violence, 19*(12), 1435–1463.

Lee, B., & Gilligan, J. (2005). The Resolve to Stop the Violence Project: Transforming an in-house culture of violence through a jail-based programme. *Journal of Public Health, 27*(2), 149–155.

Liebmann, M., & Wootton, L. (2010). *Restorative justice and domestic violence/abuse: A report commissioned by JMP.* Cardiff, Wales: Home Office Crime Reduction Unit. Retrieved from: www.restorativejustice.org.uk/resource/restorative_justice_and_ domestic_violenceabuse.

Love, C. (2000). Family group conferencing: Cultural origins, sharing, and appropriation—A Maori reflection. In G. Burford & J. Hudson (Eds.), *Family group conferencing: New directions in community-centered child and family practice* (pp. 13–30). New York: Aldine de Gruyter.

McCold, P. (2006). The recent history of restorative justice: Mediation, circles, and conferencing. In D. Sullivan & L. Tifft (Eds.), *Handbook of restorative justice: A global perspective* (pp. 23–51). London: Routledge.

Miller, S.L. (2011). *After the crime: The power of restorative justice dialogues between victims and violent offenders.* New York: New York University Press.

Mills, L.G., Barocas, B., & Ariel, B. (2013). The next generation of court-mandated domestic violence treatment: A comparison study of batterer intervention and restorative justice programs. *Journal of Experimental Criminology, 9*(1), 65–90.

Mogul, J.L., Ritchie, A.J., & Whitlock, K. (2011). *Queer (in)justice: The criminalization of LGBT people in the United States.* Boston, MA: Beacon Press.

Nixon, P., Burford, G., & Quinn, A., with Edelbaum, J. (2005). *A survey of international practices, policy & research on family group conferencing and related practices.* Washington, DC: American Humane Association. Retrieved from: www.americanhumane.org/assets/pdfs/children/fgdm/pc-fgdm-practices-survey.pdf.

Peachey, D.E. (2003). The Kitchener experiment. In G. Johnstone (Ed.), *A restorative justice reader: Texts, sources, context* (pp. 178–186). Portland, OR: Willan Publishing.

Pelikan, C. (2000). *Victim offender mediation in domestic violence cases: A research report.* Paper presented at the United Nations Crime Congress, Ancillary Meeting on Implementing Restorative Justice in the International Context, Vienna. Retrieved from: www.restorativejustice.org/10fulltext/pelikan-christa.-victim-offender-mediation-in-domestic-violence-cases-a-research-report.

Pelikan, C. (2002). Victim-offender-mediation in domestic violence cases—A comparison of the effects of criminal law intervention: The penal process and mediation. Doing qualitative research. *Forum: Qualitative Sozialforschung/Forum: Qualitative Social Research, 3*(1), n.p.

Pelikan, C. (2010). On the efficacy of victim—offender—mediation in cases of partnership violence in Austria, or: Men don't get better, but women get stronger: Is it still true? Outcomes of an empirical study. *European Journal on Criminal Policy and Research, 16*(1), 49–67.

Pennell, J. (2005). Safety for mothers and their children. In J. Pennell & G. Anderson (Eds.), *Widening the circle: The practice and evaluation of family group conferencing with children, youths, and their families* (pp. 163–181). Washington, DC: NASW Press.

Pennell, J. (2006). Stopping domestic violence or protecting children? Contributions from restorative justice. In D. Sullivan & L. Tifft (Eds.), *Handbook of restorative justice: A global perspective* (pp. 286–298). London: Routledge.

Pennell, J., & Anderson, G. (Eds.) (2005). *Widening the circle: The practice and evaluation of family group conferencing with children, youths, and their families.* Washington, DC: NASW Press.

Pennell, J., & Burford, G. (1994). Widening the circle: The family group decision making project. *Journal of Child & Youth Care, 9*(1), 1–12.

Pennell, J., & Burford, G. (2000). Family group decision making: Protecting children and women. *Child Welfare, 79*(2), 131–158.

Pennell, J., & Burford, G. (2002). Feminist praxis: Making family group conferencing work. In H. Strang & J. Braithwaite (Eds.), *Restorative justice and family violence* (pp. 108–127). Cambridge: Cambridge University Press.

Pennell, J., & Francis, S. (2005). Safety conferencing: Toward a coordinated and inclusive response to safeguard women and children. *Violence Against Women, 11*(5), 666–692.

Pennell, J., & Koss, M.P. (2011). Feminist perspectives on family rights: Social work and restorative practices for stopping abuse of women. In E. Beck, N.P. Kropf, & P.B. Leonard (Eds.), *Social work and restorative justice: Skills for dialogue, peacemaking, and reconciliation* (pp. 195–219). New York: Oxford University Press.

Ptacek, J., & Frederick, L. (2008). Restorative justice and intimate partner violence. *VAWnet*. Retrieved from: http://new.vawnet.org/Assoc_Files_VAWnet/AR_RestorativeJusticeIPV.pdf.

Richie, B.E. (2012). *Arrested justice: Black women, violence, and America's prison nation*. New York: New York University Press.

Roberts, T. (1995). *Evaluation of the victim offender mediation project, Langley, BC: Final Report*. Victoria, BC: Focus Consultants.

Shapland, J., Robinson, G., & Sorsby, A. (2011). *Restorative justice in practice: Evaluating what works for victims and offenders*. London: Routledge.

Sharpe, S. (1998). *Restorative justice: A vision for healing and change*. Edmonton, AL: Edmonton Victim Offender Mediation Society.

Sherman, L.S., Strang, H., & Woods, D.J. (2000). *Recidivism patterns in the Canberra reintegrative shaming experiments*. Canberra: Center for Restorative Justice, Research School of Social Sciences, Australian National University.

Smith, A. (2010). Beyond restorative justice: Radical organizing against violence. In J. Ptacek (Ed.), *Restorative justice and violence against women* (pp. 255–278). New York: Oxford University Press.

Strang, H. (2002). *Repair or revenge: Victims and restorative justice*. Oxford: Clarendon Press.

Strang, H., Sherman, L.W., Mayo-Wilson, E., Woods, D., & Ariel, B. (2013). Restorative justice conferencing (RJC) using face-to-face meetings of offenders and victims: Effects on offender recidivism and victim satisfaction: A systematic review. *Campbell Systematic Reviews, 9*(12), 1–59.

Stuart, B. (1992). *Reasons for sentencing, Regina versus Philip Moses*. Yukon Territory: Territorial Court, CanLII 2814.

Stuart, B. (1997). *Building community justice partnerships: Community peacemaking circles*. Ottawa: Department of Justice Canada.

Stubbs, J. (2002). Domestic violence and women's safety: Feminist challenges to restorative justice. In H. Strang & J. Braithwaite (Eds.), *Restorative justice and family violence* (pp. 42–61). Cambridge: Cambridge University Press.

Stubbs, J. (2004). Restorative justice, domestic violence, and family violence. *Australian Domestic & Family Violence Clearinghouse, Issues Paper 9*, 1–23.

Stubbs, J. (2010). Restorative justice, gendered violence, and indigenous women. In J. Ptacek (Ed.), *Restorative justice and violence against women* (pp. 103–122). New York: Oxford University Press.

Tonry, M. (2011). *Punishing race: A continuing American dilemma.* New York: Oxford University Press.

Umbreit, M., & Armour, M.P. (2010). *Restorative justice dialogue: An essential guide for research and practice.* New York: Springer.

Umbreit, M., Vos, B., & Coates, R. B. (2006a). *Restorative justice dialogue: Evidence-based practice.* Minneapolis, MN: Center for Restorative Justice & Peacemaking. Retrieved from: www.cehd.umn.edu/ssw/RJP/PDFs/RJ_Dialogue_Evidence-based_Practice_1-06.pdf.

Umbreit, M., Vos, B., Coates, R.B., & Armour, M.P. (2006b). Victims of severe violence in mediated dialogue with offender: The impact of the first multi-site study in the US. *International Review of Victimology*, *13*(1), 27–48.

Victim Offender Mediation Association (2014). *Restorative justice FAQ: What is VOMA?* St Paul, MN: Victim Offender Mediation Association. Retrieved from: www.voma.org/rjfaq.shtml.

EIGHT

Justice as a Tertiary Prevention Strategy

Leigh Goodmark

Introduction

Tertiary prevention strategies are intended to minimize problems once they have been identified as causing harm; in the context of intimate partner violence (IPV), tertiary prevention strategies "emphasize the identification of [IPV] and its perpetrators and victims, control of the behavior and its harms, punishment and/or treatment for the perpetrators, and support for the victims" (Wolfe & Jaffe, 1999, p. 136). In the US, using the law as tertiary prevention has largely meant deploying the criminal legal system (CLS) in cases of IPV—an approach that has prioritized the control and punishment aspects of tertiary prevention. Implementing strong laws against IPV also serves an expressive function, clearly identifying IPV as a harm society intends to remedy, though the impact of that expression is hard to measure. What the research suggests, however, is that the CLS's ability to deter future violence is limited. Mandatory arrest policies, which require police to make arrests whenever they have probable cause to do so, have had a minimal impact on recidivism (Stover et al., 2010). Moreover, despite 40 years of investment in the criminal legal response to IPV and the implementation of policies designed to ensure that more perpetrators come into the CLS, prosecution rates continue to vary significantly across jurisdictions, most crimes of IPV are prosecuted as misdemeanors, and sentences have not appreciably increased (Klein, 2009). Although rates of IPV declined steadily from 1994–2000, that decline was consistent with an overall decrease in the crime rate. From 2000–2010, rates of IPV fell more slowly than the continuing decrease in the crime rate (Catalano, 2012). The evidence suggests that the criminal legal response is having little impact on controlling IPV. It has also been suggested that it is impossible to know what the real impact of the CLS could be on rates of IPV, because a robust criminal legal response has yet to be fully implemented.

Nonetheless, for some people subjected to IPV, law—via the CLS—serves its function as a tertiary prevention strategy by punishing their perpetrators. Even for those people who decide not to prosecute, the existence of the legal system can provide support for people subjected to IPV if they are able to control how the legal system is deployed (using the threat of prosecution to secure needed resources or compel behavior from a partner, for example) (Ford, 1991). The legal system can also support people subjected to IPV through the provision of victim/witness advocates and crime victim compensation funds.Law fails to serve a tertiary prevention function for many others, though, because of their serious concerns about engaging with the legal system. Among those concerns is the inability of the legal system to deliver justice. As survivor Mary Walsh warned those contemplating criminal prosecution of their abusive partners, "For your own peace of mind, be prepared to throw any illusions about 'justice' you might have had out the window" (Herman, 2005, p. 582). For those who are seeking justice rather than a legal solution, what the law can provide may be secondary to finding justice through other venues.

What is justice?

To find justice requires having some sense of what the concept means. Philosophers have been exploring the meaning of justice since the beginning of recorded history, without a definitive answer. Philosopher Jeffrie Murphy (1988) describes justice as "the regular enforcement of the rules that make social stability (and thus social life) possible" (p. 182). Professor Kenneth Ehrenberg (2003) explains that "[j]ustice is about situations of actual or potential conflict and the outcomes to these conflicts or the distributions made based on the resolution of these conflicts" (p. 168). Justice may not be subject to static definitions; as Professors Harvey M. Weinstein and Eric Stover (2004) explain, "[j]ustice is a process—often a contentious one—that can evolve into different forms over time" (p. 12). In the context of crime, Professor Sophie Evekink (2013) suggests, justice should mean doing right by all stakeholders: victims, offenders, the state, families, and communities. For political systems and states, justice is often defined through the ability to impose criminal and civil sanctions on wrongdoers. Justice can be substantive or procedural, distributive or retributive, restorative or transformative. Justice can require recognition and it can require reparation. Justice can be found through the state, outside of the state, and through some combination of both. Given the diversity in the understandings of justice and the types of justice available to people subjected to IPV, it seems shortsighted and unduly restrictive to limit them to finding justice through one avenue.

Procedural v. substantive justice

Before discussing what justice means to people subjected to IPV, it is important to be clear about the type of justice at issue. Justice is often divided into two categories: substantive and procedural. Procedural justice refers to the means by which conflicts are resolved: the process used to determine the outcome (was the trial fair?). The rightness of the resolution of the conflict itself is substantive justice.

While most philosophers are concerned with substantive—or outcome—justice, philosopher Kenneth Ehrenberg makes a case for the importance of procedural justice, arguing that faith in the process can overcome concerns about the rightness of a particular result. Ehrenberg points to three ways that institutions can fail to provide procedural justice: in scope (by either failing to adjudicate cases within their scope, or reaching beyond their scope); through procedure (by using improper means to resolve conflict); or in outcome (by reaching an unjust result despite acting within the proper scope and using appropriate procedure) (Ehrenberg, 2003).

Procedural justice has a great deal of value in cases involving IPV. As Professor Deborah Epstein (2002) has explained, people who abuse are more likely to comply with protective orders and other judicial decrees when they believe the process for entering such orders has been fair. Process is also important for people subjected to IPV. A just process ensures that individuals are able to articulate their positions, goals, and concerns to a finder of fact. Moreover, just process may ensure that people subjected to IPV are able to reach their substantive justice goals. The concepts of procedural and substantive justice are, in fact, intertwined; whether the process can be deemed just may depend in large measure upon what outcome an individual hopes to achieve.

Retributive justice

Justice in the US is most often understood retributively. A crime or wrong is committed. The police identify, investigate, and arrest the perpetrator. A judge, after an appropriate process, finds that the perpetrator is responsible and sentences the perpetrator to some appropriate punishment as a result of that wrong. Retributive justice is administered through the state in the form of judges, who determine guilt and mete out punishment, and through state-run penal systems, which enforce those punishments. In retributive justice regimes, law and justice are enmeshed; law becomes a way of delivering justice

Punishment is central to retributive justice. Righting the wrong done through crime requires more than simply knowing who committed that crime. It requires that perpetrators suffer as a consequence of their actions. Punishment has value in and of itself, as a formal response to a wrong that cannot be superseded by other methods of accountability or the simple recognition that a crime has been committed. Formalizing punishment ensures that societal norms are upheld by expressing society's condemnation of the act committed and sending a message to others contemplating such wrongdoing that it will not be tolerated. Retributive justice acts as a check on individuals seeking revenge in response to a crime. Ensuring that punishments are given, and relegating the work of punishment to judges, prevents individuals from seeking vengeance by "transferring the responsibility for apportioning blame and punishment from victims to a court that acts according to the rule of law" (Weinstein & Stover, 2004, p. 14).

Restorative justice

Whereas retributive justice is concerned with punishment, restorative justice's goals are the repair and healing of relationships damaged by conflict and other harms. Proponents of restorative justice reject the language of crime, arguing that "the state and the law should not have a monopoly on defining injury" (Harris, 2011, p. 47). Instead, restorative justice seeks to repair harms caused by the actions of offenders by asking offenders to acknowledge the harm they have caused and identify ways to redress that harm. In lieu of punishment, offenders are held accountable for their actions through reparations and rehabilitation, with an eye toward reintegrating both offenders and their victims into their communities. Undergirding restorative justice efforts is the belief that social norms are best reinforced through social shaming rather than state-imposed sanction on offenders. "After appropriate rituals of guilt, responsibility, and penance," restorative justice proponents argue, offenders should be reintegrated into society (Harris, 2011, p. 41).

Restorative justice is also noteworthy for centralizing the needs and goals of victims of crimes in its processes. As a result of this victim-centeredness, research finds high levels of victim satisfaction with restorative justice. Offenders also report perceiving restorative justice as fair in both process and outcome. Restorative justice is widely used as an alternative to criminal prosecution in New Zealand; restorative practices have also been used to augment or substitute for CLS intervention in more limited forms in Australia, Canada, and the US. Restorative practices include sentencing circles, conferencing, and victim–offender mediation, and can be used both within (in diversion programs, at sentencing) and outside the CLS.

While feminist antiviolence efforts and restorative justice share a number of principles, feminists have expressed concern about using restorative justice in cases of IPV. Sociologist James Ptacek (2010; see also Chapter 7 in this book) groups those concerns into three general categories: safety, accountability, and political concerns. First, feminists worry that restorative justice practitioners fail to understand and respect the unique characteristics of and dangers posed by IPV, and as a result do not account for those factors in their programs. Second, feminists express skepticism that offenders will actually be held accountable for their actions through restorative justice, viewing such initiatives as "cheap justice" (Coker, 2002). Third, feminists fear that turning to restorative justice and other alternatives to the CLS risks undermining the treatment of IPV as a crime and decreases the power of women to demand action from the CLS.

Nonetheless, restorative justice could provide an alternative to what some characterize as an ineffectual CLS response in cases involving IPV. In recent years, feminist antiviolence advocates have shown a greater willingness to consider restorative alternatives—both because of concerns about the effectiveness of the CLS and because of the harm the CLS has caused some people subjected to violence (for example, increased arrest rates among women subjected to abuse resulting from the adoption of mandatory arrest policies) (Belknap & McDonald, 2010). Sociologist Lawrence Sherman (2000), who published some of the earliest research on arrest policy in cases involving IPV, pointed out: "Since there is no evidence that standard justice is any more effective than doing nothing in response to an incident of domestic violence, the only challenge to restorative justice is to do better than doing nothing" (p. 281). Moreover, studies suggest that restorative justice processes may provide greater procedural justice for people subjected to IPV than the traditional CLS.

Transformative justice

Transformative justice shares some of the core beliefs of restorative justice: skepticism about the effectiveness of the CLS, and a commitment to the idea that harm, not crime, should be the touchstone for intervention. Professor Angela Harris notes crucial differences between the two, however. First, transformative justice is explicitly centered on principles of anti-subordination. As Harris (2011) writes: "The aim of transformative justice is to recognize and grapple with the complicated ways in which race, gender, and other modes of domination are mutually entwined . . . each incident of personal violence should be understood in a larger context of structural violence" (p. 58). Second, Harris explains, transformative justice recognizes that restorative justice's reliance on the state and on institutions like "community" or "family" may be problematic, given the power imbalances that inhere in these institutions. While transformative justice is focused on security, it recognizes that no one vision of security will address the needs of all who suffer harm. Professor Erin Daly (2002) has suggested that another essential component of transformative justice is contextuality; transformative justice is deeply rooted in the time, place, and particular circumstances of the community seeking justice.

In the context of IPV cases, transformative justice is concerned with creating communities—defined not through traditional institutions, but by people subjected to IPV. Those communities are charged with supporting the autonomy of people subjected to IPV. While reintegration of people who abuse into the community may be a goal, that goal is secondary to the restoration of their partners' autonomy. Transformative justice projects consider the relationship between abusers' own oppression and their use of abusive tactics, but do not excuse such behavior as a result of economics, racism, heterosexism, or other oppressive factors. Coker (2002) sees transformative justice as expanding the range of responses available to people subjected to IPV without exposing them to the dangers inherent in the CLS and traditional restorative justice practices.

Creative Interventions, for example, is a California organization dedicated to community-based transformative justice efforts. Creative Interventions provides community members with the tools they need to craft individualized interventions with and for people subjected to abuse. One example: A woman sought help from her community after her police officer partner became abusive; she did not feel that the CLS could effectively protect her, given her partner's employment. Friends and supporters came together to help her find ways to feel safe in her home. Her friends set up a schedule to ensure that she was never home alone, then found someone (her mother) to intervene with her partner. They created a phone list of people she could call for assistance. These efforts addressed both the woman's immediate safety and her longer-term goal of ending the relationship without violence. They treated the problem as a community—rather than her individual—issue, asking: "How are we going to make sure that there's not harm happening in our community?" (Creative Interventions, 2012). Transformative justice invests communities with responsibility for addressing violence and provides the tools they need to effectuate change.

Justice as recognition

Justice as recognition is also concerned with the undervaluing of marginalized groups. Recognition is a response to cultural injustice, manifested through cultural domination, non-recognition, and disrespect. Remedying cultural injustice (like racism, sexism, and heterosexism) requires cultural or symbolic change. Professor Nancy Fraser (1997) explains:

> This could involve upwardly revaluing disrespected identities and the cultural products of maligned groups. It could also involve recognizing and positively valorizing cultural diversity. More radically still, it could involve the wholesale transformation of societal patterns of representation, interpretation and communication in ways that would change everybody's sense of self. (p. 15)

For example, Fraser (1997) argues, counteracting sexism requires "changing the cultural valuation[s] . . . that privilege masculinity and deny equal respect to women"—valuations that permit and facilitate violence against women. Changing these valuations requires more than simply recognizing they exist; rather, it requires rooting out the "legal and practical expressions" of such valuations as well (pp. 18–19).

Justice as recognition relies on narrative to shift harmful cultural valuations. In the context of transitional justice, Elizabeth Kiss (2000) describes justice as recognition as "acknowledging the distinctive identity of the other, striving to repair damage done to him or her through violence, stigmatization and disrespect, and including his or her stories in our collective histories" (p. 73). Victims of harm play an active role in processes designed to provide justice as recognition. Victim participation is essential to achieving justice as recognition, because the harm cannot be named and exposed without hearing the victim's story. As Professor Frank Haldemann (2008) explains: "The victim will have a chance to explain how the crime affected him, speaking in tones that are not the neutral tones of bare description, but tones that communicate to the perpetrator his righteous hurt and anger" (pp. 702–03). Empowerment, then, is a crucial component of justice as recognition; only an empowered victim will be prepared to engage in this kind of testimony. Moreover, justice as recognition envisions storytelling unconstrained by the rules and mores that govern trials in the adversarial legal system; that means contemplating stories told with emotion and guided by what the victim, rather than a court, deems relevant. Justice as recognition provides validation for victims and imposes burdens on perpetrators as a means of recognizing their wrongdoing.

In the context of IPV, justice as recognition would require a shift in the attitudes and norms that foster and excuse that violence. Moreover, justice as recognition requires processes that allow for unfettered storytelling of the kind that does not happen (consistent with concerns about procedural justice) in the CLS. But justice as recognition could dovetail with restorative and transformative justice efforts; the transformative justice organization Creative Interventions created the StoryTelling and Organizing Project (STOP) to allow people to share their stories of ending violence through community-based alternatives.

Parallel justice

Parallel justice derives from Professor Susan Herman's observation that justice is most often defined by what is done to the offender, both in terms of process and punishment, rather than what is done for the victim. But, Herman writes, "true justice requires attention to the needs of those who have suffered, as well as those who violated the law. A just society would seek to heal the wounds that crime has caused, keep victims safe, and empower them to reengage fully in society" — goals that cannot necessarily be achieved through the CLS (Herman, 2010, p. 2). Herman envisions a justice system for victims of crime that runs parallel to and does not require engagement with the CLS, but that charges the state with keeping victims safe and preventing revictimization. In Herman's system:

> All victims would be offered immediate support, compensation for their losses, and practical assistance. When their more urgent needs have been met, they would be offered opportunities to describe the harms they have experienced and set forth what they need to get their lives back on track. Government officials would marshal as many resources as possible to meet their short- and long-term needs. (Herman, 2010, p. 56)

The government is responsible for taking the lead to ensure a victim's needs are met. In partnership with the private sector and the community, parallel justice case managers with governmental authority would be made available to hear victims' stories and help victims access needed resources.

Parallel justice and restorative justice share a victim-centered orientation, but Herman highlights important differences between the two. Many restorative justice programs are housed within the CLS. Because so few crimes are reported, and so few victims of crime have contact with the CLS, most victims will not be served by those programs. Moreover, many restorative justice programs require the offender to admit responsibility for the crime before the programs will intervene. Parallel justice, by contrast, does not require any action by the offender to trigger its services and supports for the victim of crime. Finally, the resources available through restorative justice programs are often limited to what the offender and the community can provide. A strength of parallel justice is that it brings the considerable resources of the state to the table for the victim (Herman, 2010).

Parallel justice is intended to meet the goals of both the victim and society. Safety is parallel justice's overriding concern, although Herman never discusses what safety means, or what happens when victims of crime define safety differently to the government. Although Herman recognizes that some victims of crime will not be interested in or able to access the CLS, parallel justice nonetheless requires victims of crime to interact with the government in some way in order to receive services and supports. Parallel justice assumes a benign, helpful government that victims of crime will be willing to approach; it fails to consider the ways in which the state is a harmful and intrusive force for many low-income people, people of color, and undocumented people—

and the reluctance of those groups to ask the state for assistance as a result. While its goal is "to provide justice to victims by helping them rebuild their lives" (Herman, 2010, p. 75), the path to that justice runs through the state.

Defining justice in the context of IPV

Psychologist Judith Herman (2005) suggests that, in the realm of IPV, there are a number of:

> basic questions about the meaning of justice: How can the truth be made known? How should offenders be held accountable? What is appropriate punishment? Can the harm be repaired, and if so, what would be required to repair it? How can victims and offenders go on living in the same community? Is reconciliation possible? (p. 571)

Interestingly, only one of these questions specifically references the idea of retributive justice. Yet the focus of law and policy on IPV in the US has long been on retributive justice, via the CLS. The declaration in the 1980s that IPV was a crime rather than a private family dispute; the criminalization of IPV through law; the development of policing and prosecutorial techniques specifically designed to address IPV; and the subsequent devotion of millions of dollars in federal funds to the CLS through the Violence Against Women Act (VAWA), all attest to the retributive orientation of law and policy on IPV.

For a number of reasons, however, the CLS is an imperfect vehicle for finding justice for many people subjected to IPV. People subjected to IPV may feel unheard in the CLS. Because courts must ensure procedural justice for offenders, they adhere to strict evidentiary requirements that mediate victims' stories. As Herman explains, however, "[v]ictims need an opportunity to tell their stories in their own way, in a setting of their choice; the court requires them to respond to a set of yes–or–no questions that break down any personal attempt to construct a coherent and meaningful narrative" (2005, p. 574). Witnesses must keep their testimony short and focused; this control over victims' stories can distort the underlying narrative and leave victims unsatisfied with the experience of testifying. Skillful cross-examination can call into question the credibility of even the most truthful witness.

Some victims of crime believe they will receive validation through the CLS, but often want a kind of validation that the system cannot provide. The bedrock of the CLS is the presumption of innocence. Until a verdict has been rendered, judges cannot suggest that they believe a witness's testimony or affirm the merits of a case. Judges and juries may appear skeptical of or even hostile to a victim's claims in their attempts to adhere to the presumption of innocence. While judges may be able to provide some validation once the case is completed—and while some victims are gratified by hearing judges describe the harm those victims have suffered when making sentencing determinations—that validation may not be sufficient to mitigate the trauma of the court process.

Moreover, notwithstanding the truthfulness of the individual's claims, conviction rates for IPV still vary significantly. Even if individuals do seek justice through the CLS, they may be disappointed in the outcome. Trials simply fail to provide justice to some people subjected to IPV and can exacerbate their injuries. As Herman states: "[I]f one set out intentionally to design a system for provoking symptoms of traumatic stress, it might look very much like a court of law" (2005, p. 574).

The state's goals in responding to IPV may differ significantly from the individual's. The goal of police and prosecutors is to enforce IPV laws—police by gathering evidence and making arrests, and prosecutors by trying those cases and winning convictions. Like other victims of crime, however, some people subjected to IPV are not interested in either arrest or prosecution.

This clash in priorities can have problematic results. Police have told people to "press charges or shut up," or threatened that "there would be no one there" when they called for help the next time if they failed to cooperate (Erez & Belknap, 1998, p. 256). Prosecutors, too, have their own goals for intervention. Prosecutor Michelle Kaminsky (2011) explains:

> Prosecutors are public officials who arc held publicly accountable. If a woman is injured because we failed to follow through on a case, regardless of a victim's wishes, we will be held responsible. I would be a liar if I didn't acknowledge how this truth affects my decision making process. (p. 114)

Prosecutors concerned about their accountability sometimes take extreme measures to ensure that people subjected to IPV testify.

Kaminsky (2011) describes one prosecutor who bragged to an audience at a national domestic violence conference that she had people arrested and jailed when they did not cooperate with her, explaining: "I was just covering my ass" (p. 114). Former prosecutor and law professor Michelle Madden Dempsey argues that prosecutors should force people subjected to IPV to participate in cases where the violence is serious, ongoing, and reinforces patriarchy within the relationship and in society; prosecution is likely to reduce the violence and strong community interests are served by requiring the testimony (Dempsey, 2009). This stance means actively disregarding the preferences of those people subjected to IPV who want to avoid the CLS and who do not believe they will find justice through that system. When prosecutors' and individuals' goals are at odds, an individual's goals may be subsumed by the state. Because their goals do not align with law enforcement's, people subjected to IPV may not only fail to find justice through the criminal system, but may also be harmed by the system.

Some people subjected to IPV are simply not interested in retribution. Retribution—accomplished through the operation of the criminal law—enables society to express its anger, resentment, and hatred, and legitimizes society's desire for revenge. But some people subjected to IPV are not seeking punishment or revenge and do not feel hatred or resentment. They simply want to continue their relationships, albeit without the abuse. Studies have repeatedly shown that people subjected to IPV opt out of the legal system because they love their partners and want to maintain relationships with them. In a recent study of the Bennington, VT Integrated Domestic Violence Court, 70% of the couples who came through the system were either still involved in their relationships or planned to continue them (Suntag, 2014). The CLS's focus on punishment is inconsistent with that goal.

Finally, some people subjected to IPV do not believe that the CLS is a place where justice can be found. People of color—who are overrepresented in the CLS—may have concerns about asking the state for help, fearing that the state will instead intervene punitively against them. Parents of color who engage the CLS sometimes find their children being removed by child protective services for failing to protect them from exposure to IPV. People with undocumented partners fear the deportation of their partners and the loss of economic, parenting, and other forms of support if they become involved with law enforcement. Undocumented immigrants may also justifiably fear their own arrest and deportation if they report violence to police. Lesbian, gay, bisexual, and particularly transgender people experience significant rates of harassment and abuse by police, even when reporting

IPV. For many people subjected to IPV, the "process [of the CLS] is the punishment" (Feeley, 1979). As Herman (2005) concludes, "The victim's version of justice is nowhere represented in the conventional legal system" (p. 575).

What, then, constitutes justice for people subjected to IPV? Few studies have addressed that question, but Herman's work provides a starting point for its consideration. Herman (2005) conducted in-depth interviews with 22 people subjected to violent crime (sexual and domestic violence). Participants were asked about "their experiences of victimization, their efforts to seek redress, and their views of what would be required to set things right" (p. 579). For Herman's subjects, validation and vindication were their two most important justice-related goals. Herman (2005) defines validation as "an acknowledgment of the basic facts of the crime and an acknowledgment of harm," either from the perpetrator or—equally or more importantly for some individuals—from bystanders: their immediate families, the legal authorities, or the wider community (p. 585). Vindication requires communities "to take a clear and unequivocal stand in condemnation of the offense" (Herman, 2005, p. 585). Vindication "transfer[s] the burden of disgrace from victim to offender," restoring a victim's status within the community (Herman, 2005, p. 585). Justice could also involve voice: the ability to tell one's story as a means of repairing harm. In the literature reviewing truth and reconciliation processes after genocide and other human rights atrocities, voice recurs as a central theme. A man who was blinded by a police officer during South Africa's apartheid era compared his appearance before the Truth and Reconciliation Commission to having his physical injuries healed, explaining: "I feel like what has been making me sick all the time is the fact that I couldn't tell my story. But now I—it feels like I got my sight back by coming here and telling you the story" (Minow, 1998, p. 67). Justice seems to be a highly individualized concept, requiring strategies tailored to the particular context of each person subjected to IPV.

For lawyers working with people subjected to abuse, then, the challenge is to determine what constitutes justice for that client. Lawyers and clients must collaborate to make individualized assessments of what clients most need, remembering that a client's non-legal needs may outweigh the desire for a legal outcome. For some clients, retribution, achieved through the CLS, will be the goal. For others, economic relief—acquired through the civil legal system or through outside sources—community support, or a place to be heard may be more important. Accepting that justice is an individualized concept means acknowledging that the CLS, as currently constituted, cannot meet the needs of all people subjected to abuse.

The notion that justice is an individualized, contextual concept is consistent with the research on empowerment and IPV. Although empowerment is central to work with people subjected to IPV, the term has been "rarely measured or even consistently defined" (Goodman et al., 2015). In recent years, scholars have argued that empowerment must be conceptualized across different populations, settings, and specific domains of action, and must be flexible enough to allow for variation among people's goals. The process of achieving empowerment involves developing goals, amassing resources and skills to achieve those goals, and seeing progress (Cattaneo & Goodman, 2015). Similarly, finding justice could mean the process of setting and achieving justice-related goals, which might be enmeshed with empowerment goals.

How a person subjected to IPV defines justice should dictate the services and supports provided. For victims whose needs are grounded more in voice, validation, and vindication through the community, restorative and transformative justice strategies might be appropriate. Restorative justice focuses on the repair and healing of relationships damaged by conflict and other harms. Transformative justice marries those concerns with attention to the ways in which intersecting identities shape the experience of harm and a broad notion of community beyond entrenched institutions. Although little research on transformative justice exists, research finds high levels of victim satisfaction with restorative justice. People who engage in restorative processes report decreased fear and anxiety and increased feelings of dignity, self-respect, and self-confidence. While retributive justice focuses on the separation of victims and perpetrators, restorative and transformative justice provide space to acknowledge that the relationships between victims and perpetrators may continue because they have children in common, live in the same small communities, or still love each other. For people subjected to IPV who will continue to have some contact with their partners, restorative and transformative justice can help create a vision of—and concrete strategies for—what those relationships will look like going forward. Restorative and transformative strategies can also enable people subjected to IPV to achieve some sense of closure by confronting their partners with the harm that has been done and hearing them describe how they will take responsibility for their actions. The retributive system gives limited voice through victim impact statements, but does not provide the kind of two-way communication that some people want.

Process is an essential component of restorative justice. A variety of processes can be employed to serve the justice needs of people subjected to IPV. The majority of the limited scholarship on restorative justice and IPV has focused on conferencing. Conferences bring together people subjected to IPV, their partners, and supportive members of the parties' communities to discuss how the offender's violence affected everyone in the circle, and what can be done to repair that harm and prevent future damage. Conferences can be designed in any way that provides people subjected to IPV with the security and support they need to feel comfortable in the process.

For all of the aforementioned reasons, few restorative justice practitioners or domestic violence service providers are engaging people subjected to IPV in conferencing. In Canada, however, Gale Burford and Joan Pennell used conferencing to create plans for families in the child welfare system experiencing both child maltreatment and IPV. No new violence occurred during the time that conferences were held, both adult and child abuse declined in the families, and two thirds of the families reported being better off after the conference (Pennell, 2005; Pennell & Burford, 2000). In a study in New Zealand, a majority of the people subjected to IPV who engaged in restorative justice conferences reported satisfaction with the process. They were positive about their partners taking responsibility for their actions through the process, and would recommend conferencing to others (Kingi, 2014). Interest in such programs as an alternative to what some see as a punitive and ineffectual CLS response is growing.

A second restorative process—post-conviction dialogs—has been successful in helping people subjected to IPV experience empowerment, voice, and validation long after convictions have been obtained. During post-conviction dialogs, individuals can discuss their feelings about the crime and its aftermath and ask questions they continue to have. These conversations are designed to be therapeutic, and do not substitute for punishment via the CLS. As a result, offenders are often motivated to participate not to lessen their punishment, but rather to respond to affected individuals and relieve them of any sense of responsibility for the harm.

Miller and Iovanni (2013) stress the importance of timing of post-conviction dialogs: "The victim needs to be ready to reap the benefits of facing the offender and the offender must have had time to develop empathy and take responsibility" (p. 255). During the extensive preparation that occurs prior to post-conviction dialogs, victim advocates can help victims gauge their readiness to participate, and offender intervention specialists can help facilitators determine whether the offender has, in fact, developed empathy—as well as whether the offender's acceptance of responsibility is genuine. In their case study of a post-conviction dialog between Laurie and her abusive husband Paul, Miller and Iovanni (2013) describe how Laurie was able to confront Paul with her unanswered questions and to show him how different she was from the person he had repeatedly battered. Laurie was also able to hear her husband say that she had done nothing to merit his abuse and that he deserved to be arrested (p. 259). The experience gave Paul insight into what Laurie had endured and a desire to work with other abusers, and spurred him to make a number of commitments to ensure Laurie's continued safety and wellbeing after his release. The post-conviction dialog helped Paul to make behavioral change—something that rarely happens through other interventions with those who abuse their partners.

Restorative and transformative justice processes can engage not only those immediately affected by IPV, but also the wider community. Building on the example of the truth commissions created in the wake of human rights violations in countries including South Africa, Sierra Leone, Peru, Canada, and the US, as well as community-based courts in India and Rwanda, community-based justice forums could involve communities in the provision of justice to people subjected to IPV. Law professor Brenda Smith recommended that community-based justice forums be established in a variety of community spaces—child care centers, schools, churches, recreation centers, barber shops, and hair salons—to ensure that justice is visible on the ground (Smith, 2003). These forums would not be tied to the state and would not be bound by the rules of the adversarial system. This independence from the CLS would deny community-based justice forums the use of tools like subpoenas to collect information, but securing voluntary participation might be more valuable than compelling attendance. The goal of these proceedings would be to create both physical and psychic space for—and to facilitate the telling of stories about—IPV, and to provide redress other than criminal punishment, particularly for marginalized communities. Restorative transitional justice mechanisms have enabled voices that have traditionally been subjugated to come to the fore. Community justice forums could create new spaces to hear the voices of people subjected to IPV and of those who abuse.

Members of the community justice forum could reach out to potential participants through neighborhood information sources (newspapers and online forums), community organizations, and service providers. Participants would have to affirmatively opt in to the processes thereby assuaging concerns about the claims of women and other marginalized groups being devalued by being forced into alternative adjudicatory forums, and about the manipulation of informal justice systems by abusive partners. The proceedings would recognize the needs of the range of people subjected to IPV, including but not limited to women, and tailor their processes accordingly. Testimony could be given publicly or on camera, orally or in writing, anonymously or by name. Abusers would be permitted to provide testimony, but only after admitting and accepting responsibility for their abusive behavior, and only with the permission of their partners. Providing public testimony increases the accountability of perpetrators to the community. Perpetrators also feel more accountable when they are able to play an active role in the healing process. Hearing from abusers may be central to meeting the justice goals of individual people subjected to IPV, and is a crucial component in analyzing the ways in which the community may have enabled violence to occur.

Community justice forums might also facilitate dispute resolution for those people subjected to IPV who have specific issues that they want to address. Such efforts would have to be explicitly driven by people subjected to intimate partner violence; no one would be pressured or coerced into participating or accepting a resolution that did not meet their goals. A commitment to achieving the justice goals of people subjected to IPV may require this type of close negotiation with those who use violence, particularly when people choose to remain in relationships with their partners who abuse, or when couples have children in common. Community justice forums could provide a venue outside of the legal system for engaging in that work.

Community-based justice forums could be empowered to make recommendations for reparation and reform. Reparations are a concrete means of alleviating pain and redressing harm, as well as a symbol of the community's recognition of that harm. Moral reparations include apologies and acknowledgments of harm—the validation sought by some people subjected to abuse. Material reparations can be monetary (such as reimbursing the costs of medical care, lost employment time and opportunities, property damage, and housing), or can provide victims with the services they need (such as health care, mental health counseling, or employment training). The CLS in the US has been reluctant to provide victims of crime with reparations; a move toward community-based justice might make such forms of relief more readily available.

Community support and participation are essential to the success of these systems. Community-based justice forums could be staffed by local IPV organizations—those with the expertise to provide support and services to participants. After appropriate training on IPV, other community members would be engaged to witness the stories of participants. Transparency of process and sensitivity to stories of violence would be essential in the selection of witnesses. Involving the community as hearers serves a number of goals. Community members can convey the message that IPV will not be tolerated and can set community standards for responding to IPV through their responses (both verbal and in the form of individual remedies) to individuals' stories. Moreover, community members would be charged with unearthing and acknowledging the community's own complicity in perpetuating IPV, as well as with determining what changes the community might make in response to the stories it hears.

Community-based justice forums would provide people subjected to IPV with the opportunity to explore both individual and collective accountability for that violence. Participants would be encouraged to detail not only what their partners did, but also how the community and/or the state reacted—or failed to react—in ways that exacerbated the person's suffering. Community-based justice forums would explore the interconnections between the actions of individual perpetrators and the community or state, helping the community to identify sites for structural change as well as individual reparation.

Restorative and transformative justice processes, both individual and community-based, have limitations and potential dangers. Ensuring that restorative and transformative practitioners have deep expertise in IPV is essential to the success of these efforts. The requirement that offenders accept responsibility before engaging in the process will mean that many cases involving IPV will be ineligible. These efforts depend on community engagement and support, which may be difficult to cultivate. Community norms on the unacceptability of IPV may not shift enough to ensure that offenders are truly held accountable for their actions. Restorative and transformative processes are time consuming, and may not be available in cases of immediate acute violence. Finally, these types of efforts will be difficult and costly to bring to scale—and in bringing them to scale, there is the danger that those characteristics that make restorative and transformative justice unique will be lost.

Economic justice

Justice can also be cast in terms of substantive areas in which people subjected to IPV seek support and assistance. For example, economic stability is a primary concern of most people subjected to IPV. Rates of IPV are higher in economically vulnerable couples (Fox & Benson, 2006), and women whose partners do not have stable employment are more likely to experience abuse (Benson & Fox, 2004). Economics also traps people subjected to IPV in their relationships. Violence may be the price that those who are economically dependent upon their abusive partners are forced to pay for avoiding homelessness or poverty. Economics both contributes to abuse and serves as a mechanism for abuse. The vast majority of people subjected to IPV report some form of economic abuse, defined as tactics that: "control a woman's ability to acquire, use, and maintain economic resources, thus threatening her economic security and potential for self-sufficiency" (Adams et al., 2008, p. 564). These tactics might include preventing individuals from working, taking resources from women, dictating how money is spent, stealing money or property, building debt in a partner's name, and squandering family resources. Notwithstanding its destructive impact, few laws in the US provide any recourse for people subjected to intimate partner economic abuse. Only one state—Michigan— includes a narrow definition of economic abuse in its civil protection order law, permitting a court to issue a protective order if it believes a person is interfering with the petitioner at her place of employment or education or otherwise engaging in conduct that impairs employment or education. By contrast, India's Protection of Women from Domestic Violence Act of 2005 provides explicit protection and expansive remedies for people subjected to economic abuse.

Focusing on economics could provide substantive justice to people subjected to IPV. Ensuring economic stability for both partners in the relationship could work as a preventive measure, helping to decrease rates of IPV. Providing economic resources could help people subjected to IPV to leave abusive relationships in which they would otherwise be entrapped. Justice could entail attempts to ensure people subjected to IPV have their basic economic needs met, without interference from their partners, so that their choices about the future of their relationships are not constrained by economic necessity. Economic justice could also mean providing job opportunities and support to the partners of economically vulnerable individuals; stability of employment could serve a preventive function. Ensuring economic justice could do the work of tertiary prevention by supporting economically marginalized people subjected to IPV and preventing further victimization. One way to provide economically vulnerable people subjected to IPV with support is through reparations, which, as mentioned, are frequently used in restorative justice processes. In conferences or community justice forums, individuals could explain how their economic wellbeing was jeopardized by the action or inaction of their partners or communities. Individual offenders and communities would hear such testimony, consider appropriate responses, and provide reparations to people subjected to IPV in acknowledgment of their roles in destabilizing a partner's economic position. Using restorative processes involving the community to determine reparations would help to ensure both that individual offenders are held accountable for honoring their commitments to their partners and that the larger structural issues that contributed to the victimization are recognized and remedied.

Economic remedies have drawbacks, particularly if employed in isolation. Economic support does little to address an immediate incident of violence or hold an offender accountable. Some research suggests that increasing victims' economic empowerment might actually spur violence, as those who abuse feel their control of their partners slipping. The logistics of putting economic resources directly into the hands of people subjected to abuse will be challenging at best, and vulnerable to claims of misuse of funds. Focusing resources on those who abuse is likely to be unpopular, given the limited funding available to address IPV and especially if that funding is diverted from victim services or law enforcement.

Conclusion

Justice could be an effective tertiary prevention strategy if we abandoned the cramped current retributive understanding of justice. Rather than simply seeking the punishment of offenders, our conception of justice should center on providing support for people subjected to IPV in a variety of ways. Shifting the definition could enable us to engage in a wide array of efforts that could constitute tertiary prevention. Whether such efforts might be more successful than the current system in providing justice is mere speculation, however, without a clear understanding of what justice means to people subjected to IPV. Research is needed to answer that question and to inform efforts to provide justice. Until that research exists, designing tertiary prevention strategies using a justice system—whether that system is retributive, restorative, transformative, economic, or something else altogether— may be a futile effort.

References

Adams, A.E., Sullivan, C.M., Bybee D., & Greeson, M.R. (2008). Development of the scale of economic abuse. *Violence Against Women, 14,* 563–588.

Belknap, J., & McDonald, C. (2010). Judges' attitudes about and experiences with sentencing circles in intimate-partner abuse cases. *Canadian Journal of Criminology & Criminal Justice, 52*(4), 369–395.

Benson, M.L., & Fox, G.L. (2004). *When violence hits home: How economics and neighborhood play a role.* NIJ Research in Brief. Washington, DC: US Department of Justice, National Institute of Justice. Retrieved from: https://www.ncjrs.gov/pdffiles1/nij/205004.pdf.

Catalano, S. (2012). *Intimate partner violence, 1993–2010* (NCJ 239203). US Department of Justice. Retrieved from: http://149.101.16.41/content/pub/pdf/ipv9310.pdf.

Cattaneo, L.B., & Goodman, L.A. (2015). What is empowerment anyway? A model for domestic violence practice, research and evaluation. *Psychology of Violence, 5,* 84–94.

Coker, D. (2002). Transformative justice: Anti-subordination practices in cases of domestic violence. In H. Strang & J. Braithwaite (Eds.), *Restorative justice and family violence* (pp. 128–152). Cambridge: Cambridge University Press.

Creative Interventions (2012). *Creative interventions toolkit: A practical guide to stop interpersonal violence.* Retrieved from: www.creative-interventions.org/wp-content/uploads/2012/06/CI-Toolkit-Complete-Pre-Release-Version-06.2012-.pdf.

Daly, E. (2002). Transformative justice: Charting a path towards reconciliation. *International Legal Perspectives, 12,* 73–83.

Dempsey, M.M. (2009). *Prosecuting domestic violence: A philosophical analysis.* Oxford: Oxford University Press.

Ehrenberg, K.M. (2003). Procedural justice and information in conflict resolving institutions. *Albany Law Review, 67,* 167–210.

Epstein, D. (2002). Procedural justice: Tempering the state's response to domestic violence. *William and Mary Law Review, 43,* 1843–1906.

Erez, E., & Belknap, J. (1998). In their own words: Battered women's assessment of the criminal processing system's responses. *Violence and Victims, 13,* 251–268.

Evekink, S. (2013). *Retributive or restorative? Prospects for justice for those who live side-by-side with their aggressors (working paper).* Retrieved from: http://papers.ssrn.com/sol3/papers.cfm?abstract_id=2209959.

Feeley, M. (1979). *The process is the punishment: Handling cases in a lower criminal court.* New York: Russell Sage Foundation.

Ford, D.A. (1991). Prosecution as a victim power resource: A note on empowering women in violent conjugal relationships. *Law and Society Review, 25*, 313–334.

Fox, G.L., & Benson, M.L. (2006). Household and neighborhood contexts of intimate partner violence. *Public Health Reports, 121*, 419–427.

Fraser, N. (1997). *Justice interruptus: Critical reflections on the "postsocialist" condition.* New York: Routledge.

Goodman, L.A., Cattaneo, L.B., Thomas, K., Woulfe, J., Chong, K.C., & Smith, K.F. (2015). Advancing domestic violence program evaluation: Development and validation of the measure of victim empowerment related to safety (MOVERS). *Psychology of Violence, 5*, 355–366.

Haldemann, F. (2008). Another kind of justice: Transitional justice as recognition. *Cornell International Law Journal, 41*, 675–738.

Harris, A.P. (2011). Heteropatriarchy kills: Challenging gender violence in a prison nation. *Washington University Journal of Law and Policy, 37*, 13–65.

Herman, J.L. (2005). Justice from the victim's perspective. *Violence Against Women, 10*, 571–602.

Herman, S. (2010). *Parallel justice for victims of crime.* Washington, DC: National Center for Victims of Crime.

Kaminsky, M. (2011). *Reflections of a domestic violence prosecutor: Suggestions for reform.* CreateSpace Independent Publishing Platform.

Kingi, V. (2014). The use of restorative justice in family violence: The New Zealand experience. In A. Hayden, L. Gelsthorpe, V. Kingi & A. Morris (Eds.), *A restorative approach to family violence: Changing tack* (pp. 145–158). London: Routledge.

Kiss, E. (2000). Moral ambition within and beyond political constraints: Reflections on restorative justice. In R. Rotberg & D. Thompson (Eds.), *Truth v. justice: The morality of truth commissions* (pp. 68–98). Princeton, NJ: Princeton University Press.

Klein, A.R. (2009). *Practical implications of current domestic violence research: For law enforcement, prosecutors and judges.* Washington, DC: BiblioGov.

Miller, S., & Iovanni, L. (2013). Using restorative justice for gendered violence: Success with a postconviction model. *Feminist Criminology, 8*, 247–268.

Minow, M. (1998). *Between vengeance and forgiveness: Facing history after genocide and mass violence.* Boston, MA: Beacon Press.

Murphy, J. G. (1988). Mercy and legal justice. In J.G. Murphy & J. Hampton (Eds.), *Forgiveness and mercy* (pp. 162–186). New York: Cambridge University Press.

Pennell, J. (2005). Safety for mothers and their children. In J. Pennell & G. Anderson (Eds.), *Widening the circle: The practice and evaluation of family group conferencing with children, youths, and their families* (pp. 163–181). Washington, DC: NASW Press.

Pennell, J., & Burford, G. (2000). Family group decision making: Protecting women and children. *Child Welfare, 79*, 131–158.

Ptacek, J. (2010). Resisting Co-optation: Three feminist challenges to antiviolence work. In J. Ptacek (Ed.), *Restorative justice and violence against women* (pp. 5–36). New York: Oxford University Press.

Sherman, L.W. (2000). Domestic violence and restorative justice: Answering key questions. *Virginia Journal of Social Policy and Law, 8*, 263–281.

Smith, B.V. (2003). Battering, forgiveness and redemption. *American University Journal of Gender, Social Policy and the Law, 11*, 921–962.

Stover, C.S., Berkman, M., Desai, R., & Marans, S. (2010). The efficacy of a police-advisory intervention for victims of domestic violence: 12 month follow-up data. *Violence Against Women, 6*, 410–425.

Suntag, D. (2014). *DV and the traditional court model: Why we fail & what we can do about it.* Burlington, VT: Restorative Justice, Responsive Regulation and Complex Problems.

Weinstein, H.M., & Stover, E. (2004). Introduction: Conflict, justice and reclamation. In E. Stover & H.M. Weinstein (Eds.), *My neighbor, my enemy: Justice and community in the aftermath of mass atrocity* (pp. 1–26). New York: Cambridge University Press.

Wolfe, D.A., & Jaffe, P.G. (1999). Emerging strategies in the prevention of domestic violence. *The Future of Children, 9*, 133–144.

NINE

Innovative Programs to Economically Empower Women and Prevent Intimate Partner Violence Revictimization

Claire M. Renzetti, Diane R. Follingstad, and Diane Fleet

Introduction

The negative consequences of intimate partner violence (IPV) are well documented in the empirical literature, and include not only physical injuries but also mental health concerns, such as anxiety, depression, post-traumatic stress disorder (PTSD), lowered self-esteem, and a diminished sense of self-efficacy (Perez et al., 2012; Sutherland et al., 2002). Domestic violence shelters were established to provide women fleeing IPV with emergency housing, psychological counseling, and legal assistance. Over the past three decades, shelter staff have developed a variety of additional programs, expanding the services offered to residents to include transitional housing and relocation services, educational programs, drug and alcohol treatment, and employment assistance (Macy et al., 2009; Sullivan, 2012). Increasingly, domestic violence advocates and researchers are urging service providers to focus more attention on providing programs that economically empower victims (Goodman & Epstein, 2009). These domestic violence experts recognize that financial instability and the threat or actual experience of poverty, in addition to the negative mental health impacts of IPV, are among the factors that motivate women to return to abusive partners, thus increasing the risk of revictimization (Brush, 2011; Farber & Miller-Cribbs, 2014; Goodman & Epstein, 2009; Hamby & Bible, 2009; Moe & Bell, 2004; Pruitt, 2008). Economic empowerment programs, then, may be an important component of tertiary prevention. Economic empowerment has three dimensions:

- Financial literacy—the knowledge and skills necessary to make sound financial decisions and acquire resources;
- Economic self-efficacy—a person's beliefs about and confidence in their ability to achieve financial security and economic success (regardless of how they define "success");
- Economic self-sufficiency—an individual's ability to independently meet the needs of daily life. (Postmus, 2010)

Postmus (2010, p. 1) maintains that "economic empowerment programs and economic advocacy strategies represent efforts to help survivors gain or regain their financial footing during and after abuse." Such assistance may be especially critical for women who have experienced various forms of economic abuse and exploitation—women whose partners, for example, kept them from going to work or harassed them at work; hid financial information or resources; stole money or property; or ran up debt on joint credit cards (Adams et al., 2008; Postmus et al., 2015; Sanders, 2014). Furthermore, there is evidence that economic empowerment programs not only help to financially stabilize women who have experienced abuse, but also have health benefits (Glass et al., 2014).

This chapter discusses several economic empowerment programs that were specifically designed for women who have experienced various forms of trauma and abuse, or that have been adapted for use with this population. Of course, we cannot cover all of the many types of programs currently available; instead, we offer examples of those we consider especially innovative and we highlight one, based in therapeutic horticulture, with which we have been personally involved. The chapter also reviews the available empirical evidence regarding the outcomes of these programs and implications for prevention of revictimization. It will become clear, however, that considerably more research is needed to demonstrate the effectiveness of these various programs.

Financial literacy programs

The most common economic empowerment programs for women who have experienced abuse are financial literacy programs. Financial literacy programs typically cover such topics as financial goal setting, saving and investment strategies, bill paying, credit cards, interest rates, and predatory lending practices. Postmus (2010) adds that financial literacy programs specifically for IPV survivors also usually include educating the women about economic abuse and the complex financial and safety issues they face, such as "how to disentangle joint financial relationships with an abusive partner, how to repair credit damaged by an abuser, and how to identify resources to assist with financial and safety challenges" (p. 5).

Few financial literacy programs for IPV survivors have been empirically evaluated, although those that have undergone evaluation show some promising outcomes. For example, Postmus and Plummer (2010) conducted an evaluation of the Moving Ahead through Financial Management program, developed by the Allstate Foundation and implemented in partnership with the National Network to End Domestic Violence, Inc. Postmus and Plummer (2010) report that IPV survivors who participated in the Moving Ahead program showed significant gains on all three measures of economic empowerment—financial literacy, economic self-efficacy, and economic self-sufficiency. Although these findings are encouraging, it is important to note that this evaluation used a fairly small, non-random sample. It may not be possible to conduct a randomized controlled trial of this program[1], but evaluations with larger, more diverse samples are needed to confirm the positive results obtained by Postmus and Plummer (2010).

Postmus (2010) notes that a growing trend at shelters and victim advocacy organizations is to combine financial literacy programs with asset building programs (for example, matched savings programs or small loans), which are particularly helpful in promoting economic self-sufficiency among women who have experienced trauma and abuse—a point to which we will return shortly (see also Christy-McMullen, 2000; Sullivan, 2012). Some programs also incorporate employment assistance (for example, résumé writing or practice interviewing). But many IPV survivors lack job references and have spotty résumés at best, because their abuse experiences have interrupted their work history. Economic empowerment programs may prove more efficacious if they integrate opportunities for work experience into general IPV programming. For example, time spent healing from IPV while in residence at a shelter might include work opportunities, such that when the survivor is ready to leave, she leaves with some employment history and a job reference.

We turn now to an innovative program that is attempting to address some of these issues, integrating economic empowerment and recovery from trauma, and ultimately reducing the risk of revictimization.

GreenHouse17: Therapeutic horticulture and economic empowerment

GreenHouse17 (formerly the Bluegrass Domestic Violence Program, Inc.) is a shelter for battered women that serves Lexington (Fayette County), KY, and 16 surrounding counties in the state (see www. greenhouse17.org). GreenHouse17 serves approximately 230 women and their children each year, offering standard shelter services (for example, a 24-hour crisis line, safe emergency housing, legal assistance, counseling, and referrals) for both residential and nonresidential clients. But one program that makes GreenHouse17 unique relative to other victim service agencies for battered women is that it operates a working farm. Domestic violence shelters are often located in physical environments that are separated from nature (Stuart, 2005). But GreenHouse17 is situated on 40 acres of rich farmland and surrounded by other working farms, including horse farms. In 2010, faced with budget constraints, shelter administrators and staff began to consider potential revenue–generating activities as well as ways to raise awareness of the shelter's work in the community. A variety of "cottage industries" were discussed, but ultimately shelter administrators and staff felt that cultivating the land could address several issues simultaneously:

- Reduce the shelter's food budget, while improving nutrition for residents and staff;
- Raise revenue through the sale of produce at local farmers markets;
- Connect the shelter with the larger community through the shared value of land preservation and the "buy local" movement; and
- Provide residents with opportunities for physical exercise, socializing, and quiet reflection and meditation, thereby facilitating healing[2].

What became known as the "farm program" is an example of tertiary IPV prevention through economic empowerment using therapeutic horticulture.

Therapeutic horticulture

The term "therapeutic horticulture" (TH) applies to interventions that use nature or plant-related activities to improve participants' physical, psychological, and social wellbeing. TH is distinguished from horticultural therapy, in that the latter is typically administered in a structured setting by trained therapists. In contrast, TH is defined as exposure to plants and horticulture for enhancement of wellbeing. It can be found in a broad range of settings by a variety of service providers and practitioners, often as an adjunct to other services (Gonzalez et al., 2009). The improvement of "wellbeing" for individuals in TH programs is expected to be achieved through structured outcomes (for example, the attainment of employment and social contact), through indirect outcomes (for example, an increased sense of self-esteem), or through subjective emotional benefits (for example, peacefulness and belonging) (Sempik et al., 2003). Although there is a dearth of well-executed experimental evaluations of TH programs, qualitative accounts and the philosophical underpinnings of TH (Morreau, 1979) have led to the development of these programs for diverse populations; these include juvenile offenders, individuals with substance abuse disorders, military veterans diagnosed with PTSD, people diagnosed with schizophrenia, and clinically depressed persons (Annerstedt & Währborg, 2011; Gonzalez et al., 2009, 2011; Horowitz, 2012; Sempik et al., 2005).

Much of the early focus of TH was to promote rehabilitation of physical injuries or conditions (for example, Colson, 1944), but the expectation that nature is beneficial for psychological and emotional relief has a long history in the healing arts (Sempik et al., 2003). Benjamin Rush, the father of TH, wrote in the late 1700s about the benefits for persons with mental health problems of working in gardens or on farms, citing the importance of the activity of the body as well as the emotions that can be generated by involvement in agriculture for promoting mental health (Rush, 1812). A number of European countries developed programs starting in the mid-1800s, which used farm work as a treatment for individuals with psychiatric disorders, individuals with learning disabilities, and disadvantaged groups. For example, one of the earliest reports was of Johann Christian Reil, a Prussian reformer who advocated for the inclusion of "agriculture, cattle-breeding, and horticulture" to be included in asylum programs (Neuberger, 1995). TH efforts led to discussions in psychiatric journals during the later 1800s as to the pros and cons of this approach, which was promoted through "Agricultural Colonies" for individuals with learning disabilities (Neuberger et al., 2006). In North America, the first recorded TH program occurred in 1886 with the establishment of the Canadian Berkshire Farm Centre and Services for Youth, which served troubled children and their families. Around the same time, numerous psychiatric institutions in the US incorporated gardens into their programs, and gardening or landscaping historically has been a common activity in prisons and psychiatric hospitals (Sempik et al., 2003).

Professional interest in TH was not consistently maintained over the years because of the emergence of medications and psychotherapy in the early 1900s, but a resurgence of programs occurred as professionals recognized that medications and psychotherapy might have limited effectiveness—as well as pose other health risks (Neuberger et al. 2006)—suggesting that a broader perspective might be more efficacious. Italy developed social cooperatives in response to the closure of psychiatric institutions in the 1980s. Slovenian practitioners introduced social care and agriculture into privatized social service and care practices in the late 1990s. Similarly, in France and the Flanders, social farming initiatives were linked to citizens' desires to respond to the needs of particular disadvantaged groups (Di Iacovo & O'Connor, 2009). In contemporary Europe, most social farming and associated care programs are conducted by small-scale private farm owners; this is not the case in Germany where scientifically planned programs are funded by the state but implemented by a variety of interest groups (Di Iacovo & O'Connor, 2009). The Netherlands boasts more than 500 care farms, where clinicians send their clients as part of their prescribed therapy (Borchers & Bradshaw, 2008). Thus, TH continues to be considered a viable alternative program or adjunct to programs for individuals with mental health problems, particularly in Europe.

Use of the term "therapeutic" implies that the primary benefits of these horticulture programs are either physical or psychological rehabilitation. However, it is important to note that program developers are keenly aware of the vocational potential implicit in TH programs (Haller, 2003). Development of skills and work experience is often the next needed step for individuals with physical or mental difficulties, and TH programs are recognized as potentially providing clients with horticulture work experience that could later be directly applied in other occupational settings that involve working with plants, or that provides other benefits of a work experience that are still valuable in different job settings (for example, small business skills, accounting, marketing skills, meeting job expectations, and working on a team). TH programs, then, can potentially empower program recipients with economic benefits beyond the physically or psychologically therapeutic aspects of the programs.

The theoretical and empirical underpinnings of TH

Different forms of TH have been developed for specific purposes: social farms for social services, vocational training, and care; therapeutic gardens for cultivation of healing plants; healing gardens within health care facilities where individuals may go to relax and reflect; horticultural gardens designed for a targeted group of individuals to meet their therapeutic needs; community gardens designed to connect members of a local area as well as provide nutritional benefits; and restorative gardens to provide a space conducive to reducing stress and regaining mental strength. TH may exist as a structured program or as one in which participants are given more autonomy to be creative in their horticulture experience.

Most of the conceptual work and research into the impact of TH has focused on the psychological aspects that appear positively affected by the experience. Although the preference for the natural world may arise from our evolutionary background and cultural associations that people have developed in their interaction with nature, there are likely multifaceted explanations for why TH is hypothesized to produce psychological reduction of stress and actual restoration of mental functioning (Sempik et al., 2003). The proposition that working with plants in a natural environment may produce psychological benefits derives from various theoretical perspectives. One theory, *attention restoration theory*, draws on research showing that trauma and stress reduce an individual's attentional capacity and increase negative thoughts and rumination, which in turn lead to difficulties in problem-solving and effectively carrying out everyday activities (Kaplan, 1995). A restorative environment has been hypothesized to provide:

- escape from typical or troubling aspects of life;
- fascination through growing things and producing beauty;
- a feeling of being in a meaningful and orderly world; and
- an affinity with nature and the environment. (Kaplan & Kaplan, 1990)

Working in a garden, on a farm, or in another natural setting, then, is thought to give traumatized individuals psychological and emotional distance from negative distractions and reminders, thereby restoring their ability to heal and to attend to functional tasks (Gonzalez et al., 2009; Hartig et al., 1997). A second relevant theory, *conservation of resources (COR) theory*, maintains that traumatic life events—such as physical violence and psychological abuse in intimate relationships—produce "resource loss" for victims. Lost resources may include housing and income, social interaction with family and friends, and/or a reduced sense of self. These losses cause physical and psychological distress; however, according to COR theory, wellbeing can be improved through "resource gain," such as re-establishing safety, developing skills, and restoring self-efficacy (Hobfoll, 2001; Sullivan, 2012). By providing opportunities for resource gain, therefore, TH may improve participants' physical, psychological, and social wellbeing. In the case of IPV victims, such resource gains may translate into greater self-sufficiency and self-efficacy, and reduced risk of revictimization (Sullivan & Bybee, 1999).

Research evaluating TH programs in diverse settings has generally found them to be effective for reducing stress, depression, and negative feelings, and in promoting relaxation, social inclusion, and self-confidence. In a systematic review of 35 controlled studies and three meta-analyses, Annerstedt and Währborg (2011) found that "nature-assisted therapies" have three main types of positive outcomes: 1) short-term recovery from stress and mental fatigue; 2) faster recovery from illness; and 3) long-term overall improvement in health and wellbeing.

For example, Stigsdotter and Grahn (2004) studied residents of "high stress" urban neighborhoods and found that those with access to a garden had significantly lower "sensitivity to stress" (an index measure of stress, irritation, and fatigue) than those without access to a garden, and that participants who simply visited a garden experienced a reduction in sensitivity to stress. In two prospective studies with samples of Norwegian individuals identified as clinically depressed, Gonzalez et al. (2009, 2011) reported that a 12-week TH program significantly reduced depression scores for participants, both during the intervention and at 3-month follow-up. And in the most extensive evaluation of TH programs for vulnerable groups to date, Sempik et al. (2005) found that such interventions improve nutrition and dietary habits; raise self-esteem and perceptions of self-worth through the status gained from being a "gardener" or "worker"; increase self-confidence and satisfaction by learning new skills, acquiring knowledge, and producing food or craft objects; and reduce social isolation through group activities (see also Son et al., 2004; Yamane et al., 2004).

These outcomes suggest that a sense of accomplishment, focused attention away from the negative, development of potential skills, social contact, tangible products, and a sense of meaning may all derive from exposure to TH—all potentially useful outcomes for victims of IPV. But the research literature to support the *social benefits* of engaging in TH is limited and mostly anecdotal, and the variability in groups for whom TH has been employed reduces the ability to know whether this benefit is actually more likely to occur with *particular* targeted groups. In addition, the type of TH employed may differentially affect social benefits; community gardens, for example, are more likely to facilitate social contact (Sempik, et al. 2003). Although there is some empirical support for psychological benefits from TH, evidence to date does not demonstrate support for improvements in physical functioning in physically impaired individuals who engage in TH. Unfortunately, it is difficult to compare across programs using TH to address specific physical conditions or impairments, because they target a vast range of physical functioning—from cardiovascular problems to obesity to musculoskeletal pain. However, *general* physical benefits from TH, agrotherapy, or farm work in various groups exposed to TH have not been empirically assessed.

Applicability of TH to domestic violence shelters

Domestic violence shelters could potentially employ several forms of TH to address the restorative needs of residents, generate a food supply and enhance nutrition, and provide work experiences that could economically empower abused women. Shelter staff recognize that battered women arrive with multiple problems that must be addressed if their shelter stay is to be successful and their post-shelter decisions are not determined by the problems present when they arrived. TH, with its physical, mental, and skill-building components, may contribute to the wellbeing of shelter residents through a variety of direct and indirect impacts.

The model by which we hypothesize that a range of beneficial outcomes may result for domestic violence shelter residents participating in a TH program—above and beyond the shelter's standard programming—asserts that "working the land," or even simply using farm products in daily or creative activities, encompasses many elements or dimensions that individually have the potential to impact a range of physical, psychological, and functional outcomes (Figure 2). The multiplicity of potential outcomes that could be beneficial to shelter residents come from the aspects of TH that involve physical activity, the process of cultivating and producing food, an attentional component, a sensory experience in nature, skill development, and opportunities for informal social contact. The immediate and basic mechanisms arising from these dimensions are an altered self-view in terms of increased self-esteem and self-sufficiency due to participants' accomplishments; a complex of restoration, tranquility, and distraction leading to mental recovery; and a sense of belonging. These, in turn, may impact physical wellbeing; reduce anxiety, depression, and cognitive disruption—all of which affect mental wellbeing; improve social inclusion; and increase skills, including financial literacy and marketable job skills.

Interestingly, there is evidence that TH programs are beginning to be developed for IPV victims, particularly those who have taken refuge at shelters. One program in California—Project GROW—was piloted from Spring 1999 to Winter 2000, with the goals of increasing the food security of the shelters while simultaneously contributing to the healing and empowerment of shelter residents (Stuart, 2005). An evaluation of this program, however, had serious methodological limitations (for example, survey or interview data were collected from only 5% of program participants), making the findings ungeneralizable. Nevertheless, those who supplied feedback regarding their experience in the program were positive about its impact, suggesting that TH may have promise for producing beneficial outcomes in domestic violence shelter settings (see also Lee et al., 2008). Domestic violence shelters that are considering adding horticulture in some form to their standard programming need to assess:

- Specifically, which outcomes from TH might be useful for victims of IPV;
- Whether incorporating horticulture into one's programming is actually effective in producing desired changes in the *shelter's* targeted outcomes;
- Whether this potential addition to a shelter's programming is different from introducing other economically empowering strategies to shelter residents; and
- Whether inclusion of horticulture can actually generate a unique environment resulting in stronger and wider ranging therapeutic effects than standard programming.

These questions have yet to be answered.

Figure 2: Model of Hypothesized Mechanisms and Outcomes Resulting from TH Project Conditions of Physically Working the Land or Using Farm Products

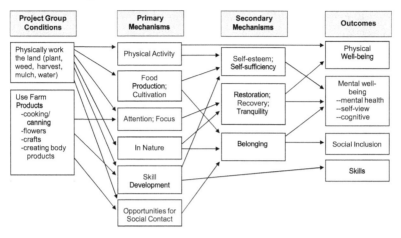

GreenHouse17

As noted, GreenHouse17, a battered women's shelter located in Lexington, KY, has established a farm program that draws on the principles of TH to provide residents with a variety of potentially beneficial activities[3]. Under the supervision of a paid professional farmer and farm manager (whose responsibilities include farm-to-table utilization of the harvest), residents are offered voluntary opportunities to participate in farming activities, and those who wish to actively work the land (for example, prepare beds, mulch, plant, water, weed, harvest) may commit to 9 hours of labor per week in exchange for a small stipend as compensation. Residents who do not wish to engage directly in farming may participate in farm-related activities, such as cooking farm-to-table, arranging flowers, and making crafts and body products from harvested products. The harvested produce and flowers are sold at local farmers' markets. Community members have the option of ordering flower arrangements for special events (such as weddings), or purchasing body products (for example, lip balm or soap) at farmers' markets, pop-up sales, or online. In addition to being able to earn income, shelter residents gain financial literacy and entrepreneurial and marketing skills, and have an employer who can provide them with a reference for other jobs. The farm is also an adjunct to the therapeutic services offered at the shelter, in that its mission is to create an agriculture-based therapeutic environment with the potential to improve residents' physical, psychological, and emotional wellbeing.

Thus, the farm program at GreenHouse17 is designed to provide: physical activity, companionable social interaction, and serenity for IPV victims; a source of nutritional and seasonal field-to-table food for shelter residents; and opportunities for self-sufficiency and microenterprise. All of these program elements may reduce the negative effects of IPV victimization, while promoting financial stability, self-efficacy, self-sufficiency, and improved physical and mental health—which, in turn, may reduce the risk of revictimization.

To what extent has the farm program achieved these goals? An evaluation of the program is currently underway. The first phase of the evaluation, which focused largely on shelter staff's perceptions of the impact of the farm program, suggested positive outcomes for program participants (Renzetti & Follingstad, 2015). Many staff were initially skeptical of the farm program; some openly worried that it would detract from the primary mission of the shelter—that is, to provide a safe, healing home environment to women fleeing abuse. But staff's direct observations of the program's significant physical, psychological, and social benefits for shelter residents led them to overcome these early reservations. Benefits to residents reported by the staff include economic empowerment, exercise, better nutrition, stress reduction, increased self-esteem, sustained sobriety, and reduced social isolation. In addition, staff perceived several benefits to themselves—the most important being expanded opportunities to deliver services. And staff maintain that the farm program has resulted in unexpected benefits for the shelter as a whole, because it has garnered favorable media attention for the shelter and increased community awareness of the problem of IPV and the need for and impact of shelter services.

These findings, though, are anecdotal. The second phase of the evaluation thus includes a quasi-experimental study to collect data from residents, which will allow us to compare the physical, psychological, social, and economic effects of direct farm program participation with participation in farm-related activities and no farm program participation. Data will also be collected post-shelter-stay to help evaluate the impact of program participation on revictimization experiences.

Given that few shelters are located on farmland, some observers may object that a TH shelter–based program will have limited utility in most communities. Importantly, however, TH programs similar to the one at GreenHouse17 can be adapted and implemented in a variety of environments, including urban areas, via techniques such as container gardening and rooftop gardening.

The importance of cultural competence: Pigs for Peace (PFP)

There has been considerable debate about whether economic empowerment is always beneficial to women, given that some researchers have found that labor force participation and financial decision making may actually precipitate or worsen IPV in some contexts (Grzywacz et al., 2009; MacMillan & Gartner, 1999; Tsai, 2016; Schuler et al., 2016). Studies of women participating in microfinance programs, for example, have obtained mixed findings. Some researchers report that the increased independence and elevated status that women experience as a result of successful microfinance participation are perceived by their husbands as undermining men's authority and dominance, which consequently leads to greater IPV (see, for instance, Schuler et al., 2016). Others, though, report a decrease in IPV following successful microfinance participation, and still others show no change in IPV (Murshid & Zippay, 2016). As Murshid and Zippay (2016) point out, microfinance programs, with their goals of socially and economically empowering women and promoting gender equality, are accessed by millions of poor women throughout the developing world. They are, in fact, the "cornerstone of anti-poverty efforts" in many countries (Murshid & Zippay, 2016, p. 2); therefore, research to evaluate their impact on IPV victimization is clearly warranted.

Glass and her colleagues (Glass et al, 2012, 2014) have been evaluating a microfinance program in eastern Democratic Republic of Congo (DRC) that appears to both economically empower women and improve their mental health following severe trauma, which includes sexual and gender-based violence (for example, war rape and IPV). The program, Pigs for Peace (PFP), is the product of a collaboration between a Congolese microfinance organization and the Johns Hopkins School of Nursing, Baltimore, MD. Like other microfinance programs, PFP provides a loan to a household—in this case, prioritizing the economic empowerment of women and their families[4]. But unlike most other microfinance programs, PFP's loan is not in the form of money; rather, it is a 2–4-month-old female pig. The loan recipient assumes primary responsibility for caring for the pig, including building a pen, providing it with adequate food, and ensuring its health. PFP agents assist, and also provide male pigs to impregnate the female pigs. When the piglets are born (twice a year, with 6–12 piglets per litter), loan recipients repay the loan by giving two piglets from the first litter to PFP, which, in turn, uses them to bring more households into the program.

To evaluate the impact of the program, Glass et al. (2012, 2014) used a lottery to randomly assign eligible women to the PFP program or a delayed control group[5]. Nearly all participants had experienced multiple conflict-related traumatic events, as well as a high rate of IPV. Not surprisingly, baseline measures showed that symptoms of PTSD, chronic stress, and depression were widespread and severe among participants. Post-intervention data, however, showed significant reductions of all symptoms.

Several aspects of the PFP program are especially noteworthy. First, as Glass et al. (2012, 2014) pointed out, livestock such as pigs are a traditional rural asset. They are raised, bred, and sold, serving not as a direct source of food, but rather as a "savings account"—a liquid asset that can be used as needed for economic opportunities (for example, to pay school fees or to build or repair a home) or in emergencies (for example, the illness or death of a family member). Consequently, PFP provides access to and control over an income-generating activity that helps women rebuild the financial stability of their families. PFP is particularly beneficial to women, because in DRC—as in many economically undeveloped and/or conflict-stricken areas—women have few, if any, assets that could be used as collateral for traditional types of loans, including microfinance or microcredit.

The use of pigs as the livestock in this intervention also demonstrates the program's attention to cultural competence. Specifically, there are no religious or cultural taboos in the DRC against raising and breeding pigs. Perhaps more importantly, raising, breeding and selling pigs is a gender-neutral economic activity in which both women and men can participate "to improve social, health and economic outcomes for their family" (Glass et al., 2014, p. 11). The cultural competence of the program, then, may be a critical component in terms of preventing IPV, although there are currently no data available to test this hypothesis.

The evaluation research that has been conducted indicates that the social and health benefits of the PFP program for women stem from their ability to provide for their families, which strengthens their self-esteem and also raises their status in the larger community. Despite these positive outcomes, though, a single livestock/animal asset program is not going to ameliorate the severely detrimental effects of trauma and violence in women's lives, which Glass and her colleagues (2014) readily acknowledge. In addition, as we have noted, there is a need for continued evaluation to determine if the PFP program helps to reduce women's *revictimization* by gender-based violence—which is, after all, the goal of tertiary prevention (see also Pronyk et al., 2006).

Conclusion

Shelters and victim advocacy programs have been leaders in tertiary IPV prevention efforts for more than three decades. Over the years, the services offered by shelters and advocacy programs have expanded to include economic empowerment programs. This is in recognition of the fact that financial hardship and instability play a significant role in motivating women who have experienced IPV to return to abusive partners, which substantially increases their risk of revictimization.

In this chapter, we discussed several types of economic empowerment programs, including a financial literacy program, a TH program, and a microfinance program. Early evaluation findings indicate that these programs appear to have financial and social benefits for IPV survivors, but their success as tertiary prevention strategies is still undetermined. At least one evaluation, using a quasi-experimental design, is underway to examine the tertiary prevention effects of a shelter-based TH program. Clearly, however, additional, rigorously designed research is needed to tease out the preventative impact of economic empowerment programs on IPV revictimization.

Notes

1. The randomized control trial (RCT) is considered the "gold standard" in evaluation research design. However, because of ethical, legal, and sometimes financial concerns it often is not possible to implement an RCT, especially when the study sample is from a highly vulnerable population.
2. The ordering of these goals is not intended to reflect a hierarchy of the shelter's priorities.
3. A brief history of the development of the GreenHouse17 farm program is provided by Renzetti and Follingstad (2015).
4. Individuals aged 16 and older are eligible to participate if they are the responsible householder (for example, if they are married, responsible for younger siblings because of the death of parents, or widowed). They must also be permanent residents of the participating villages, and express a commitment to and understanding of microfinance principles (for example, repayment of the loan). Although women are targeted, men are not excluded. Many microfinance programs, however, are open only to women, because research has shown that women are more likely than men to use the income they earn for their families and meeting household needs (Murshid & Zippay, 2016).
5. Those in the delayed control group eventually received a loan, but only after the initial participants in the PFP program had repaid their loans.

References

Adams, A.E., Sullivan, C.M., Bybee, D., & Greeson, M.R. (2008). Development of the Scale of Economic Abuse. *Violence Against Women, 14*, 563–588.

Annerstedt, M., & Währborg, P. (2011). Nature-assisted therapy: Systematic review of controlled and observational studies. *Scandinavian Journal of Public Health, 39*, 371–388.

Borchers, J.G., & Bradshaw, G.A. (2008, December). How green is my valley—and mind: Ecotherapy and the greening of psychology. *Counseling Today*, 38–41.

Brush, L.D. (2011). *Poverty, battered women, and work in US public policy*. New York: Oxford University Press.

Christy-McMullin, K. (2000). An analysis of the Assets for Independence Act of 1998 for abused women. *Violence Against Women, 6*, 1066–1084.

Colson, J.H.C. (1944). *The rehabilitation of the injured*. London: Cassell.

Di Iacovo, F., & O'Connor, D. (Eds.) (2009). *Supporting policies for social farming in Europe: Progressing multifunctionality in responsive rural areas*. Florence, Italy: ARSIA.

Farber, N., & Miller-Cribs, J.E. (2014). Violence in the lives of rural, southern, and poor white women. *Violence Against Women, 20*, 517–538.

Glass, N., Perrin, N.A., Kohli, A., & Remy, M.M. (2014). Livestock/animal assets buffer the impact of conflict-related traumatic events on mental health symptoms for rural women. *PLoS ONE, 9*(11): e111708. doi: 10.1371/journal.pone.0111708.

Glass, N., Ramazani, P., Tosha, M., Mpanano, M., & Cinyabuguma, M. (2012). A Congolese–US participatory action research partnership to rebuild the lives of rape survivors and their families in eastern Democratic Republic of Congo. *Global Public Health, 7*(2), 184–195.

Gonzalez, M.T., Hartig, T., Patil, G.G., Martinsen, E.W., & Kirkevold, M. (2009). Therapeutic horticulture in clinical depression: A prospective study. *Research and Theory for Nursing Practice, 23*, 312–328.

Gonzalez, M.T., Hartig, T., Patil, G.G., Martinsen, E.W. & Kirkevold, M. (2011). A prospective study of group cohesiveness in therapeutic horticulture for clinical depression. *International Journal of Mental Health Nursing, 20*, 119–129.

Goodman, L.A., & Epstein, D. (2009). *Listening to battered women: A survivor-centered approach to advocacy, mental health and justice*. Washington, DC: American Psychological Association.

Grzywacz, J.G., Rao, P., Gentry, A., Marin, A., & Acury, T.A. (2009). Acculturation and conflict in Mexican immigrants' intimate partnerships: The role of women's labor force participation. *Violence Against Women*, *15*(10), 1194–1212.

Haller, R. (2003). Vocational, social, and therapeutic programs in horticulture. In S. Simson & M. Straus (Eds.), *Horticulture as therapy: Principles and practice* (pp. 43–68). Boca Raton, FL: CRC Press.

Hamby, S., & Bible, A. (2009). Battered women's protective strategies. *VAWnet*. Retrieved from: www.vawnet.org.

Hartig, T., Korpela, K., Evans, G.W., & Gärling, T. (1997). A measure of restorative quality in environments. *Scandinavian Housing & Planning Research*, *14*, 175–194.

Hobfoll, S.E. (2001). The influence of culture, community, and the nested-self in the stress process: Advancing conservation resource theory. *Applied Psychology*, *50*, 337–370.

Horowitz, S. (2012). Therapeutic gardens and horticultural therapy: Growing roles in health care. *Alternative and Complementary Therapies*, *18*, 78–83.

Kaplan, R., & Kaplan, S. (1990). Restorative experience: The healing power of nearby nature. In M. Francis & R.T. Hester (Eds.), *The meaning of gardens* (pp. 238–243). Cambridge, MA: MIT Press.

Kaplan, S. (1995). The restorative benefits of nature: Toward an integrative framework. *Journal of Environmental Psychology*, *15*, 169–182.

Lee, S., Kim, M.S., & Suh, J.K. (2008). Effects of horticultural therapy on self-esteem and depression of battered women at a shelter in Korea. *Acta Horticulturae*, *790*, 139–142.

MacMillan, R., & Gartner, R. (1999). When she brings home the bacon: Labor force participation and risk of spousal violence against women. *Journal of Marriage and the Family*, *61*, 947–958.

Macy, R.J., Giattina, M., Sangster, T.H., Crosby, C., & Montijo, N.J. (2009). Domestic violence and sexual assault services: Inside the black box. *Aggression and Violent Behavior*, *14*, 359–373.

Moe, A.M., & Bell, M.P. (2004). Abject economics: The effects of battering and violence on women's work and employability. *Violence Against Women*, *10*, 29–55.

Morreau, L.E. (1979). Methods for developing charting skills and evaluative techniques. Presented at the 7th Annual Conference of the National Council for Therapy and Rehabilitation Through Horticulture, Mt Vernon, VA.

Murshid, N.S., & Zippay, A. (2016). Microfinance participation and marital violence in Bangladesh: A qualitative inquiry. *Violence Against Women.* doi: 10:1177/1077801216665480 (Epub ahead of print).

Neuberger, K.R. (1995). Pedagogics and horticultural therapy: The favorite task of Mr Huber., digging up potatoes. *Acta Horticulturae, 391,* 241–248.

Neuberger, K., Stephan, I., Hermanowski, R., Flake, A., Post, F-J., & Van Elsen, T. (2006). Farming for health: Aspects from Germany. In J. Hassink & M. van Dijk (Eds.), *Farming for health* (pp. 193-211). Netherlands: Springer.

Perez, S., Johnson, D.M., & Wright, C.V. (2012). The attenuating effect empowerment on IPV-related PTSD symptoms in battered women living in domestic violence shelters. *Violence Against Women, 18,* 102–117.

Postmus, J.L. (2010). Economic empowerment of domestic violence survivors. *VAWnet.* Retrieved from: www.vawnet.org.

Postmus, J.L., & Plummer, S.B. (2010). *Validating the Allstate Foundation's national model on helping survivors of violence achieve economic self-sufficiency: Final report.* New Brunswick, NJ: Rutgers University School of Social Work, Center on Violence Against Women and Children.

Postmus, J.L., Plummer, S.B., & Stylianou, A.M. (2015). Measuring economic abuse in the lives of survivors: Revising the Scale of Economic Abuse. *Violence Against Women.* doi: 1077801215610012 (Epub ahead of print).

Pronyk, P.M., Hargraves, J.R., Kim, J.C., Morison, L.M., Phetla, G., Watts, C., et al. (2006). Effect of a structural intervention for the prevention of intimate partner violence and HIV in rural South Africa: A cluster randomised trial. *Lancet, 368,* 1973–1983.

Pruitt, L.R. (2008). Place matters: Domestic violence and rural difference. *Wisconsin Journal of Law, Gender and Society, 23,* 346–416.

Renzetti, C.M., & Follingstad, D.R. (2015). From blue to green: The development and implementation of a therapeutic horticulture program for residents of a battered women's shelter. *Violence and Victims, 30,* 676–690.

Rush, B. (1812). *Medical inquiries and observations upon diseases of the mind.* Philadelphia: Kimber & Richardson.

Sanders, C.K. (2014). Economic abuse in the lives of women abused by an intimate partner: A qualitative study. *Violence Against Women, 21,* 3–29.

Schuler, S.R., Lenzi, R., Badal, S.H., & Bates, L.M. (2016). Women's empowerment as a protective factor against intimate partner violence in Bangladesh. *Violence Against Women*. doi: 10.1177/1077801216654576 (Epub ahead of print).

Sempik, J., Aldridge, J., & Becker, S. (2003). *Social and therapeutic horticulture: Evidence and messages from research*. Lougborough: Loughborough University Media Services.

Sempik, J., Aldridge, J., & Becker, S. (2005). *Health, well-being and social inclusion: Therapeutic horticulture in the UK*. Bristol: Policy Press.

Son, K.C., Song, J.E., Um, S.J., Lee, S.J., & Kwack, H.R. (2004). Effects of visual recognition of green plants on the changes of EEG in patients with schizophrenia. *Acta Horticulurae, 639*, 193–199.

Stigsdotter, U.A., & Grahn, P. (2004). *A garden at your doorstep may reduce stress: Private gardens as restorative environments in the city*. Proceedings of the "Open space: People space" conference on inclusive outdoor environments, Edinburgh, Scotland.

Stuart, S.M. (2005). Lifting spirits: Creating gardens in California domestic violence shelters. In P.F. Barlett (Ed.), *Urban place: Reconnecting with the natural world* (pp. 61–88). Cambridge, MA: MIT Press.

Sullivan, C.M. (2012). *Examining the work of domestic violence programs within a "social and emotional well-being promotion" conceptual framework*. Harrisburg, PA: National Resource Center on Domestic Violence. Retrieved from: www.dvevidenceproject.org/publications/.

Sullivan, C.M., & Bybee, D.I. (1999). Reducing violence using community-based advocacy for women with abusive partners. *Journal of Consulting and Clinical Psychology, 67*, 43–53.

Sutherland, C.A., Bybee, D.M., & Sulivan, C.M. (2002). Beyond bruises and broken bones: The joint effects of stress and injuries on battered women's health. *American Journal of Community Psychology, 30*, 609–636.

Tsai, L.C. (2016). Household financial management and women's experiences of intimate partner violence in the Philippines: A study using propensity score methods. *Violence Against Women*. doi: 10.1177/1077801216642869 (Epub ahead of print).

Yamane, K., Kawashima, M., Fujishige, N., & Yoshida, M. (2004). Effects of interior horticultural activities with potted plants on human physiological and emotional status. *Acta Horticulturae, 639*, 37–43.

TEN

Preventing Intimate Partner Violence: Thinking Forward[1]

Shamita Das Dasgupta

Introduction

The anti-violence against women movement in the US gathered force in the 1970s, with the focus on assisting battered women and victims of rape to escape abusive relationships and seek justice (Bograd, 1988; Pence & Shepard, 1999; Schechter, 1982, 1988; Tierney, 1982). Internationally, this trajectory was repeated in various countries in the 1970s and 1980s, with the objectives of not only responding to individual violence against women but also establishing structural changes to equalize power between the genders. Quite rightly, the central motivation of the burgeoning movement in the US was to ensure safety as well as care for victims. Emerging from the feminist movement, much of the early endeavors were individual and collective efforts that received little or no official recognition or support at the time. The activism to end battering and rape developed its own feminist philosophy and interdisciplinary methods of intervention that gave primacy to victims' voices and needs (French et al., 1998; Hall, 2015; Pence, 1999). The movement struggled to bring a common experience to the public that was hitherto considered private, and simultaneously challenged the state to take responsibility for the safety of its female citizenry. Activists realized that the movement must channel the formidable authority of the state to equalize the social power differentials between the genders (read: perpetrator and victim), which rendered women vulnerable to intimate abuse (for example,

Anderson, 2005; Kaur & Garg, 2010; Naved & Persson, 2010; Pence & Paymar, 1993; World Health Organization, 2009). It is due to the pioneering activism of battered and sexually abused women and their allies that domestic relationships and women's right to be safe everywhere, especially in their homes, are no longer considered beyond the purview of the state.

As the state was urged to protect women from abuse by their loved ones through legal sanctions, women mobilized to establish safe residences and helplines for those who were fleeing violent relationships and homes (Barner & Carney, 2011; Saathoff & Stoffel, 1999; Tierney, 1982; Williamson & Abrahams, 2014). With the availability of state funding, these early shelters expanded into advocacy organizations to assist battered and sexually assaulted women to negotiate legal and social service systems that victims often found unsympathetic, baffling, and harsh. Consequently, groups of ancillary advocacy organizations began to challenge institutional policies and practices, and reshape them to centralize battered and sexually violated women's safety and needs (DePrince et al., 2012; Pence, 1999; Pence & McDonnell, 1999; Pence & Shepard, 1988; Shetty & Kaguyutan, 2011). The main institutions that were first targeted for reform were the law enforcement and justice systems—prominent state forces that tend to intervene in victims' lives whether they desire it or not. The idea was to rid these institutions of biases against women, which had hitherto erected barriers to safeguarding battered and sexually abused women and holding (male) perpetrators accountable. Thus, among the advocacy organizations that came forth to work exclusively with battered and sexually abused women, some concentrated on providing needed services, others on reforming critical institutions in society, and still others attempted to integrate both. However, although the expressed goal of the movement was to end violence against women, if and when organizations engaged in prevention work it was confined to community awareness raising. At times, such consciousness raising included educational programs in schools. The emphasis on raising awareness among school-age children came from the recognition that childhood socialization in gender equity and nonviolent interpersonal interactions might be the key to ending violence against girls and women.

The excessive highlighting of intervention to the detriment of prevention was mainly due to the demands of the advocacy community, which searched for ways to safeguard and heal the survivor of violence, convince the government of the need to challenge structural inequities, and coax funding agencies to meet the needs of services for victims/ survivors. As violence against women became acknowledged as a global "epidemic" (Heise, 1994; Garcia-Moreno, Jansen, Ellsberg, Heise, & Watts, 2005), and its emotional, physical, and material costs appraised, practitioners from various disciplines joined in the movement to contribute toward the ultimate ending of violence against girls and women. Feminist scholarship in various fields has also collaborated to strengthen the analyses, advocacies, and services that define the contemporary anti-violence against women movement.

This chapter sketches some thoughts on effective prevention and ways that different stakeholders may work toward reducing—and ending—domestic and sexual violence. It categorizes a few general pathways and charts issues that might facilitate or create barriers to preventing violence against girls and women. In the background of this chapter is a brainstorming meeting on prevention of violence against women that was held for two days in 2014. Thus, at times, the chapter draws from the collective wisdom of the participants at the gathering. In addition, it culls findings from prevention research on diverse populations in various cultures. Some of the themes on prevention that have emerged focus on systems-level reforms; others focus on vaster cultural modifications that would transform whole communities and gender norms (Bruce, 2002; Fabiano et al., 2004).

However, whether these changes would actually yield the desired outcome of preventing/ending violence against women and girls remains an open question. One of the major issues that neither research nor advocacy seems to have addressed and resolved is whether "preventing" and "ending" are conceptually distinct. Most advocates and researchers have used the terms interchangeably. This chapter considers "prevention" as a practical step toward reaching the actual goal of ending violence against girls and women. That is, any activity that *permanently* reduces or stops incidents of domestic and sexual violence is preventive. Accordingly, the term "preventing" is used to refer to an action that would lead to the objective of ultimately "ending" violence against girls and women.

Larger social modification

Shifting cultural norms and traditions

Historically, every society maintained misogynous practices of woman abuse through the justification that girls and women deserve it, and men—particularly husbands, fathers, brothers, and other male relatives—are entitled to "discipline" recalcitrant women and girls.

Thus, men were (and in many societies still are) allowed to "chastise" girls and women to rectify their conduct—"chastisement" that usually escalated into injurious violence. More frequently than not, such violence was perpetrated with impunity. Over time, although many societies have endeavored to stop this trend (particularly in the West), violence against girls and women still continues unabated in most countries around the globe. In every region of the world, girls and women are still routinely harassed, beaten, maimed, sexually violated, burned alive, stabbed, shot, doused in acid, genitally mutilated, and killed outright—because they are viewed as deserving of abuse. Such "correcting" is exemplified by the "religious police" in many countries that publicly beat and torture women perceived to be defying the "good woman" moral code.

Even where such flagrant public mistreatment is frowned upon, more subtle forms of coercive control—such as public shaming, sexual harassment, and child marriage—abound. The so-called "honor killing" of girls and women by their family members is an extreme example of a practice that purports to justifiably punish females for transgressing social and familial rules of "decent" conduct, as defined by men (Gupte, 2015; Gupte et al., 2012; Mayell, 2002; Sev'er, 2012). Advantaging males has led to selective abortion of female fetuses in many countries (Abrevaya, 2009; DasGupta & Dasgupta, 2010; Madge, 2014; Puri et al., 2011), while girls and women who are (un)fortunate enough to be born are routinely deprived of opportunities in society, confined to the home, trafficked, forced into marriage, exchanged for money and favors, coerced into prostitution, and pushed to give birth (or not). All because they are considered nothing more than chattel.

Although gender is the prime factor of vulnerability in violence against women, it is certainly not the only one. Class, caste, sexuality, disability, citizenship, and other social markers intersect with gender in complex ways (Arnold & Ake, 2013). The commonality among these factors is that all are rooted in the endeavor to maintain a hierarchy of patriarchal power and control in society.

Most cultures have generated traditions and practices that deliberately limit girls' and women's emotional, physical, sexual, and material opportunities, as well as their freedom to actualize their potential and enjoy life to the fullest. In nearly every culture, men have been ascribed both higher status than women by virtue of their gender, and the right to control girls and women by harsh means. Various cultural norms and practices that correlate with patriarchal subjugation of girls and women reinforce and/or contribute significantly to the violence against them (for example, Anton, 2005; Banyard et al., 2007;

Berkowitz, 2003; Warrier, 2005). Sex-selective abortion; restrictions on female education and mobility; dowry; female genital mutilation/cutting (FGM); child marriage; prohibitions against divorce; and early pregnancy are only a few examples of worldwide traditions that set the stage for abuse of girls and women. While no culture is monolithic, and all have traditions that cherish as well as disenfranchise the feminine, each is rife with the possibility of violence perpetrated at the whim of masculinist ideologies and structures. Societies socialize their members so profoundly in patriarchal beliefs that large numbers of men carry the attitudes of justifiable violence as a way of sanctioning women—and women themselves police their sisterhood to remain within the boundaries of these gender traditions, accepting and even condoning violence against apparent transgressors. The majority of laws and institutional practices in every society also reflect the cultural misogyny that is its legacy (Pence, 1999; Pence & McDonnell, 1999; Pence & Shepard, 1988). The inequities generated by structural unevenness contribute strongly to the relentless continuation of violence against girls and women.

The pervasive ideologies of societal misogyny that result in violence against girls and women might also render public health approaches to prevention rather ineffectual. Such approaches promote the perspective: "If people could be taught to wear seatbelts in cars within a short period of time, they could certainly learn to stop violence against girls and women." The problem with this is that it assumes violence against girls and women to be only a *behavioral* issue. Once we recognize that violence against the female arises from deeper and historically entrenched convictions about gender roles and intergender relationships, which are similar to religious dogmas—rather than more superficial behaviors and practices, such as wearing seat belts—the complexities and difficulties with prevention become obvious. It becomes apparent that, to prevent violence against women and girls, there needs to be a fundamental paradigm shift and significant resocialization in new egalitarian cultural values, beliefs, and practices.

While most researchers and activists alike agree that cultures need to be changed if the goals of preventing—and ultimately ending—violence against girls and women are to be achieved, no one is quite sure how this can be done on a grand scale. The current emphasis on "going back to the community" to find answers does not necessarily fill one with optimism. It is in the communities that women and girls were (and continue to be) abused with impunity in the first place. While modifying cultures through institutional changes is certainly an option, the process is tedious, and durability of those shifts tenuous. Progressive, women-centered laws and institutional practices remain at the mercy of the strength of convictions of the next group of legislators and other institutional authorities. From 2010 onward, women's reproductive rights, firmly established for nearly 40 years, have been deliberately and persistently curtailed in the US. We see this in opposition to women's abortion rights and rights to free contraceptives, as well as in governmental defunding of women's healthcare clinics.

Most countries are nibbling away at the edges of violence against girls and women with laws and state-sponsored services, as a result of being pushed by international bodies such as the United Nations (for example, the Convention on the Elimination of all Forms of Discrimination Against Women [CEDAW], 1979; Declaration on the Elimination of Violence against Women [DEVAW], 1993). However, deep-seated androcentric traditions and practices have not yet been seriously challenged. Part of the problem is that no one wants to throw the "baby out with the bathwater;" that is, not destroy the acceptable and nourishing traditions of a culture while dismantling the misogynist, classist, homophobic, and other discriminatory parts. However, such selective unpacking and erasure of cultural contents might be difficult to achieve. Different components of a culture and the belief systems that feed them tend to be so integrally intertwined that disassembling some but keeping other parts intact might prove to be impossible. This unacknowledged aspect of cultural change work to neutralize gender disparities needs to be interrogated and debated further to design effective strategies. It might also be the reason why most prevention activism occurs in small, well-defined areas and some of its achievements are superficial, temporary, and often subverted by rampant misogyny in a culture.

The majority of research that has been conducted on culture and sexual and domestic violence against girls and women has attempted to identify the kinds of traditions and practices that heighten women's vulnerability to abuse in the family and community; relationships and beliefs that create barriers for women wishing to leave abusive relationships or seek help; and resources available to ameliorate the situation. While most such studies conclude by indicating the need for cultural alterations that will neutralize the conditions of violence against girls and women, they do not offer fool-proof strategy details to bring about the required changes. That is, even when there is a call for massive cultural modifications, it is not clear how exactly those changes could be induced, implemented, and sustained (Casey & Lindhorst, 2009). There is little evidence-based information on effective social change that is comprehensive, profound, and permanent.

Challenging religion

Often, it is practically impossible to send out messages against gender inequality and gender-based violence (GBV) in communities and initiate gender parity due to religious beliefs that posit gender roles as divinely ordained. Most religions include ideologies that disenfranchise women, as well as principles that empower the feminine. Unfortunately, it is the anti-female tenets that have gained the stature of "cultural traditions," to the disadvantage of creeds that support women. Thus, a significant part of transforming a culture must entail analyzing religions to shed light on their misogynist traditions, and replacing these with women-affirming maxims (Anton, 2005). While Christian feminists in the US have been discussing the roles religion and faith leaders play in preventing and perhaps even ending violence against women, similar efforts are not as common in other religious communities. Nonetheless, most activists around the world are gradually recognizing the impressive power religion has in bringing about change in the lives of the observant. A case in point is the diverse religion of Islam, which has historically been dubbed as ferociously anti-women. Women Living Under Muslim Laws (n.d.) and other Islamic feminist scholars have been reinterpreting the Quran to challenge purportedly religiously sanctioned gender discrimination (Badran, 1995, 2009; Hassan, 1999; Hussain, 1984; Mernissi, 1975; Zakaria, 2014). These scholars state that the Quran provides extensive social, educational, legal, and economic rights to women, which have generally been overlooked by both the followers of the religion and outsiders.

Muslims in many communities have been struggling to establish gender-just societies in line with the feminist philosophies embedded in the Holy Book. For example, led by a group of feminist Muslim women, the Islamic Center of Long Island (ICLI) in New York took measures to equalize power in marriage. The group observed that, in their community, men frequently either sought legal divorce without giving women religious divorce, or secured a religious divorce without legally ending the marriage. The same happened with marriages where a religious wedding was not followed up with legal recognition of the union, or vice versa. The upshot of this legal and religious disjuncture was that women who were only religiously married ran into difficulties with immigration services if the marriage did not work out, and "divorced" women were actually not free from their marriages—either legally or morally. With the support of the Imam, ICLI implemented the rule that both *nikah* (Islamic marriage) and *talaq* (equivalent to divorce) must correspond with legal marriage and divorce in the US.

Furthermore, going against the tradition that only men may ask for divorce, ICLI has created a template for *nikah* contract that allows women to seek divorce independently (personal communication with Ms. Rukhsana Ayyub and Shaida Khan, past ICLI directors).

In my experience of urging Hindu and Muslim survivors of domestic and sexual violence to make changes in their lives, I found that, until I began to quote passages from scriptures that denounce GBV, women assumed that their effort to seek justice was tantamount to betraying their religions and cultures.

Educating communities

One of the methods of cultural transformation identified by researchers and activists alike is educating communities to raise awareness of the harms effected by violence against women and girls, and thus bring about changes in beliefs, attitudes, and practices. The approach is based on the idea that most communities take pride in being fair and have faith in justice and thus, if made aware, would consciously make the move to prevent GBV. As such, advocacy agencies and scholars have expended considerable efforts to design educational curricula and learning models to provoke community conscience regarding violence against women. Each curriculum is designed to have maximum impact on the target community. For instance, curricula that harken back to a community's past history of gender equality and honoring of the female are utilized to inspire the community's members to revive their revered conventions. A few examples of such efforts are *Kizhaay Anishinaabe Niin* in Ontario (n.d.); Tewa Women United in New Mexico (2016); Namelehuapono in Hawaii (Joyful Heart Foundation, n.d.); Native American Youth and Family Center in Oregon (NAYA Family Center, n.d.); and Freedom, Inc. in Wisconsin (2015). All of these programs evoke and rely on positive cultural traditions of equality to intervene, educate, and address GBV in affected communities.

As educating the public in equality of gender roles is considered a significant method of prevention, both media marketing in the larger social arena (Break the Silence Against Domestic Violence, n.d.; Breakthrough, 2012; Hamling, 2014; NO MORE, n.d.; Oregon Attorney General's Sexual Assault Task Force, 2014; V-Day, 2013) and more intimate education at the community and individual levels are deemed significant in encouraging social change. Albeit with mixed results, anti-violence against women activists have long engaged with the media to spread their messages by designing poster displays, public service announcements, and advertisement campaigns to educate people in gender equity and effects of violence against girls and women (Kabeer, 2005). Although recognized as important, evaluations of public media campaigns have yielded mixed results (Donovan & Vlaise, 2005; Learning Network, 2012). For advertisement spots that tend to be less than a minute long, the impact may be less than comprehensive and effective.

The community re-educational efforts include training teachers to integrate gender equality into the curricula of early education, high school, and colleges (Akpakwu & Terhile, 2014; Nilsson, 2007). The idea is that this education would focus on healthy gender roles, rather than only the negative aspects of a binary gender system. While the degree of success of such efforts is questionable in terms of actual change in beliefs and related behaviors, not to engage the community is also unthinkable. If nothing else, community education seems to be worthwhile as outreach to victims. If successful, however, community awareness building through education could not only shift ideologies, but also make communities accountable for girls' and women's safety.

Engaging males for deeper social change

In recent years, there has been a rise in the recognition of preventive methods that engage boys and men in anti-violence against women activities. In the last two decades, advocates and researchers have begun to acknowledge that GBV cannot be prevented—let alone ended—unless boys and men are re-educated in gender equality and actively involved in anti-violence against women work (Alemu, 2015; Casey & Smith, 2010; DeKeseredy et al., 2000; Flood, 2010; Kimball et al., 2013; Texas Council on Family Violence, n.d.; Wells et al., 2013; World Health Organization, 2009).

> Men's violence against women is now firmly on the public agenda. The last 40 years has seen a groundswell of efforts to reduce and prevent physical and sexual assault of women. Two shifts have characterized the field in recent years: a growing emphasis on the need to prevent violence against women before it occurs, and an emerging emphasis on engaging boys and men in prevention. (Flood, 2010, p. 4)

The public health definition of "prevention" entails at least primary (before abuse has occurred), secondary (while abuse is occurring), and tertiary (after abuse has occurred) foci. While programs that engage men may have different meanings and ranges of activities for different organizations, nearly all involve their target constituency in the primary prevention approach by redefining masculinity. They also work to increase knowledge about abuse and perpetrators' responsibility, build skills to recognize situations of possible abuse, advocate for women's rights, change institutional policy and practice, organize communities, and mobilize the public (Storer et al., 2016). Additionally, many groups and organizations help boys and men build skills of intervention while an incident of violence is in progress, thus teaching them to engage in secondary prevention—for example, the Bell Bajao movement (Breakthrough, 2012), the Green Dot project (Green Dot, et cetera, 2010, and the Mentors in Violence Prevention project (Katz, 1995).

Dubbed the "Ally Movement" (Casey, 2010), a number of organizations—such as the White Ribbon Campaign (n.d.) in Canada; Stepping Stones in South Africa (Jewkes et al., 2008); CONNECT (n.d.), National Organization for Men against Sexism (1975– 2015), and Mentors in Violence Prevention (2016) in the US; Men Against Violence and Abuse (2014) in India; and the global MenEngage Alliance (n.d.)—intentionally involve men and boys in anti-violence against women activism, with the idea that men can unlearn abusive behavior, internalize gender-sensitive conduct, and stop future violence. In collaboration with feminist advocacy organizations, male engagement efforts are committed to developing their own agenda and methods to reduce, if not eradicate, violence against girls and women (Kimball et al., 2013). The emergence of international networks and conferences on men's violence prevention work indicate an expanding gender-based movement across the world. Many funding agencies are now insisting on boys- and men-focused components in the women's service provision programs they support. While the premise of engaging men in anti-violence work is attractive due to the amount of material resources and efforts being diverted to the cause, the efficacy of these activities needs to be carefully critiqued for their actual potential to further prevention of violence against girls and women.

Historically, men's concerns with anti-violence against women work have been supportive as well as detracting. Some of the programs, such as batterer intervention programs (BIP) and treatment for sexual aggressors, have focused on re-educating teens and men who have used violence against female partners and sexually assaulted women. Designed and established by anti-violence against women organizations, the goal of these re-education programs is for men to recognize the historicity and inhumanity of their misogynist attitudes and abusive actions and learn ways to disengage from violence. These programs are now a well-recognized component of the anti-violence against women movement.

Among the major detractors of the anti-violence against women movement are men's and fathers' rights groups (in the US and around the globe), which claim that men face unprecedented legal and social discrimination due to the influence of feminist activism-instigated pro-women laws and policies. Their complaint goes further, adding that women lie about the abuse they experience in intimate relationships to manipulate legal outcomes, especially to unjustifiably secure child custody and alimony (Flood, 2010). Consequently, instead of being privileged, men are actually the disadvantaged group in society and their rights—familial, financial, social, and legal—are generally ignored and crushed (Crowley, 2008; Doyle, 2004; Dragiewicz, 2011; Flood, 2007, 2009). A line of research on violence against women also claims that GBV is a myth. Rather, in heterosexual relationships, both men and women use violence against each other, and that is the essential nature of intimate relationships. Women are equally—if not more—violent toward their male partners as are men toward women (Hamberger & Potente, 1994; Morse, 1995; Steinmetz & Lucca, 1988; Straus, 1993, 1997; Straus et al., 1980). Thus, the key to preventing violence against women is to end violence initiated by women against their intimate partners, as it encourages reactive male violence (Straus, 1997, 1999). Following this argument, a few organizations engaging men have rejected the theoretical notion of gender asymmetry in social power and abuse (Casey et al., 2013; Flood, 2015), in opposition to the foundational philosophy of the majority of similar organizations.

In exception to these two outlying branches of thought, the mainstream of men's and boys' engagement with prevention of GBV consistently draws from theories and strategies that underscore amending the social norms of sexist, misogynist, and masculinist ideologies (Sundaram, 2016). In fact, activists propose that boys' and men's involvement could influence violence against women in at least three ways: committing men to personally refrain from abusing and controlling girls and women; teaching boys and men to intervene in or stop violence by other boys and men; and changing cultural norms of hegemonic masculinity to end violence against girls and women (Berkowitz, 2004a, 2004b; Edwards et al., 2000; Flood, 2010, 2011; Fulu et al., 2013; Gadd, 2012; Gidycz et al., 2011; Minerson et al., 2011; Storer et al., 2016; World Health Organization, 2004). Although the prospect of boys and men modifying culture by changing standards of masculinity seems attractive, its actual viability as a preventive strategy requires further research and evaluation.

Generally, the majority of organizations that work to engage men have shared the basic feminist understanding of the root causes of violence against women: gender hierarchy and aggressive androcentrism. Thus, among other approaches prevention efforts have entailed programs to build empathy for women, as well as to challenge traditional masculinity and replace it with egalitarian gender roles (Advocates for Youth, 2010; Bridges, 2010; Casey & Smith, 2010; Minerson et al., 2011; Wall, 2014; World Health Organization, 2009). The degree of change in attitudes of the men and boys engaged in anti-violence work has generally been considered an index of success (Banyard, 2014; Banyard et al., 2007; Potter et al., 2011). However, attitude modifications do not necessarily indicate changes in behavior. Whether the attitude alteration of men and boys who have participated in anti-violence programs translates to actual conduct that surrenders power and control over girls and women has not yet been completely settled. Ricardo et al.'s (2011) evaluation of 65 methodologically strong (that is, utilizing randomized and quasi-randomized controlled methodologies) studies conducted internationally with early-teen boys and young men indicate little correspondence between attitude change and reduction of sexual and non-sexual violence against women. The authors state: "While behaviour change theories suggest the possibility of a strong link between increased education and changes in attitudes and a subsequent change in behaviour, this link is still, to a large degree, an empirical question" (Ricardo et al., 2011, p. 31).

The issue of behavior becomes critical when boys and men are witnesses to abuse perpetrated by others. At that point, they may either accept the responsibility of intervening to stop the violence, or become complicit by their silence and inaction. In stopping sexual assault, particularly on college campuses, teaching bystander intervention to young men has been considered an important strategy of intervention—for example, the Mentors in Violence Prevention (MVP) model and Green Dot project in the US. Derived from the notion of bystander effect on apathy and diffusion of responsibility in groups (Darley & Latané, 1968), bystander intervention in the form of the MVP model (Banyard et al., 2004; Coker et al., 2011; Katz, 1995; Katz et al., 2011) has become a popular tool to teach boys and men (and at times also women) to intercede in situations of violence against women.

Although promising, such prevention education has not yielded consistently positive results (see, Burn, 2009; Cook & Reynald, 2016; Katz et al., 2011; Sundaram, 2016). Some studies have found that many teens and young men presume violence is unpreventable, a part of human—particularly male—nature, and even justifiable in various situations of intimate relationships (Bhanot & Senn, 2007; Burton & Kitzinger, 1998; Lau & Stevens, 2012; McCarry, 2010; Sundaram, 2016). Research also indicates that the effects of prevention education are not longlasting, and might need frequent booster shots (Flood, 2015; Gibbons, 2013). Furthermore, age, social hierarchy, uncertainty about an event, loyalty to friends, privacy boundaries, not knowing what to do, and possible negative consequences of intervention (including violence, as well as aspersions cast on interveners' sexuality and masculinity) may act as barriers for men in situations of violence against women (Cook & Reynald, 2016; Corboz et al., 2016; Flood, 2011; Towns & Terry, 2014). Even when intervention skills have been built and positive attitude modifications have occurred, it is not certain that changes in behavior have consistently followed (Flood, 2011; Gibbons, 2013; Gidycz et al., 2011; Katz et al., 2011). It is even questionable whether certain gender-sensitizing efforts that are becoming popular in the US—such as Walk A Mile In Her Shoes—produce the desired goal of developing empathy in participants, or actually reproduce and reinforce their patriarchal beliefs and attitudes (Bridges, 2013).

Another criticism of bystander intervention programs is that the curricula tend not to pay adequate attention to interveners' safety. Most such programs on campuses—such as Green Dot (Green Dot, et cetera, 2010) and MVP (Mentors in Violence Prevention, 2016)—recommend a buddy system, being in a supportive peer group, and diversion instead of direct confrontation to ensure individual safety. However, it is unclear how effective such safety programs are in uncontrolled situations of real life and in different country conditions, particularly where law enforcement responses are slow or inactive. An illustration may be drawn from the murders of two young men in Mumbai, both killed while interrupting a situation of sexual harassment (Shantanu, 2016). The young men had done everything right—they were with a group of friends in front of a crowded restaurant, and had supposedly called the police. They were killed by the perpetrators and their friends as a group of spectators watched. This is not a solitary case of interveners becoming victims of violence; yet we know little of how to ensure the safety of individuals who are entrusted to intervene. Thus, it is imperative that research and activism identify and build in safety measures in bystander intervention programs that engage boys and men in anti-violence work.

Limited and tangible social change

Intensifying institutional modification

The most vital part of the anti-violence against girls and women agenda has been to modify institutions in society that intervene in survivors' lives, particularly law enforcement and the judiciary. Even when victims may be reluctant to seek help from institutions, many enter their worlds when called in by neighbors, relatives, or children, or when victims seek healthcare or other essential services out of necessity (see *The story of Rachel*, Praxis International, 2010). Perhaps the most progress that has been made in global responses to violence against women is in the area of drafting and passing laws designed to enhance victims' safety and hold perpetrators of violence accountable. Often encouraged by treaties such as CEDAW (UN Women, 1979) and DEVAW (UN General Assembly, 1993) and agendas of international bodies such as the United Nations, countries have passed anti-domestic violence laws and legal measures to prosecute crimes of sexual violence that minimize hardship to victims (for example, rape shield laws). Although there is still a gender gap in laws worldwide (Ford & Anderson, 2015), in 2016, 137 countries around the world had passed some kind of legal measure against domestic violence (Rubiano-Matulevich, 2016). Additionally, an effort to enact the International Violence Against Women Act (IVAWA) (Amnesty International, 2015) to commit international governments to preventing woman abuse is slowly gaining momentum. While implementation of these laws may be inconsistent, their mere presence signals to perpetrators, victims, and communities that abuse of girls and women is unacceptable and carries legal consequences.

Even when helpful laws have been passed in a country (for example, On Measures against Violence in Family Relations in the Republic of Albania; Prevention of Domestic Violence Act in Sri Lanka; Protection of Women from Domestic Violence Act 2005 in India; and The Punjab Protection of Women against Violence Act 2016 in Pakistan), victims often cannot easily access such laws to seek legal justice due to lack of information, finances, and legal advocacy, as well as the pervasive social stigma of compromising family privacy. It is imperative that barriers to accessing legal recourses be removed for victims who choose to seek justice through the courts. To strengthen the message that GBV is not only morally repugnant but also a crime, reliable implementation of laws is essential, as is providing victims with uninterrupted access to legal and social support. However, in societies that attach stigma to victims of intimate abuse by assuming wrongdoing on the victims' part, and oppose police intervention in "private" family matters, victims might self-restrict their interactions with legal justice systems. Instituting full accessibility to legal recourses would entail a cultural shift to reposition intimate abuse as a public concern, along with the removal of other obstacles to accessibility, which include financial hardship, police and judiciary ignorance and biases, and lack of sustained legal advocacy. Such preventive programs must be integrated into the service provision systems. Culturally competent services, tailormade for various communities, could actually move toward cultural change by empowering women to access legal recourses (Flood, 2015; Moynihan et al., 2011; Shlash, 2009). Additionally, these services would need to include campaigns to destigmatize law enforcement and divorce, as well as improve services during the "leaving" process and enhance coordination among community-based organizations and official systems.

However, improvements of such complexity are only possible with state-supported public welfare for anti-violence programs and survivors, and unfortunately such support is being gradually reduced in most developed countries. "[E]ffective response to violence against women requires multisectoral coordination, committed resources, and support from the highest levels of government" (Morrow et al., 2004, p. 359). Relying on private resources and "pull up by the bootstraps" philosophy weakens anti-violence organizations and hobbles survivors and their children from progressing to end violence in their lives. By exercising some control over state resources, materials, and policies, survivors of domestic and sexual violence can also reclaim some of their social rights, which violence has wrested from them. Governments paring down financial sponsorship for domestic and sexual violence services and diluting policies that support feminist agendas of gender equity sends a message that is not conducive to preventing or ending violence against women (Morrow et al., 2004).

In recent years in the US, many advocates and activists working in communities of color have been protesting overreliance on the criminal legal system (CLS) for solving community problems, including in relation to the prevention of woman-abuse (Bhattacharjee, 2001; Eng, 2003; Incite!, 2001; Silliman & Bhattacharjee, 2002). Recognizing the debilitating and punitive consequences of state involvement in survivors' lives, Abraham and Tastsoglou (2016a) write:

> [T]he rights and autonomy of women facing domestic or intimate partner violence appear to be translated by neoliberal patriarchal states into intervention through

> criminalization, and forms of state regulation that result in an uneasy co-habitation of women and the state. Framing the issue in this way has complex consequences for women's lives and, also, deflects attention from the social, economic, and political realities that contribute to abuse: the consequences of which are also particularly salient in the context of immigration. (p. 569)

In addition, activists questioning legal recourses as the main solution to violence against women claim that biases against Black and brown people—integral to the legal system in the US—have created a pipeline to prison for men of color. That is, implementation of stringent and often unnecessary laws against domestic violence and sexual assault (for example, mandatory arrest and no-drop prosecution policies) only exacerbate the problem of high incarceration rates of Black and Latino men (Coker, 2004; Richie, 2012).

Instead of involving the CLS in every situation, use of alternative approaches—such as restorative justice (Center for Justice and Reconciliation, n.d.) and Panchayat arbitration (Ashoka Changemakers, n.d.)—might be acceptable alternatives to deal with perpetrators and victims of abuse. Although not all cases are suitable for these substitute interventions, abusers who have not necessarily utilized extreme violence or been assessed as highly dangerous may benefit from being involved in these. The alternatives may require perpetrators to mend their ways through re-education, enforcing the obligation with the threat of turning to more formal legal systems in cases of noncompliance. Whether utilizing formal legal or alternative systems of justice, engagement of interdisciplinary crisis response teams that include community leaders might be a good way of circumscribing perpetrators' behaviors and shifting community norms about violence and victims.

In addition, an issue that is rarely seriously addressed in GBV prevention is the omnipresence of state violence, which is not only directed toward its own citizens (Bhattacharjee, 2001; Goodmark, 2013; Silliman & Bhattacharjee, 2002) but also directed internationally. In response to the rise in terrorism internationally, all countries are witnessing an increase in draconian—and often unjustified—law enforcement measures domestically. In the US, police killings (Mapping Police Violence, 2016), particularly of Black men, have led to massive protests and demands for police accountability from movements like Black Lives Matter (Black Lives Matter, n.d.; Cobb, 2016). In addition to creating a police force more sensitive to minority communities, we need to neutralize governments' modeling of violence as a method of resolving conflicts. The US is especially guilty of such aggressive overreaction in rhetoric and action to real or perceived threats to the nation. However, the US is not singular in its stance. Reacting severely to international terrorism, most governments are placing enormous emphasis on surveillance and punishment (Choudhury & Fenwick, 2011; McCahill, 2007; Spalek & Lambert, 2007)—a posture that must be replaced by nurturing, re-education, and healing of communities. Government is a powerful educational tool that sanctions the use of violence against others (Abraham & Tastsoglou, 2016b). Unless dismantled with deliberation, states inevitably reproduce (even if imperceptibly) power structures that reinforce hierarchies, such as asymmetrical gender relationships and violence, in order to maintain the status quo.

Future research and conclusion

Research on violence against women has generally highlighted types and corollaries of violence, identified effective intervention methods, and presented theoretical analyses and various therapeutic approaches that might repair the harm caused by intimate abuse. It is still important to document and articulate evidence-based information on the nuances of the dynamics of domestic and sexual violence to enhance the appropriateness and quality of services provided by advocates. Until recently, little consistent attention was paid to preventive measures that might actually *end* violence against women. In the last decade or so, other efforts—such as identifying culture-based strategies, transnational cross-pollination of laws, and engaging men and the larger community in preventing violence against women—have gained prominence. Nonetheless, the overwhelming gaps in research on prevention are still far from being fully addressed.

In engaging boys and men, recent research and activism have begun to focus on radical solutions for the problem of violence against women. This choice of subject matter has emerged to interrupt the persistence of violence against girls and women and the continuation of the status quo globally. In addition, the preventive measures that are being explored are wide-ranging, and involve factors in transforming institutions, structures, cultures, gender roles, and gender inequities. Although this stream of research is growing, certain gaps need to be recognized and addressed. For example, much of the emerging research is still based on white communities and located in the Global North.

We know little about communities of color, immigrant populations, sexual minorities, and cultures in the Global South. For that matter, we hardly understand how to bring about deep cultural changes altogether. We need interdisciplinary research on how large-scale cultural shifts, which could ultimately enrich prevention programs, may be instigated. It is unlikely that prevention research findings in narrow subject areas, with dominant white populations of mostly college age and located in the Global North, are generalizable to demographically different populations in varied societies. Even in the West, research involving dominant communities may not have explanatory power for the conditions of immigrant communities of color. Keeping methodological limitations in mind, it might thus be necessary to research the same question in multiple populations. A quick fix here would be to convince funding sources to support targeted research that actually supports practical intervention strategies.

Investigations into wider cultural changes must be nuanced, with a recognition of various layers of cultures and their intersections with social markers of identities that include "race", gender, sexualities, class, caste, disability, citizenship, and history of colonization. A case in point is preventive work to re-educate men in non-aggressive gender roles to prevent violence against women. Masculinity is not monolithic; it is distinct in different social contexts and historical periods, requiring subtle understanding and application. For example, during the colonial period, the British defined Indian men as less than men, while the western male was deemed ideal in masculinity (Nandy, 1983; Sinha, 1995). To resuscitate the nation's self-esteem and rescue it from western denigration, masculinity in India was rebuilt around "protective" aggression and quiet competency (Dasgupta, 2015). Furthermore, male dominance and female subjugation in intimate relationships became eroticized in India to nourish this masculine gender role (Derné, 1999). Scholars have linked the rise of masculinity in India with concurrent increases in violence against women—embodied in sex-selective female feticide, dowry-related abuse, control of female sexuality, and heterosexism (Vijayan, 2012). Over the years, the bellicosity ingrained in this brand of masculinity was revived in times of national crises. In recent years, in recognition of the assimilatory forces of globalization, it has been ratcheted up again by conservative religious, nationalist and political movements. Challenging masculine gender roles in India, associated with postcolonial nationalism, is likely to meet with high levels of resistance and be viewed as a western imperialist conspiracy to weaken the country. Investigations into masculinities in India and other postcolonial nations, as well as development of successful gender role re-education curricula, have to be informed by such historical–cultural backgrounds.

In general, prevention research could focus on two categories:

- Larger and overall shifts, which would be time consuming but would bring in-depth and permanent changes such as cultural transformations and changes in gender roles.
- Smaller and specific changes, which may be quick and limited but would make significant shifts in current conditions such as policies, laws, and other institutional regulations.

Additionally, more investigations into trends in violence and its causes must be encouraged. Research in developing life-course prevention curricula could actually yield practical information that helps us understand and implement effective prevention programs. Involvement of researchers and activists in policy making might also help enhance efficacy of policies. The bulk of research in violence against women highlights the abuse that is perpetrated, particularly the types of violence and factors that exacerbate abuse. While this is necessary to fathom the scope and breadth of violence, we need to develop good understanding of what positive features of a culture make that culture at least disinclined to (if not immune from) violence against girls and women. This is an area that has been woefully neglected in research. We need to identify societies that have low rates of violence against women, and isolate salient factors that inure them to woman abuse. From the vantage point of current knowledge, we must recognize that no other method seems to even decrease the rates of violence against women—let alone prevent it—except strict CLS interventions. Yet, we can hardly depend on the CLS to deliver equal justice for all (Delgado & Stefancic, 2001).

It is important to nurture the thinner stream of preventive research to move toward ending domestic and sexual violence. We need to rigorously evaluate the different approaches to preventing the historically and culturally rooted behaviors of domestic and sexual violence—public health, feminist, and others. It is important to move away from the dominant western understanding of violence against women as intimate partner abuse, toward exploring violence by poly-perpetrators and the factors that contribute to it. Investigators have to expand their research location and population base to include different cultures, conditions, and communities. Focusing on a campus-based, white, young population in the West may not necessarily bring us closer to the goal of preventing—and thereby ending—violence against girls and women.

Note

1. I am deeply grateful to Dr. Sherry Hamby for her advice and suggestions in writing this chapter.

References

Abraham, M., & Tastsoglou, E. (2016a). Addressing domestic violence in Canada and the United States: The uneasy co-habitation of women and the state. *Current Sociology*, *64*, 568–585.

Abraham, M., & Tastsoglou, E. (2016b). Interrogating gender, violence and the state in national and transnational contexts: Framing the issues. *Current Sociology*, *64*, 517–534.

Abrevaya, J. (2009). Are there missing girls in the United States? Evidence from birth data. *American Economic Journal: Applied Economics*, *1*, 1–34.

Advocates for Youth (2010). *Gender inequity and violence against women and girls around the world.* Retrieved from: www.advocatesforyouth. org/storage/advfy/documents/gender_bias_fact_sheet_2010.pdf.

Akpakwu, O.S., & Terhile, B.F. (2014). Gender equality in schools: Implications for the curriculum, teaching and classroom interaction. *Journal of Education and Practice*, *5*, 7–12.

Alemu, B.S. (2015). *Working with men and boys to end violence against women and girls: Approaches, challenges, and lessons.* United States Agency for International Development (USAID). Retrieved from: https:// www.usaid.gov/sites/default/files/documents/1865/Men_VAW_ report_Feb2015_Final.pdf.

Amnesty International (2015). *The International Violence Against Women Act (IVAWA)*, Issues Brief. Retrieved from: https:// aaf1a18515da0e792f78-c27fdabe952dfc357fe25ebf5c8897ee. ssl.cf5.rackcdn.com/1839/IVAWA+Issue+Brief+spring+2015. pdf?v=1427740907000.

Anderson, K.L. (2005). Theorizing gender in intimate partner violence research. *Sex Roles*, *52*, 853–865.

Anton, J. (Ed.) (2005). *Walking together: Working with women from diverse religious and spiritual traditions.* Seattle, WA: FaithTrust Institute.

Arnold, G., & Ake, J. (2013). Reframing the narrative of the battered women's movement. *Violence Against Women*, *19*, 557–578.

Ashoka Changemakers (n.d.). *No private matter! Ending abuse in intimate and family relations.* Retrieved from: www.changemakers.com/competition/endabuse/entries/women-law-and-social-change-action-indias-mahila.

Badran, M. (1995). *Feminists, Islam, and nation: Gender and the making of modern Egypt.* Princeton, NJ: Princeton University Press.

Badran, M. (2009). *Feminism in Islam: Secular and religious convergences.* London: Oneworld Press.

Banyard, V.L. (2014). Improving college campus-based prevention of violence against women: A strategic plan for research built on multipronged practices and policies. *Trauma, Violence, and Abuse, 15,* 339–351.

Banyard, V.L., Moynihan, M.M., & Plante, E.G. (2007). Sexual violence prevention through bystander education: An experimental evaluation. *Journal of Community Psychology, 35,* 463–481.

Banyard, V.L., Plante, E.G., & Moynihan, M.M. (2004). Bystander education: Bringing a broader community perspective to sexual violence prevention. *Journal of Community Psychology, 32,* 61–79.

Barner, J.R., & Carney, M.M. (2011). Interventions for intimate partner violence: A historical review. *Journal of Family Violence, 26,* 235–244.

Berkowitz, A. (2003). Fostering men's responsibility for preventing sexual assault. In P.A. Schewe (Ed.), *Preventing violence in relationships: Interventions across the lifespan* (pp. 163–196). Washington, DC: American Psychological Association.

Berkowitz, A. (2004a). Working with men to prevent violence against women: An overview (Part 1). *VAWnet.* Retrieved from: www.vawnet.org.

Berkowitz, A.D. (2004b). Working with men to prevent violence against women: Program modalities and formats (Part 2). *VAWnet.* Retrieved from: www.vawnet.org.

Bhanot, S., & Senn, C.Y. (2007). Attitudes towards violence against women in men of South Asian ancestry: Are acculturation and gender role attitudes important factors? *Journal of Family Violence, 22,* 25–31.

Bhattacharjee, A. (2001). *Whose safety? Women of colour and the violence of law enforcement.* Philadelphia, PA: American Friends Service Committee.

Black Lives Matter (n.d.). Retrieved from: http://blacklivesmatter.com/.

Bograd, M. (1988). Feminist perspectives on wife abuse: An introduction. In K. Yllö & M. Bograd (Eds.), *Feminist perspectives on wife abuse* (pp. 11–27). Newbury Park, CA: Sage.

Break the Silence Against Domestic Violence (n.d.). *Social media campaigns*. Retrieved from: www.breakthesilencedv.org/social-media-campaigns/.

Breakthrough (2012). *Bell bajao movement*. Retrieved from: www.bellbajao.org/.

Bridges, T.S. (2010). Men just weren't made to do this: Performances of drag at "walk a mile in her shoes" marches. *Gender & Society*, *24*, 5–30.

Bruce, S. (2002). The "a man" campaign: Marketing social norms to men to prevent sexual assault. *The Report on Social Norms: Working Paper #5*. Little Falls, NJ: PaperClip Communications.

Burn, S.M. (2009). A situational model of sexual assault prevention through bystander intervention. *Sex Roles*, *60*, 779–792.

Burton, S., & Kitzinger, J. (1998). *Young people's attitudes towards violence and sex in relationships*. Glasgow, UK: University of Glasgow.

Casey, E. (2010). Strategies for engaging men as anti-violence allies: Implications for ally movements. *Advances in Social Work*, *11*, 267–282.

Casey, E.A., Carlson, J.C., Fraguela-Rios, C., Kimball, E., Neugut, T., Tolman, R.M., & Edleson, J. (2013). Context, challenges, and tensions in global efforts to engage men in the prevention of violence against women: An ecological analysis. *Men and Masculinities*, *16*, 228–251.

Casey, E.A., & Lindhorst, T.P. (2009). Toward a multi-level, ecological approach to the primary prevention of sexual assault. *Trauma, Violence, and Abuse*, *10*, 91–114.

Casey, E., & Smith, T. (2010). "'How can I not?'": Men's pathways to involvement in anti-violence against women work. *Violence Against Women*, *16*, 953–973.

Center for Justice and Reconciliation (n.d.). *RJ in the criminal justice system*. Retrieved from: http://restorativejustice.org/restorative-justice/rj-in-the-criminal-justice-system/.

Choudhury, T., & Fenwick, H. (2011). *The impact of counter-terrorism measures on Muslim communities: Project report*. Manchester: Equality and Human Rights Commission.

Cobb, J. (2016). The matter of black lives: A new kind of movement found its moment. What will its future be? *The New Yorker*, March 14. Retrieved from: www.newyorker.com/magazine/2016/03/14/where-is-black-lives-matter-headed.

Coker, A.L., Cook-Craig, P.G., Williams, C.M., Fisher, B.S., Clear, E.R., Garcia, L.S., & Hegge, L.M. (2011). Evaluation of Green Dot: An active bystander intervention to reduce sexual violence on college campuses. *Violence Against Women*, *17*, 777–796.

Coker, D. (2004). Race, poverty, and crime-centered response to domestic violence. *Violence Against Women, 10*, 1331–1353.

CONNECT (n.d.). Retrieved from: www.connectnyc.org/.

Cook, A., & Reynald, D. (2016). Guardianship against sexual offenses: Exploring the role of gender in intervention. *International Criminal Justice Review, 26*, 98–114.

Corboz, J., Flood, M., & Dyson, S. (2016). Challenges of bystander intervention in male-dominated professional sport: Lessons from the Australian football league. *Violence Against Women, 22*, 324–343.

Crowley, J.E. (2008). *Defiant dads: Fathers' rights activists in America.* Ithaca, NY: Cornell University Press.

Darley, J.M., & Latané, B. (1968). Bystander intervention in emergencies: Diffusion of responsibility. *Journal of Personality and Social Psychology, 8*, 377–383.

DasGupta, S., & Dasgupta, S.D. (2010). Motherhood jeopardized: Reproductive technologies in Indian communities. In W. Chavkin & J. Maher (Eds.), *The globalization of motherhood: Deconstructions and reconstructions of biology and care* (pp. 131–153). New York: Routledge.

Dasgupta, S.D. (2015). (Un)holy connections? Understanding woman abuse in Hinduism. In A.J. Johnson (Ed.), *Religion and men's violence against women* (pp. 371–382). New York: Springer-Verlag.

DeKeseredy, W.S., Schwartz, M.D., & Alvi, S. (2000). The role of profeminist men in dealing with woman abuse on the Canadian college campus. *Violence Against Women, 6*, 918–935.

Delgado, R., & Stefancic, J. (2001). *Critical race theory: An introduction.* New York: New York University Press.

DePrince, A.P., Belknap, J., Labus, J.S., Buckingham, S.E., & Gover, A.R. (2012). The impact of victim-focused outreach on criminal legal system outcomes following police-reported intimate partner abuse. *Violence Against Women, 18*, 861–881.

Derné, S. (1999). Making sex violent: Love as force in recent Hindi films. *Violence Against Women, 5*, 548–575.

Donovan, R. J., & Vlais, R. (2005) *VicHealth review of communication components of social marketing/public education campaigns focusing on violence against women.* Melbourne, Australia: Victorian Health Promotion Foundation.

Doyle, C. (2004). The fathers' rights movement: Extending patriarchal control beyond the marital family. In P. Herrmann (Ed.), *Citizenship revisited: Threats or opportunities of shifting boundaries* (pp. 57–88). New York: Nova Science Press.

Dragiewicz, M. (2011). *Equality with a vengeance: Men's rights groups, battered women, and antifeminist backlash.* Boston, MA: Northeastern University Press.

Edwards, R.W., Jumper-Thurman, P., Plested, B.A., Oetting, E.R., & Swanson, L. (2000). Community readiness: Research to practice. *Journal of Community Psychology, 28,* 291–307.

Eng, P. (2003). *Safety and justice for all: Examining the relationship between the women's anti-violence movement and the criminal legal system.* New York: Ms. Foundation for Women.

Fabiano, P., Perkins, H.W., Berkowitz, A.B., Linkenbach, J., & Stark, C. (2004). Engaging men as social justice allies in ending violence against women: Evidence for a social norms approach. *Journal of American College Health, 52,* 105–112.

Flood, M. (2007). *Background document for preventing violence before it occurs: A framework and background paper to guide the primary prevention of violence against women in Victoria.* Victoria: Victorian Health Promotion Foundation. Retrieved from: www.dvvic.org.au/attachments/2007_vichealth_pvaw.framework.pdf.

Flood, M. (2009). *Father's rights and family law.* Seminar. Victoria: Women's Legal Service, September 21. Retrieved from: http://angelzfury.blogspot.com/2009/09/fathers-rights-and-family-law-michael.html

Flood, M. (2010). Where men stand: Men's roles in ending violence against women. *White Ribbon Prevention Research Series, 2.* Sydney: White Ribbon Foundation.

Flood, M. (2011). Building men's commitment to ending sexual violence against women. *Feminism and Psychology, 21,* 262–267.

Flood, M. (2015). Work with men to end violence against women: A critical stocktake. *Culture, Health and Sexuality, 17,* 159–176.

Ford, L., & Anderson, M. (2015). Women's prospects limited by law in 155 countries, finds World Bank study, *Global development: Women's rights and gender equality. The Guardian,* September 9. Retrieved from: www.theguardian.com/global-development/2015/sep/09/women-business-and-the-law-2016-getting-to-equal-world-bank-report.

Freedom Inc. (2015). *Our community is our campaign.* Retrieved from: http://freedom-inc.org/.

French, S.G., Teays, W., & Purdy, L.M. (1998). *Violence against women: Philosophical perspectives.* Ithaca, NY: Cornell University Press.

Fulu, E., Warner, X., Miedema, S., Jewkes, R., Roselli, T., & Lang, J. (2013). *Why do some men use violence against women and how can we prevent it? Quantitative findings from the United Nations multi-country study on men and violence in Asia and the Pacific.* Bangkok: UNDP, UNFPA, UN Women, and UNV.

Gadd, D. (2012). Domestic abuse prevention after Raoul Moat. *Critical Social Policy, 32,* 495–516.

Garcia-Moreno, C., Jansen, H. A. F. M., Ellsberg, M., Heise L., & Watts, C. (2005) *WHO multi-country study on women's health and domestic violence against women: Initial results on prevalence, health outcomes and women's responses.* Geneva, Switzerland: World Health Organization.

General Assembly resolution 48/104, *Declaration on the elimination of violence against women,* A/RES/48/104 (20 December 1993). Retrieved from: www.unhchr.ch/huridocda/huridoca.nsf/ (Symbol)/A.RES.48.104.En?Opendocument.

Gibbons, R.E. (2013). The evaluation of campus-based gender violence prevention programming: What we know about program effectiveness and implications for practitioners. *VAWnet.* Retrieved from: www.vawnet.org.

Gidycz, C.A., Orchowski, L.M., & Berkowitz, A.D. (2011). Preventing sexual aggression among college men: An evaluation of a social norms and bystander intervention program. *Violence Against Women, 17,* 720–742.

Goodmark, L. (2013). Transgender people, intimate partner abuse, and the legal system. *Harvard Civil Rights–Civil Liberties Law Review, 48,* 51–104.

Green Dot, et cetera, Inc. (2010). *Greendot.* Retrieved from: www. livethegreendot.com/index.html.

Gupte, M. (2015). *The role of honor in violence against South Asian women in the United States.* Manavi Occasional Paper No. 11. New Brunswick, NJ: Manavi.

Gupte, M., Awasthi, R., & Chickerur, S. (Eds.) (2012). *"Honour" and women's rights: South Asian perspectives.* Pune: MASUM.

Hall, R.J. (2015). Feminist strategies to end violence against women. In R. Baksh and W. Harcourt (Eds.), *The Oxford handbook of transnational feminist movements* (pp. 394–417). New York: Oxford University Press.

Hamberger, L.K., & Potente, T. (1994). Counseling heterosexual women arrested for domestic violence: Implications for theory and practice. *Violence and Victims, 9,* 125–137.

Hamling, A. (2014). Eight inspiring campaigns to end violence against women. *Amnesty International.* Retrieved from: www.amnesty.org. au/features/comments/36107/.

Hassan, R. (1999). Feminism in Islam. In A. Sharma & K.K. Young (Eds.), *Feminism and world religions* (pp. 248–278). New York: State University of New York Press.

Hussain, F. (1984). Introduction: The ideal and the contextual realities of Muslim women. In F. Hussain (Ed.), *Muslim Women* (pp. 1–7). London: Croom Helm Press.

Incite! (2001). *Gender violence and the prison industrial complex.* Retrieved from: www.incite-national.org/page/incite-critical-resistance-statement.

Jewkes, R., Nduna, M., Levin, J., Jama, N., Dunkle, K., & Puren, A. (2008). Impact of stepping stones on incidence of HIV and HSV-2 and sexual behaviour in rural South Africa: Cluster randomised controlled trial. *British Medical Journal, 337,* 391–395.

Joyful Heart Foundation (n.d.). *Namelehuapono.* Retrieved from: www.joyfulheartfoundation.org/programs/healing-wellness/survivor-programming/namelehuapono-wahine.

Kabeer, N. (2005). Gender equality and women's empowerment: A critical analysis of the third millennium development goal. *Gender and Development, 13,* 13–24.

Katz, J. (1995). Reconstructing masculinity in the locker room: The Mentors in Violence Prevention project. *Harvard Educational Review, 65,* 163–174.

Katz, J., Heisterkamp, H.A., & Fleming, W.M. (2011). The social justice roots of the Mentors in Violence Prevention model and its application in a high school setting. *Violence Against Women, 17,* 684–702.

Kaur, R., & Garg, S. (2010). Domestic violence against women: A qualitative study in a rural community. *Asia-Pacific Journal of Public Health, 22,* 242–251.

Kimball, E., Edleson, J.L., Tolman, R.M., Neugut, T.B., & Carlson, J. (2013). Global efforts to engage men in preventing violence against women: An international survey. *Violence Against Women, 19,* 924–939.

Kizhaay Anishinaabe Niin [I am a kind man] (n.d.). Retrieved from: www.iamakindman.ca/IAKM/about-us-kizhaay-anishinaabe-niin.html.

Lau, U., & Stevens, G. (2012). Textual transformations of subjectivity in men's talk of gender-based violence. *Feminism and Psychology, 22,* 423–442.

Learning Network (2012). *Report on the evaluation of violence against women public education campaigns: A discussion paper.* London, Ontario, Canada: Centre for Research & Education on Violence Against Women & Children.

Madge, V. (2014). Gestational surrogacy in India: The problem of technology and poverty. In S. DasGupta & S.D. Dasgupta (Eds.), *Globalization and transnational surrogacy in India: Outsourcing life* (pp. 45–66). Lanham, MD: Lexington.

Mapping Police Violence (2016). Retrieved from: http://mappingpoliceviolence.org/reports/.

Mayell, H. (2002). Thousands of women killed for family "honour". *National Geographic News* (February 12). Retrieved from: http://news.nationalgeographic.com/news/2002/02/0212_020212_honorkilling.html.

McCahill, M. (2007, Summer). Us and them: The social impact of "new surveillance" technologies. *CJM: Criminal Justice Matters, 68,* 14–15.

McCarry, M. (2010). Becoming a "proper man": Young people's attitudes about interpersonal violence and perceptions of gender. *Gender and Education, 22,* 17–30.

Men Against Violence and Abuse (MAVA) (2014). *Empowering women through humanization of men.* Retrieved from: www.mavaindia.org/.

MenEngage Alliance (n.d.). Retrieved from: http://menengage.org/.

Mentors in Violence Prevention (MVP). (2016). Retrieved from: www.mvpnational.org/.

Mernissi, F. (1975). *Beyond the veil: Male-female dynamics in modern Muslim society.* Cambridge, MA: Schenkman.

Minerson, T., Carolo, H., Dinner, T., & Jones, C. (2011). *Issue brief: Engaging men and boys to reduce and prevent gender-based violence.* Retrieved from: http://whiteribbon.ca/wp-content/uploads/2012/12/wrc_swc_issuebrief.pdf.

Morrow, M., Hankivsky, O., & Varcow, C. (2004). Women and violence: The effects of dismantling the welfare state. *Critical Social Policy, 24,* 358–384.

Morse, B.J. (1995). Beyond the conflict tactics scale: Assessing gender differences in partner violence. *Violence and Victims, 10,* 251–272.

Moynihan, M.M., Banyard, V.L., Arnold, J.S., Eckstein, R.P., & Stapleton, J.G. (2011). Sisterhood may be powerful for reducing sexual and intimate partner violence: An evaluation of the bringing in the bystander in-person program with sorority members. *Violence Against Women, 17,* 703–719.

Nandy, A. (1983). *The intimate enemy: Loss and recovery of self under colonialism*. Delhi: Oxford University Press.

National Organization for Men against Sexism (NOMAS) (1975–2015). Retrieved from: http://nomas.org/.

Naved, R.T., & Persson, L.A. (2010). Dowry and spousal physical violence against women in Bangladesh. *Journal of Family Issues*, *31*, 830–856.

NAYA Family Center (n.d.). *Native American youth and family center*. Retrieved from: http://nayapdx.org/.

Nilsson, J. (2007, October). *Sweden case study report 2: Developing a school curriculum for gender equality*. Malmö: School of Teacher Education, Malmö University.

NO MORE (n.d.). *NO MORE Print Ads*. Retrieved from: http://nomore.org/public-service-announcements/nomoreexcusespsas/print-ads/.

Oregon Attorney General's Sexual Assault Task Force, The (2014). *A best practice: Using social media for sexual violence prevention*. The Prevention and Education Subcommittee. Retrieved from: http://oregonsatf.org/wp-content/uploads/2011/02/ORSATF-Using-Social-Media-for-Sexual-Violence-Prevention-FINAL.pdf.

Pence, E., & Paymar, M. (1993). Theoretical framework for understanding battering. In E. Pence & M. Paymar (Eds.), *Education groups for men who batter: The Duluth model* (pp. 1–15). New York: Springer.

Pence, E. L. (1999). Some thoughts on philosophy. In M. F. Shepard & E. L. Pence (Eds.), *Coordinating community responses to domestic violence: Lessons from Duluth and beyond* (pp. 23–40). Thousand Oaks, CA: Sage.

Pence, E.L., & McDonnell, C. (1999). Developing policies and protocols. In M.F. Shepard & E.L. Pence (Eds.), *Coordinating community responses to domestic violence: Lessons from Duluth and beyond* (pp. 41–64). Thousand Oaks, CA: Sage.

Pence, E.L., & Shepard, M.F. (1988). Integrating feminist theory and practice: The challenge of the battered women's movement. In K. Yllö & M. Bograd (Eds.), *Feminist perspectives on wife abuse* (pp. 282–298). Newbury Park, CA: Sage.

Potter, S.J., Moynihan, M.M., & Stapleton, J.G. (2011). Using social self-identification in social marketing materials aimed at reducing violence against women on campus. *Journal of Interpersonal Violence*, *26*, 971–990.

Praxis International (2010). *The story of Rachel*. Available from: http://praxisinternational.org/product/the-story-of-rachel/.

Puri, S., Adams, V., Ivey, S., & Nachtigall, R.D. (2011). "There is such a thing as too many daughters, but not too many sons": A qualitative study of son preference and fetal sex selection among Indian immigrants in the United States. *Social Science & Medicine*, 72, 1169–1176.

Ricardo C., Eads, M., & Barker, G. (2011). *Engaging boys and men in the prevention of sexual violence: A systematic and global review of evaluated interventions.* Pretoria, South Africa: Sexual Violence Research Initiative (SVRI).

Richie, B.E. (2012). *Arrested justice: Black women, violence, and America's prison nation.* New York: New York University Press.

Rubiano-Matulevich, E. (2016, May 13). Gender equality: What do the data show in 2016? *The World Bank.* Retrieved from: http://blogs. worldbank.org/opendata/gender-equality-what-do-data-show-2016.

Saathoff, A.J., & Stoffel, E.A. (1999). Community-based domestic violence services. *The Future of Children*, 9(Winter), 97–110.

Schechter, S. (1982). *Women and male violence: The visions and struggles of the battered women's movement.* Boston, MA: South End Press.

Schechter, S. (1988). Building bridges between activists, professionals, and researchers. In K. Yllö & M. Bograd (Eds.), *Feminist perspectives on wife abuse* (pp. 299–312). Newbury Park, CA: Sage.

Sev'er, A. (2012). *Patriarchal murders of women: A sociological study of honour-based killings in Turkey and in the West.* Lewiston, NY: Edwin Mellen.

Shantanu, S. (2016). They died for trying to save their friends: 9 things you need to know about the Keenan-Reuben case. *India Today* (May 5). Retrieved from: http://indiatoday.intoday.in/story/keenan-reuben-murder-case-9-things-you-need-to-know/1/659707.html.

Shetty, S., & Kaguyutan, J. (2011). Immigrant victims of domestic violence: Cultural challenges and available legal protections. *VAWnet. org.* Retrieved from: www.vawnet.org/applied-research-papers/print-document.php?doc_id=384.

Shlash, A. (2009). Women's empowerment: A misunderstood process. *Social Watch.* Retrieved from: www.socialwatch.org/node/858.

Silliman, J., & Bhattacharjee, A. (2002). *Policing the national body: Race, gender, and criminalization.* Cambridge, MA: South End Press.

Sinha, M. (1995). *Colonial masculinity: The "manly" Englishman and the "effeminate" Bengali in the late nineteenth century.* Manchester, UK: Manchester University Press.

Spalek, B., & Lambert, B. (2007, Summer). Muslim communities under surveillance. *CJM: Criminal Justice Matters*, 68, 12–13.

Steinmetz, S.K., & Lucca, J.S. (1988). Husband battering. In V.B. Van Hasselt, R.L. Morrison, A.S. Bellack & M. Hersen (Eds.), *Handbook of family violence* (pp. 233–246). New York: Plenum Press.

Storer, H.L., Casey, E.A., Carlson, J., Edleson, J.L., & Tolman, R.M. (2016). Primary prevention is? A global perspective on how organizations engaging men in preventing gender-based violence conceptualize and operationalize their work. *Violence Against Women, 22*, 249–268.

Straus, M.A. (1993). Physical assaults by wives: A major social problem. In R.J. Gelles & D.R. Loseke (Eds.), *Current controversies on family violence* (pp. 67–87). Newbury Park, CA: Sage.

Straus, M.A. (1997). Physical assaults by women partners: A major social problem. In M.R. Walsh (Ed.), *Women, men and gender: Ongoing debates* (pp. 210–221). New Haven, CT: Yale University Press.

Straus, M.A. (1999). The controversy over domestic violence by women: A methodological, theoretical, and sociology of science analysis. In X.B. Arriaga & S. Oskamp (Eds.), *Violence in intimate relationships* (pp. 17–44). Thousand Oaks, CA: Sage.

Straus, M.A., Gelles, R.J., & Steinmetz, S.K. (1980). *Behind closed doors: Violence in the American family*. New York: Anchor.

Sundaram, V. (2016). "You can try, but you won't stop it. It'll always be there": Youth perspectives on violence and prevention in schools. *Journal of Interpersonal violence, 31*, 652–676.

Tewa Women United (2016). Retrieved from: http://tewawomenunited.org/.

Texas Council on Family Violence (n.d.). *Guide to engaging men and boys in preventing violence against women and girls*. Austin, TX: Men's Nonviolence Project. Retrieved from: http://tcfv.org/pdf/mensguide/EngagingMenandBoys.pdf.

Tierney, K.J. (1982). The battered women's movement and the creation of the wife beating problem. *Social Problems, 29*, 207–220.

Towns, A.J., & Terry, G. (2014). "You're in that realm of unpredictability": Mateship, loyalty, and men challenging men who use domestic violence against women. *Violence Against Women, 20*, 1012–1036.

UN Women (1979). *Convention on the elimination of all forms of discrimination against women (CEDAW)*. Retrieved from: www.un.org/womenwatch/daw/cedaw/text/econvention.htm.

V-Day (2013). *One billion rising*. Retrieved from: http://2013.onebillionrising.org/news/entry/v-days-one-billion-rising-is-biggest-global-action-ever-to-end-violence-aga.

Vijayan, P.K. (2012). *Making the pitribhumi: Masculine hegemony and the formation of the Hindu nation.* Unpublished doctoral dissertation, International Institute of Social Studies, Erasmus University, Rotterdam.

Wall, L. (2014). *Gender equality and violence against women: What's the connection?* Australian Center for the Study of Sexual Assault (ACSSA) Research Summary. Retrieved from: https://aifs.gov.au/sites/default/files/publication-documents/ressum7.pdf.

Warrier, S. (2005). *Culture handbook.* San Francisco, CA: Family Violence Prevention Fund.

Wells, L., Lorenzetti, L., Carolo, H., Dinner, T., Jones, C., Minerson, T., & Esina, E. (2013). *Engaging men and boys in domestic violence prevention: Opportunities and promising approaches.* Calgary, AB: University of Calgary, Shift: The Project to End Domestic Violence.

White Ribbon Campaign (n.d.). Retrieved from: www.whiteribbon.ca/.

Williamson, E., & Abrahams, H. (2014). A review of the provision of intervention programs for female victims and survivors of domestic abuse in the United Kingdom. *Affilia, 29*, 178–191.

Women Living Under Muslim Laws (n.d.). Retrieved from: www.wluml.org/.

World Health Organization (WHO) (2004). *Preventing violence: A guide to implementing the recommendations of the world report on violence and health.* Geneva: WHO. Retrieved from: http://apps.who.int/iris/bitstream/10665/43014/1/9241592079.pdf.

World Health Organization (WHO). (2009). *Violence prevention the evidence: Promoting gender equality to prevent violence against women.* Geneva: WHO. Retrieved from: www.who.int/violence_injury_prevention/violence/gender.pdf.

Zakaria, R. (2014). Feminism in faith: Zainah Anwar's quest to reinterpret the Qur'an's most controversial verse. *Buzzfeed News* (March 7). Retrieved from: www.buzzfeed.com/rafiazakaria/feminism-in-faith-islam-1?utm_term=.agyRPW7NB#.qfO8XVoR4.

Index

Please note: IPV refers to intimate partner violence; GBV to gender-based violence.

A

abortion of females 232–3
Abraham, M. & Tastoglou, E. 243–5
Abrevaya, J. 232
acculturation levels and IPV 25
Acierno, R. et al 108
active bystanding interventions 8
Adams, A.E. et al 203, 210
advertisement anti-violence campaigns 236–7
advocacy organizations 230
Advocates for Youth 240
Affordable Care Act-2010 (US) 9, 107
Africa
  incidence of IPV 1–2
  IPV/GBV programs 78, 86–7
  self-defence programs 46
African American cultures
  disclosure of IPV 25–6
  on physical aggression 138
  primary prevention programs, with adolescents 20
Ahmad, F. et al 105
Ahrens, C.E. et al 51
Akpakwu, O. & Terhile, B. 237
Alemu, B. 237
Ally Movement (Casey) 238
Amnesty International 242
animal husbandry projects 221–3
Annerstedt, M. & Wahrborg, P. 216
Anton, J. 235
Arnold, G. & Ake, J. 232
arrest policies 129–32, 185

and women's arrests 130–2, 140, 189–90
athletics coaching and mentoring programs 83, 86
attention restoration theory 215–16
Australia
  IPV/GBV programs 80
  programs for women 146
Austria, VOM programs 168–70
awareness raising campaigns 236–7, 243
  "universal-women" argument 7–9
  see also bystander-based prevention programs; school-based programs

B

Badran, M. 235
Bair-Merritt, M.H. et al 104–5
Ball, B. et al 22–3
Baltimore Responsible Fatherhood Project (BRFP) 80
Bancroft, L. et al 78
Banyard, V.L./et al 18–20, 39–40, 48–9, 52, 91, 232, 240
Barner, J.R. & Carney, M.M. 230
batterer intervention programs (BIPs) 8–9, 135, 238–9
Batterer Intervention Standards (Michigan) 148–9
Because We Have Daughters program 81
Belknap, J. & McDonald, C. 189
Belknap, R.A. et al 21
Bell Bajao movement 238

amongst racially and ethnically diverse
  populations 25–7
face-to-face vs computer-based
  screening 105–6
privacy expectations 26
reduced rates to informal sources
  25–6
to family only 25
to same-gender relatives 21
women who use force 141–2, 145–7
Dissel, A. & Ngubeni, K. 170–1
domestic violence *see* intimate partner
  violence (IPV)
domestic violence shelters 11, 209, 230
  and economic empowerment
    programs 209–10, 211–12, 212–23
  in racially and ethnically diverse
    neighbourhoods 24
domestic violence survivorship
  programs 147–8
Donovan, R. & Vlaise, R. 237
Douglas, U. et al 81
Doyle, C. 239
Dragiewicz, M. 130–1, 239
drink-driving campaigns, bystander-
  based prevention programs 48
Dubowitz, H. et al 77
Dugan, L. et al 24
Duluth Domestic Abuse Intervention
  Project 166, 179
Dunn, J. 139
Durlak, J.A. et al 40, 59
Duroza, A. et al 177

E

"early adopters" 50
early conduct disorder as risk factor 84
economic abuse 203
economic dependency of women 26,
  169–70, 203–4
economic empowerment programs
  209–23
  financial literacy 26, 211–12
  horticulture/farming based 212–23
economic impacts of IPV 3
economic justice 202–4
Eden, K.B. et al 112–13
education programs
  for cultural transformation 26–7,
    236–7
  see also college-based programs;
    economic empowerment programs;
    GBV prevention programs; IPV
    prevention programs; school-based
    programs
Edwards, Dr. Dorothy 50
Edwards, K.M. et al 51
eHealth initiatives 111–12

case studies 112–13
Ehrenberg, K.M. 186–7
Ehrensaft, M.K. et al 75, 84
Elias-Lambert, N. & Black, B.M. 51
Elliott, L. et al 108
EMPOWER project (Kentucky) 55
empowerment
  and IPV 198
  and justice 192
  through financial literacy programs
    211–12
  through horticulture/farming
    programs 212–23
engagement of men and boys 9, 71–92,
  237–41
  aims and rationale for 71–2
  challenges and rewards of 73
  changing social norms 239–41
  developing prevention strategies 73–4
  future directions for research 89–91,
    237–41
  global efforts 84–9
  locations for 74–5
    college settings 81–4
  secondary prevention programs 238–9
  timing of 74–5
    parenthood and caregiving stages
      77–81
    transitioning to parenthood 75–6
Enhanced Assess, Acknowledge, Act
  Sexual Assault Resistance self-
  defence program 46
Ensler, E. 145–6
environmental factors, in schools 44–5
Epstein, D. 187
Erez, E. & Belknap, J. 195
Erickson, M.J. et al 116
Ethiopia, GBV/IPV programs 87–8
ethnically diverse groups *see* racially and
  ethnically diverse populations
evaluation studies *see* research
  evaluations
Evekink, S. 186–7
Expect Respect program 22–3

F

Families for Safe Dates program 18
familismo (importance of family) 25
family group conferencing 160–1,
  166–7, 199
  see also community-based justice
    forums
family group decision making (Canada)
  165–7
The Family Nurse Partnership program
  (UK) 75–6
family planning clinics 114–16